CSR, Sustainability, Ethics & Governance

Series Editors

In recent years the discussion concerning the relation between business and society has made immense strides. This has in turn led to a broad academic and practical discussion on innovative management concepts, such as Corporate Social Responsibility, Corporate Governance and Sustainability Management. This series offers a comprehensive overview of the latest theoretical and empirical research and provides sound concepts for sustainable business strategies. In order to do so, it combines the insights of leading researchers and thinkers in the fields of management theory and the social sciences – and from all over the world, thus contributing to the interdisciplinary and intercultural discussion on the role of business in society. The underlying intention of this series is to help solve the world's most challenging problems by developing new management concepts that create value for business and society alike. In order to support those managers, researchers and students who are pursuing sustainable business approaches for our common future, the series offers them access to cutting-edge management approaches.

CSR, Sustainability, Ethics & Governance is accepted by the Norwegian Register for Scientific Journals, Series and Publishers, maintained and operated by the Norwegian Social Science Data Services (NSD)

Stefano Amato • Alessia Patuelli

Family Firms and Local Roots

Implications on Economic Performance and Corporate Social Responsibility

Springer

Stefano Amato
Department of Economics and Management
University of Trento
Trento, Italy

Alessia Patuelli
Northumbria University
Amsterdam Campus
Amsterdam, The Netherlands

ISSN 2196-7075 ISSN 2196-7083 (electronic)
CSR, Sustainability, Ethics & Governance
ISBN 978-3-031-31792-7 ISBN 978-3-031-31793-4 (eBook)
https://doi.org/10.1007/978-3-031-31793-4

This Springer imprint is published by the registered company Springer Nature Switzerland AG
The registered company address is: Gewerbestrasse 11, 6330 Cham, Switzerland

Preface

DESIDERO DUE COSE AL MONDO PIÙ CHE ALCUN'ALTRA: L'UNA LA ESALTAZIONE PERPETUA DI QUESTA CITTÀ E DELLA LIBERTÀ SUA; L'ALTRA LA GLORIA DI CASA NOSTRA, NON SOLO VIVENDO IO, MA IN PERPETUO. A DIO PIACCIA CONSERVARE E ACCRESCERE L'UNA E L'ALTRA

FRANCESCO GUICCIARDINI

"*Two things I want more than anything else in the world: the first one is the perpetual exaltation of this city and its freedom; the other one is the glory of our house, not only as long as I live but forever. May Lord enshrine and enrich them both*". These are the words of Francesco Guicciardini, a member of one of the oldest Florentine families, engraved in a marble plaque hung at the entrance of the Poppiano Castle, a magnificent Medieval fortress in the hamlet of Poppiano, near Florence, in the heart of the Tuscan countryside. Guicciardini's family has owned the Poppiano Castle since 1199, and around the building extends the vineyards where the Guicciardini family has produced world-renowned wines for generations. The case of the Guicciardini exemplifies the inextricable bonds between the family, the firm, and the place. This book aims to unravel the connections between local roots and family firms. To do so, it proposes an integrated view on the economic, social, and emotional ties that families have with their home places.

Personal interests and a common research passion motivated this book. Among the former is our curiosity for authenticity and localism—that is, bounded territories conflating a unique natural, historical, and socio-cultural heritage. We are passionate about the stories of places and the people living in those places for generations. In the globalization era, local people, families, and institutions are the crucial actors that maintain place identity. Yet, even though family business research has flourished in recent decades, it has been chiefly "place-less", with the literature that has only just started to investigate the nexus between the territory and the family firm and the implications for the owning family, the business, and territory as a whole.

Bringing the territory into family business studies has required extensive work, involving a considerable effort of synthesis, reinterpretation, and the confluence of empirical evidence with research disciplines—seemingly distant constructs and perspectives. However, we believe that such an interdisciplinary approach will contribute to unravel family firms' complexity.

Debates within different research communities have contributed to the birth of this book. On the one hand, with the family business research community, which has started looking with increasing interest at the family firm-territory nexus as a promisingly novel area of investigation. On the other hand, with regional and economic geographers, who have only recently started to acknowledge family firms' distinctiveness in the study of space and the economy. This book has significantly benefitted from the several visits to firms and interviews with entrepreneurial families on their home ground, where the authors had the chance to hear stories of the families and see the places that are rooted in the distant past.

We hope this book will provide an enjoyable introduction to family business studies and provide the information the reader needs to grasp the territorial foundations of family firms and their uniqueness.

Trento, Italy Stefano Amato
Amsterdam, The Netherlands Alessia Patuelli

Acknowledgments

The authors thank Prof. Nicola Lattanzi for introducing us to the family business field and Prof. Rodrigo Basco for the fruitful and constant conversations regarding the connections between family firms and territories. The idea of this monograph comes from afar but has found fertile ground for its development in the IMT School for Advanced Studies Lucca. However, the insights expressed in this publication are those of the authors.

Contents

List of Figures

List of Tables

Chapter 1
Introduction

In the last two decades, there has been a growing interest in family firms as a particular type of business where a family, a social unit sharing legal or genetic bonds, influences the organization's goals, strategy, and processes. The provision of the means, both material and immaterial, to satisfy the primary needs of its members entails the conduct of the economic activity, that is, a set of actions consisting in the production, sale, and distribution of goods and services, and which is instrumental in this respect. Thus, the firm becomes a conventional organizational device through which the family carries out such an economic activity and, by combining production factors, becomes involved in business or, put differently, becomes an "entrepreneur."

As family firms are the most widespread form of business worldwide, family business research has progressively gained legitimacy in the scientific community, practitioners, and policymakers. The academic community's interest in family firms has increased in many areas: published articles, the schools offering family business programs, and the membership of family firm associations. Starting as an informal reunion of 30 researchers in Amsterdam in 2001, the International Family Enterprise Research Academy[1] (IFERA), is today an essential point of reference for family business research, uniting academics, researchers, and family business stakeholders worldwide. Other organizations with international reach include the European Family Businesses[2] and the Family Firm Institute,[3] with the aim of bringing together academic research, family businesses, and relevant stakeholders. The European

[1] Please visit https://ifera.org/ for more information about IFERA.

[2] The European Family Business was established in 1999. It is a federation of national associations from the European Union representing family-owned enterprises. To learn more about it and its associates, please visit https://europeanfamilybusinesses.eu

[3] The Family Firm Institute has a global reach and aims at educating, connecting, and inspiring professionals who serve family enterprises. To learn more, please visit www.ffi.org

S. Amato, A. Patuelli, *Family Firms and Local Roots*, CSR, Sustainability, Ethics & Governance, https://doi.org/10.1007/978-3-031-31793-4_1

Academy of Management[4] (EURAM) has a Strategic Interest Group and a track specifically dedicated to family business research every year. Three peer-reviewed international journals are explicitly dedicated to the field in the academic panorama. They are *Family Business Review*, the *Journal of Family Business Strategy*, and the *Journal of Family Business Management*. Thus, family business studies and educational programs have achieved today an internationally recognized status as an autonomous and mature field in academic research. Family firm studies have been continuously committed to investigating how the involvement of family members in the business uniquely shapes the behavior of these organizations. However, an inner dimension aiming at exploring the internal dynamics among family members and between the owning family and the business has traditionally prevailed. Family business research is replete with evidence of the light and dark sides of family firms. Among the former, reduced agency costs due to the coincidence of ownership and control, long-run objectives and perspective in the investment horizons (i.e., family firms as "patient capital"), emphasis on non-economic goals, faster decision-making, and an imitable social capital, among others. Among the latter are risk aversion, nepotism, resistance to change, family conflicts, and less professionalization.

With the area's growth, scholars in the family business field have recently started looking at the interplay between family firms and the geographical space as a platform where economic activity occurs, thus integrating a territorial perspective to understand family firms' uniqueness and behavior. Space has to be regarded not only in physical terms, that is, the space as a "container," but also in relational terms, that is consisting of a set of localized relationships among economic actors (e.g., people, firms, and institutions). However, space also has an emotional and symbolic value, becoming a site of meanings for the individual and group of people living and working therein. As such, space turns into place and an intricate link of economic, social, and emotional connections bind individuals, and through this, firms to territories. In the case of family firms, both the family and the business share the same relational space, developing a mutual dependence on and identification with the place the family's social life and the firm's economic activity occur. Personal experiences, memories, and a "spatial persistence" as a social group and economic actor anchor the owning family to a given location, framing the family firm's genesis, dynamics, and evolution over time. By integrating insights from regional economics, economic geography, and environmental psychology literature, this book aims to constitute a founding brick in the novel research field where family firms and territories intersect. Specifically, an attempt is made to answer two broad research questions: *What makes family firms deeply embedded in their home territory? How do the relationships between family firms and the local area influence organization' economic performance and corporate social responsibility initiatives?*

[4]EURAM was founded in 2001. It attracts members from 60 countries in Europe and beyond and aims to advance the academic field of management in Europe. To learn more, please visit https://euram.academy

To do so, the book develops a groundbreaking approach, bringing together different streams of the literature and providing a novel integrated view of family firms' relationships with territories; it develops new conceptualizations to understand how intimate connections with the local context are born and developed (e.g., Family firms' local roots in Chap. 4 and the place-based family enterprise in Chap. 5). The book also brings fresh empirical evidence, both quantitative and qualitative, to show how the links to the territory may affect family firms' economic performances and corporate social responsibility (CSR). While the literature used in the book has a global reach, the empirical part is set in Italy, a country with a strong presence and tradition of family businesses. More specifically, while the quantitative study is based on the population of active manufacturing firms, the qualitative one is set in the Chianti Classico area, a wine cluster known worldwide where the history of family firms enmeshes with the territory to create a strong identity.

This book is organized as follows. Part one is conceptual. It starts with Chap. 2 (*"Defining and Understanding the Family Firm"*), which introduces the family firm phenomenon, providing insights into the prevalence of family firms worldwide and discussing the primary literature, concepts, and theoretical approaches that explain their unique behaviors. Chapter 3 (*"The Spatial Dimension of Firm's Economic Activity"*) provides an overview of the role of space in firms' economic activity, addressing different conceptualizations of space, discussing agglomeration economies and the specific cases of industrial districts, business clusters, and peripheral areas. Chapter 4 (*"Firms in territories: the local roots of family firms"*) provides an in-depth study of the firm-territory "nexus." It disentangles the crucial concepts of place attachment and local embeddedness, which are the key to understanding how family firms are rooted in their home territory. Chapter 5 (*"Family Firms, Corporate Social Responsibility, and Place-Based Enterprises"*) brings together family firms, the territory and CSR, discussing the literature joining these three streams and introducing the concept of the place-based family enterprise. After this, part two is dedicated to empirical findings. Chapter 6 (*"Unveiling the origins of local roots: a case study in the Chianti Classico wine cluster"*) presents the results of a case study conducted in the Chianti Classico Italian wine cluster, showing the central role the family firm plays in developing and maintaining the individual and family relationships with the territory, and the natural tendency toward actions connected to CSR. Finally, Chap. 7 (*"The role of local roots on the economic performance and corporate social responsibility of family firms: a quantitative analysis"*) brings new empirical evidence of the impact of local roots on family firms' economic results and CSR, highlighting the pro-environmental attitudes of locally rooted family firms. Chapter 8 closes the manuscript by outlining the existing debate on family firms and territories, the contributions made by the book, its limitations, and future research avenues.

Chapter 2
Defining and Understanding the Family Firm

2.1 The Family Firm Phenomenon

Around the world, family businesses account for 70% of the global GDP and provide 60% of jobs. Asia is home to two-thirds of the largest family-owned businesses in the world. About two-thirds of the GDP in India is thought to be accounted for by family enterprises.[1] In the USA, there are 5.5 million family companies. Family-owned companies employ 63% of workers and 57% of the GDP.[2] More than 60% of all companies in Europe are family businesses,[3] making more than 40–50% of all jobs (Fig. 2.1).[4]

They range from small local businesses to massive global corporations. Family businesses of all sizes, whether publicly traded or privately held, contribute significantly to the economy. Family businesses are all around us, and many famous businesses worldwide are family businesses. These include Gap, Levi Strauss, Hermés (France), Zara (Spain), LG Electronics (Korea), Fiat (Italy), BMW (Germany), Ikea (Sweden), and Wal-Mart (US) (Poza, 2013).

Family businesses account for more than 85% of all businesses in Italy, generating 70% of total employment. They constitute the backbone of Italian industrial

[1] 2017 data. Please visit Accenture, at the following link, for more details: https://www.accenture.com/_acnmedia/thought-leadership-assets/pdf/accenture-family-businesses-in-asia-deepening-the-roots-of-trust.pdf

[2] Please visit the following website for more details: https://www.gvsu.edu/fobi/family-firm-facts-5.htm

[3] Please see the website of the European Commission: https://single-market-economy.ec.europa.eu/smes/supporting-entrepreneurship/family

[4] Please visit the following website for more details: https://europeanfamilybusinesses.eu/about-european-family-businesses

S. Amato, A. Patuelli, *Family Firms and Local Roots*, CSR, Sustainability, Ethics & Governance, https://doi.org/10.1007/978-3-031-31793-4_2

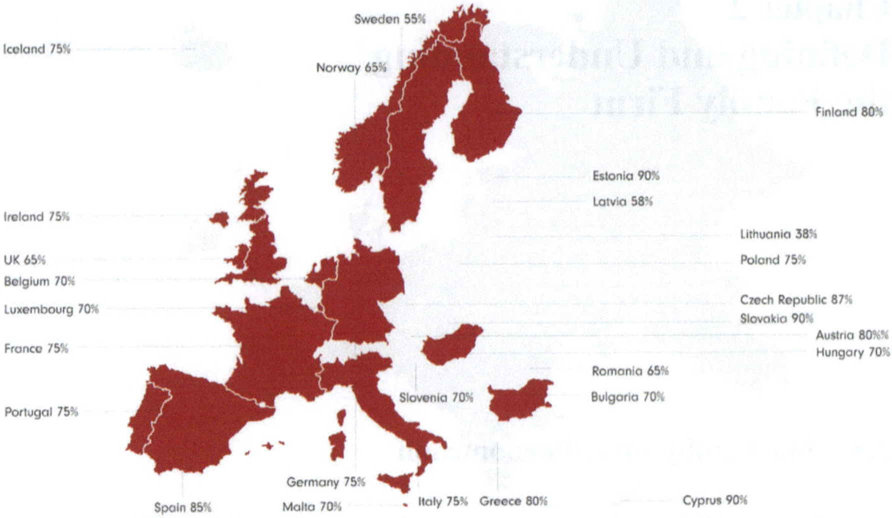

Fig. 2.1 Family firms in Europe (Source: European Family Businesses, https://europeanfamilybusinesses.eu/about-european-family-businesses)

districts[5] (AIDAF, 2018). This high presence has historical reasons and roots. During the twentieth century, Italy was considered a "latecomer" on the international scene, and the prevailing model of the small family business with low capitalization, compared to large companies across European countries, was one of the factors that explain the phenomenon (Bianchi, 2002).

Family businesses tend to be somehow different from non-family ones. The academic literature has been studying these differences extensively. Just to mention a few examples, family businesses tend to outperform non-family ones (Anderson & Reeb, 2003), and most highly innovative large European firms are family owned (Duran et al., 2016). Family businesses were resilient in facing COVID-19 (Amore et al., 2022), and they highly support their employees during financial crises (Amato et al., 2023). They are usually very active in CSR activities (Campopiano & De Massis, 2015) and global challenges, including SDGs (Patuelli et al., 2022). However, only 30% of family businesses survive with the second generation and 12% with the third generation. Finally, 3% continue to operate beyond the fourth generation.[6] Family businesses are indeed unique. What makes them so?

[5]Family firms and industrial districts are peculiarities of the Italian economy. Chapter 7 ("The Role of Local Roots on the Economic Performance and Corporate Social Responsibility of Family Firms: A Quantitative Analysis") provides a detailed analysis of family firms within Italian industrial districts.

[6]For further details, please consult the website of the Italian Association for Family Firms (AIDAF, Associazione Italiana delle Aziende Familiari) at: www.aidaf.it

Research in the social sciences (e.g., psychology) indicates that feelings and emotions motivate people to act in ways that logic would rarely approve of. [7] As a result, familial relationships or patterns, which are often charged with emotion, might take precedence over the reason behind business decisions (Poza, 2013). In a nutshell, family businesses are characterized by the coexistence of two social dimensions: the firm and the family. When the two closely related realities often overlap, their interaction can create unique synergies (Chua et al., 1999). These themes will be discussed extensively in this chapter.

This chapter gives the reader a general introduction to the family business phenomenon. First, it will define a family business. In doing so, it will also discuss what the literature calls the "definitional dilemma," discovering that there are many different definitions and concepts of the family business. It is not easy to define a family firm. However, agreeing on a generally accepted definition is essential for many reasons. First, a definition is needed to determine the number of family businesses worldwide. This takes us to the next theme this chapter will present: how many family businesses exist? Last, the chapter will dig deeper into understanding what makes family businesses unique and different from other businesses. It will present and discuss the most acknowledged concepts and theoretical frameworks essential to get a clear picture of the family business phenomenon.

2.2 Defining a Family Business

Many definitions and concepts of family business exist in the literature, making it challenging to identify the phenomenon uniquely. Scholars have been studying family businesses from multiple perspectives and according to the theoretical lenses of different disciplines (including psychology, sociology, organizational behavior, and strategy), resulting in some generalizations and mixed findings (Wortman, 1994).

In family businesses, an internal element that can be decisive for the business's success (or failure) is the *family*. Generally, when talking about family businesses, we refer to those firms that a family influences. This could happen in various ways,

[7] Accordingly, a new stream of research in economics and business developed in the 1950s. The traditional assumption in economic theory is that the human being (the *homo economicus*) is primarily driven by individualistic needs and desires and that he/she perfectly knows the environment and has (almost) perfect information. However, Herbert A. Simon argued that individuals are not rational in their choices (Simon, 1955). He coined the term "bounded rationality" to indicate that individuals are subject to cognitive limits when they make decisions. Thus, economic theory and business literature should assume that the individual does not always make the most rational choice (Simon, 2000). Later, the groundbreaking studies of Kahneman and Tversky (1979) moved further away from the rationality assumption. The authors empirically proved that individuals value their loss and gain differently when they make decisions in situations under risk. Contrasting utility theory, which argued that individuals are perfectly rational, they opened new research paths, including the role of cognition and emotions in economic and business decisions.

the most discussed ones being ownership, management, and board control (Astrachan & Zellweger, 2008). However, the family's participation in business ownership, management, and/or governance might not be enough for a firm to identify as a family business. In practice, firms that show similar structures and family participation in the governance, ownership, and management either identify or do not identify as family businesses. This reasoning gave rise to another approach. It maintains that although family involvement in the business is an effective way to operationalize the identification of family businesses, a family business is more than a firm with the presence of a family in its business structure. Identifying a family business is a matter of "essence." In a nutshell, it is not merely about the family involvement in the firm: it is about how the family influences a firm's goals, values, strategy, and structure (Chua et al., 1999).

In short, the literature distinguishes the *essence* and the *demographic* approach to identifying family businesses (Basco, 2013). The demographic approach is based on the involvement of family members in ownership, governance, and managerial positions, as well as the number of generations involved in the business. However, critics have pointed out that this approach does not consider the *effects* of the family's participation in the business. Instead, supporters of the essence approach maintain that measuring the extent to which the family influences a business in practice is crucial (Chua et al., 1999).

The growing relevance of the family firm phenomenon in recent years has involved the European Commission. The Commission tried to put an end to the definitional problem, providing a shared European definition[8] based on four founding pillars:

- The majority of decision-making rights are in possession of the natural person (s) who established the firm, or in possession of the natural person(s) who has/have acquired the share capital of the firm, or in possession of their spouses, parents, child, or children's direct heirs.
- The majority of decision-making rights are indirect or direct.
- At least one representative of the family or kin is formally involved in the firm's governance.
- Listed companies meet the definition of family enterprise if the person who established or acquired the firm (share capital) or their families or descendants possess 25% of the decision-making rights mandated by their share capital.

One of the primary revision studies of the existing definitions is by Chua et al. (1999), reviewing over 250 articles with 21 different family business definitions and highlighting the definitional problem. The authors conclude that a family business is "a business governed and/or managed with the intention to shape and/or pursue the vision of the business held by a dominant coalition controlled by members of the

[8]Please see the website of the European Commission about the EC's definition of the family business and further information about European policies in this regard: https://single-market-economy.ec.europa.eu

same family or a small number of families in a manner that is potentially sustainable across generations of the family or families" (Chua et al., 1999, p. 25).

Apart from the definitional dilemma, the variety of shades within the family firm set is worth noting. In studying family businesses, scholars face a heterogeneous group of companies that differ in size, structure, management, and governance, so the criterion chosen to define the family business phenomenon heavily influences its quantification. This heterogeneity makes it difficult to circumscribe family businesses into categories with rigid, inflexible margins.[9]

In reality, many kinds of family firms exist, and family firms are not a homogeneous phenomenon. Traditionally, the literature has focused on the family versus non-family firm's dichotomy. This was because the early research on family businesses aimed to develop a theory to differentiate them from non-family firms and grow as an autonomous research field. Research on family business heterogeneity developed later, with current studies highlighting the differences between family firm types and their consequences on multiple business dimensions. However, the theme of heterogeneity was intrinsic within the variety of definitions of the family firm phenomenon, in the sense that the variety of definitions already highlighted multiple dimensions of the family firm. The sources of heterogeneity can be very different. The main ones include goals (for example, the balance between economic and non-economic goals), governance structures (for example, the family's involvement in ownership, governance, and management), and resources. However, other factors, such as the founder's values or the firm's size and industry, can lead to heterogeneity (Chua et al., 2012).

The dichotomous approach was needed at first for the family business field to become an independent research stream. However, an approach that considers family firms' heterogeneity allows researchers to dig deeper into the factors and relationships that allow family firms to have positive outcomes on multiple dimensions[10] (Astrachan & Zellweger, 2008).

In sum, a firm is a family business not merely based on the presence of family members within it but on the extent to which family members uniquely influence the business.

---

[9]From the definitional dilemma and the heterogeneity of family firms, three streams of studies emerge, which aim to obtain operational definitions of family firms, develop measurement scales to capture family involvement, and determine the different family firm typologies (Sharma, 2004). However, this chapter does not aim to dig into the details of the different definitions. Some suggested readings are Daspit et al. (2021); Howorth et al. (2010); Neubaum et al. (2019).

[10]One of the most discussed themes is the relationship between family businesses and performances. For example, while comparing family businesses listed on the Italian Stock Market, Culasso et al. (2015) find that the firm's size influences the extent to which a family positively impacts the firm's performance. In short, they find that the family influences the firm's economic results only when the firm's size is not large. This effect does not appear when comparing large family and non-family firms.

2.3 First Approaches to Explain Family Firms' Uniqueness: From Agency Theory to Familiness

Early literature in the field questioned if and how family businesses differ from non-family businesses. There is now agreement that what sets family business studies apart from its sister disciplines is the reciprocal relationship between family and business (Zahra & Sharma, 2004). However, scholars have long debated and had difficulty agreeing on a unifying paradigm in family business studies (Wortman, 1994).

The first approaches to research on family businesses used to discuss the advantages and disadvantages of family businesses, but mostly following descriptive approaches. They argued that family businesses are not intrinsically better or worse than non-family businesses. However, the family can have a distinctive influence on the business, leading to positive and negative outcomes. Researchers had to offer insights to individuals working in family firms to help them better comprehend their circumstances and develop their courses of action (Donnelley, 1988).

The first studies in the family business field aimed at explaining the businesses' competitive advantage and unique behaviors adopted theoretical approaches descending from financial economics and strategic management. These included agency theory, stewardship theory, and the resource-based view (Berrone et al., 2012). The following paragraphs will explain them in detail.

According to agency theory, there are inherent conflicts of interest between a firm's owners and management (Jensen & Meckling, 1976). This approach describes an agency situation where one party, the principal, assigns work to another, the agent, who has to accomplish the task. However, two problems generally arise. The first occurs when the principal and the agent have opposing interests or needs; the second arises when it is costly for the principal to monitor the agent's actions. Although scholars have different perspectives about agency, this approach focuses on the relationship (contract) between the agents and the principal (Eisenhardt, 1989). It is commonly claimed that family businesses have low agency issues because the owners (principals) and management (agents) are all family members. Alternatively, they have a reduced need for formal supervision and for designing governance structures to align the interests of different parties. Thus, in this view, family businesses have a competitive advantage over non-family businesses due to lower agency costs (Schulze et al., 2001).

However, some scholars began criticizing agency theory, which only considered the relationships between principals and agents as rational and individualistic subjects. In short, agency theory did not consider the psychological and sociological aspects of organizations. In the case of family businesses, specific characteristics, such as non-economic objectives and family engagement, can result in behavior and governance changes that significantly depart from agency theory. Therefore, academics looked to stewardship theory, which furthers a deeper comprehension of the family business (Madison et al., 2016).

According to stewardship theory, individuals are not characterized by individualistic and self-serving attitudes. Instead, they act as stewards whose behavior is oriented toward altruistic, pro-organization, and collectivistic aims. In this view, a manager would be actively pursuing the organization's aims and interested in the business having high performances, rather than only maximizing what agency theory defined as the agent's utility (Davis et al., 1997). Following this reasoning, the founding family members see the business as an extension of themselves and, hence, see a connection between the enterprise's continued success and their own well-being. Eddleston and Kellermanns (2007) demonstrated that it is hard to completely comprehend family businesses' performance without considering the psychodynamic consequences of kinship. How family members interact can lead to the failure of the family business; nevertheless, interpersonal ties within the family can also be a source of benefit. Thus, stewardship theory describes family firms' competitive advantages as deriving from stewards' strong interests and commitment to maximizing the organization's objectives.

The resource-based view theory is the third mainstream approach traditionally used to explain family firms' unique behaviors. This theory describes the firm's resources as a set of tangible and intangible assets that are tied to it. These resources vary in scope and range from skilled individuals to machinery and efficient internal procedures, to mention a few (Wernerfelt, 1984). This makes the basis of the firm's position in the market, or what is called competitive advantage. In some situations, incorporating these assets into internal business procedures, human capital, or other intangible assets may give the company a competitive advantage.[11] Based on the resource-based view, Habbershon and Williams (1999) defined family businesses' unusual synergies, which emerge as extra capabilities and resources, as *familiness*. The concept is defined as "the unique bundle of resources a particular firm has because of the systems interaction between the family, its individual members, and the business" (Habbershon & Williams, 1999, p. 11) (Fig. 2.2).

Following family business literature corroborated and developed this concept, which was then considered a multidimensional construct that might affect the competitive advantage of family firms. However, families and family firms are all unique and different from one another. Families can be both an asset and a liability in constructing the business' familiness, leading to positive and negative effects on family firms' competitive advantage and performances (Zellweger et al., 2010).

[11]Research on firms' strategies and competitive positioning had significant development in the 1970s (Andrews, 1971) and further expanded with the contributions of Michael E. Porter (1985). Porter views competitive advantage as the goal of strategies. It can be expressed in the ability to offer an "original" product or service, which is able to attract demand by satisfying particular needs. In the same period, further studies helped complete the strategy concept. Henry Mintzberg (1987) proposed the five dimensions of strategy, maintaining that a company must be able to keep its stability through change. In this perspective, a strategy must contribute to the search for stability, defining the way forward.

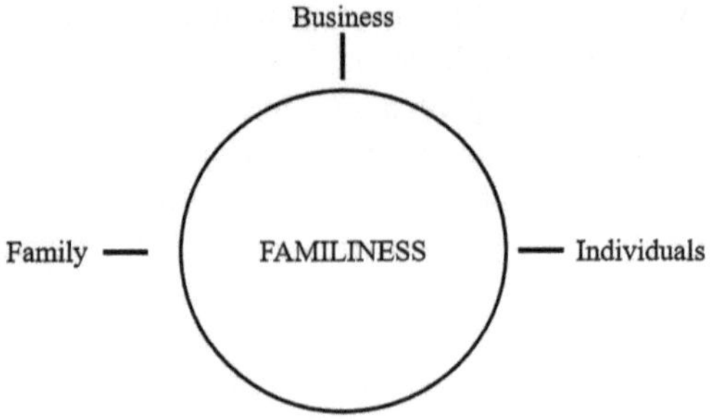

Fig. 2.2 The familiness concept (Own elaboration, adapted from Habbershon and Williams, 1999)

2.4 Developing a Unifying Paradigm: From the Three-Circle Model to Socioemotional Wealth Theory

Meanwhile, the family business literature had started developing theories to explain family firms' behaviors. One of the most recognized ones is the *three-circle model* (Tagiuri & Davis, 1996). The family business has several distinctive, ingrained characteristics, and each has advantages and disadvantages for the owning families, non-family employees, and family employees. Tagiuri and Davis (1996) refer to these characteristics as "bivalent attributes." How well these intrinsic features are managed will determine whether any family business succeeds or fails. Thus, family business owners and managers must recognize the potential contribution families can make to the firm's long-term strengths, identify the associated weaknesses, and implement organizational controls to address these issues. In their seminal paper, Tagiuri and Davis (1996) conceptualize the interactions between owners, family members, managers, and employees as three separate and overlapping circles, depicted in Fig. 2.3.

The underlying idea is that bivalent attributes emerge as distinguishing features of family firms, which result from the overlapping between family members, ownership, and management. Although they are not intrinsically good or bad for a firm, they can lead to positive and negative outcomes. Tagiuri and Davis (1996) identify these outcomes as simultaneous roles, shared identity, lifelong common history, emotional involvement and ambivalence, private language, mutual awareness and privacy, and meaning of the family company. Table 2.1 provides a brief and clear explanation, with some examples, of the bivalent attitudes.

In a family firm, family members will view issues, priorities, and difficulties in various ways. Members of the family and the company will naturally have different perspectives, given their relative roles within the system. The three-circle model depicted in Fig. 2.4 shows the different roles one can have in a business, considering the intersections between the different dimensions.

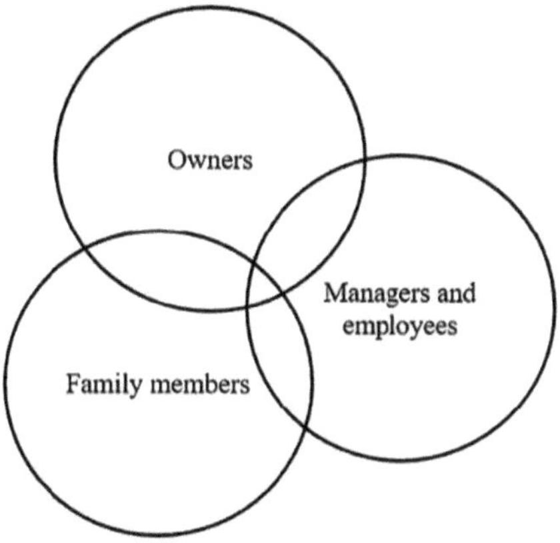

Fig. 2.3 The three-circle model (Source: Tagiuri and Davis, 1996, p. 200)

For instance, a parent who is the CEO and the company's sole shareholder (represented by position 7) will probably have a different perspective than a family member who is not involved in the management and has no ownership stake in the company (position 1). Similarly, a non-family manager (position 3) will probably have a very different viewpoint due to their particular position inside the family business organization (Poza, 2013).

The interactions between the firm and the family, and more specifically, the values that guide the family, can lead family firms to see their challenges from a *family-first*, *business-first*, or *family-enterprise-first* viewpoint (Sharma & Nordqvist, 2008; Ward, 1987), although the literature has variously classified the aspirations of family businesses (Basu, 2004). A *family-first* business believes that the family's well-being is more important than the business. Where the family comes first, employment in the family company is a birthright: family members will probably work in the firm. Sometimes, the family takes decisions that negatively affect the company, but they benefit the family. A *business-first* firm is the opposite: the firm's financial well-being has a higher value than the family's. Family members govern the firm following solid business principles—without giving priority to family values. It may happen that fewer family members are employed in these firms, as firms do not have a preference for family members—they value what is best for the business' sustainability. The *family-enterprise-first* perspective takes a mid-way. In this view, nor the family or the firm are superior to one another. The family and the firms' well-being are both treated as priorities, which is essential for their long-term survival.

The consequence of the prevalence of the family or business or the other dimension in terms of success is clearly depicted in Sharma (2004). The author defined a model to conceptualize family firms' performances based on two primary dimensions: the family and the business. At any stage of its existence, the family company's performance is defined as a high performance in its family and business dimensions. This is depicted in Fig. 2.5.

Table 2.1 Bivalent attributes in family firms (Source: Own elaboration, adapted from Tagiuri and Davis, 1996)

Attributes	Description and examples
Simultaneous roles	Family members working in the family business might simultaneously play the roles of owner, manager, and relative. This can lead to: • Increased loyalty to each other and the business (+) • Higher efficiency in decision-making (+) • Confusion between one's role (−) • Conflicts between the two dimensions (−)
Shared identity	Working together as a family fosters a feeling of identity. This can lead to: • Family members feeling that what they are doing is meaningful and important (+) • The actions of one relative can have an impact on the reputations of other family members as well as the business, in both positive (+) and negative ways (−) • Family members might feel they are controlled in their outside behaviors (−)
Lifelong common history	Family members have a common history, many shared experiences and know each other quite well. This can lead to: • Relatives relying on each other's assets and strengthen each other's deficiencies (+) • Point out a relative's shortcomings to lower that person's status within the company (−) • Easily overcoming significant difficulty and be loyal to one another if the relationship has a good foundation (+) • Have complex relationships at work due to past contrasts and disappointments (−)
Emotional involvement and ambivalence	Family members have both strong and conflicting emotions toward one another. This can lead to: • Communications evoke the same emotional reaction as they did earlier in childhood (−) • Challenging objective interpretation of one another's words and behavior (−) • Stronger motivation, loyalty, and trust among relatives (+)
Private language	Family members may communicate more effectively than most other groups of people, even close friends, by using private or "family languages". This can lead to: • Communicate openly and privately (+) • Make choices quickly (+) • Eliciting unpleasant, sensitive responses (−)
Mutual awareness and privacy	Relatives are particularly aware of one another's circumstances (e.g., the stresses they are under, the things that make them happy or furious, and how they are physically feeling). This can lead to: • Offering family members advice on how to help one another (+) • Feeling trapped or monitored too much (−)
Meaning of the family company	The business has a certain strong significance for the family who owns it. This can lead to: • A strong desire to pursue the organization's objectives (+) • Disputes between family members on the control of the organization (−)

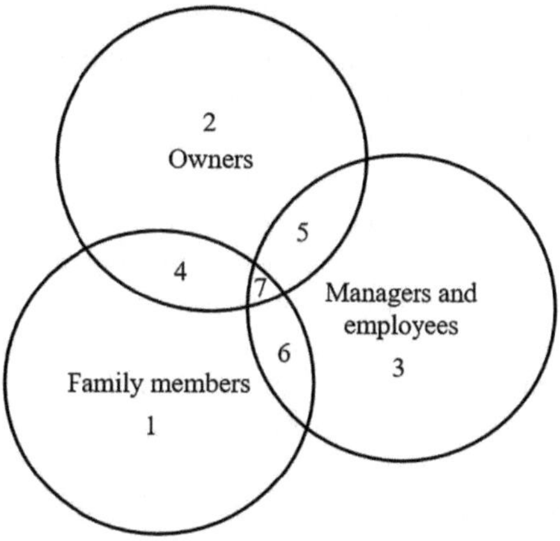

Fig. 2.4 The three-circle model (Own elaboration, adapted from Tagiuri and Davis, 1996, and Gersick et al., 1997)

		FAMILY (+)	FAMILY (-)
BUSINESS	(+)	Quadrant I *Warm Hearts* *Deep Pockets* High Emotional and Financial Capital	Quadrant II *Pained Hearts* *Deep Pockets* High Financial but Low Emotional Capital
BUSINESS	(-)	Quadrant III *Warm Hearts* *Empty Pockets* High Emotional but Low Financial Capital	Quadrant IV *Pained Hearts* *Empty Pockets* Low Financial and Emotional Capital

Fig. 2.5 Family firms' performances (adapted from Sharma, 2004)

The successful family businesses are those in Quadrant I, they enjoy prosperous businesses and good family relations. Businesses in Quadrant II are known for their commercial success. However, they may also be tense or show strained familial ties. Despite the poor performance of their enterprises, Quadrant III corporations have close familial ties. They possess significant levels of emotional capital but low levels of financial capital. Businesses in Quadrant IV have failed and performed poorly on personal and professional fronts. Although Quadrant I would be ideal for these businesses, they might need to travel via Quadrant II or III to get there. The explanation above of potential outcomes of family company performance is oversimplified because it only considers two dimensions, each of which has only two extreme positions.

In the last two decades, a new approach developed and gained recognition. In 2007, Gómez-Mejía et al. proposed the concept of socioemotional wealth to explain family firms' behavior. Today, socioemotional wealth is considered the prevalent paradigm in the family business field (Berrone et al., 2012; Brigham & Payne, 2019). This approach developed from Kahneman and Tversky's (1979) works on prospect theory and Cyert et al.'s (1963) behavioral theory of the firm. Both approaches assume that individuals are not rational while making decisions. Taking distance from classical approaches, the two theories maintain that a single individual has different risk preferences depending on the context: the risk an individual is willing to take depends on what one believes is important. In the context of family firms, this assumption refuses the traditional approach of family firms being more risk-averse than non-family firms. It proposes a new approach to family firms' decision-making.

In this view, family firms' decisions are highly driven by the non-financial components of family owners' "affective endowments." SEW theory suggests that family enterprises are frequently motivated by and devoted to the maintenance of their SEW. In this reasoning, SEW is the most crucial factor that separates a family business from other organizations. Family businesses use gains or losses in SEW as the primary point of reference to make decisions (Berrone et al., 2012). Thus, a family firm is more willing to accept economic losses than non-family firms and favor other non-economic goals. These goals refer to family aspects, such as family control and influence, dynastic succession, the preservation of family values, emotional connections, and reputation (Swab et al., 2020).

However, there is a lack of agreement about SEW's fundamental nature and definition. Specifically, this approach's limitation is the difficulty in measuring family businesses' SEW (Brigham & Payne, 2019). The most effective approach to measuring the construct is found in Berrone et al. (2012). To capture the family's affective endowment toward the firm, the authors propose the "FIBER" model, which is composed of different dimensions, namely:

- F: family control and influence
- I: identification of family members with the firm
- B: binding social ties
- E: emotional attachment of family members
- R: renewal of family bonds to the firm through dynastic succession.

2.5 Concluding Remarks

Family businesses are unique phenomena. For most of humankind's history, different forms of family businesses have been the predominant type of organizations producing commodities and services (Dodd & Dyck, 2015). This chapter aimed to give the reader a clear and straightforward picture of the family business's main literature. The family business field is indeed young but prolific. The chapter addressed the main aspects that can help to understand the family business phenomenon from different perspectives. It may not have sometimes given single points of view but preferred to show how different scholars interpreted the same phenomenon. As previous research pointed out (Madison et al., 2016), the chapter aims not to prefer a theory or an explanation to the other. Instead, it aims to provide the reader with different approaches that can coexist rather than looking for one single explanation.

This ground laid the foundation for understanding a family business, the principal concepts and theories that explain their unique behaviors and superior performance. The chapter highlighted that the presence of the family, and its interaction with the business on various dimensions, make the family business unique. Additionally, it underlined that family businesses are all different from one another. What is a source of force for a family business might be a liability for another The literature is working toward theories that generalize findings. From a practical perspective, it is essential that managers are aware of the potential and limits of their family businesses and work to transform the family into a unique asset for the business.

Family businesses also have a particular stakeholder structure: strong links with the territory, identity, relationships, and a long-term orientation. A stakeholder structure is configured for family businesses based on a distant future (temporal dimension) and strong links with the territory (spatial dimension). These considerations are particularly significant with family businesses, whose histories are rooted in the values of the family history itself.

The next chapters will dig deeper into these phenomena and their interactions with the family business.

References

AIDAF. (2018). *Dieci anni di capitalismo familiare*. X osservatorio AUB.

Amato, S., Patuelli, A., Basco, R., & Lattanzi, N. (2023). Family firms amidst the global financial crisis: A territorial embeddedness perspective on downsizing. *Journal of Business Ethics., 183*, 213. https://doi.org/10.1007/s10551-021-04930-0

Amore, M. D., Pelucco, V., & Quarato, F. (2022). Family ownership during the Covid-19 pandemic. *Journal of Banking and Finance, 135*, 106385. https://doi.org/10.1016/j.jbankfin.2021.106385

Anderson, R. C., & Reeb, D. M. (2003). Founding-family ownership and firm performance: Evidence from the S&P 500. *Journal of Finance, 58*(3), 1301–1328. https://doi.org/10.1111/1540-6261.00567

Andrews, K. R. (1971). *The concept of corporate strategy* (pp. 26–27). Dow Jones Irwin.

Astrachan, J. H., & Zellweger, T. (2008). Performance of family firms: A literature review and guidance for future research. *ZfKE – Zeitschrift Für KMU Und Entrepreneurship, 56*(1–2), 155–177. https://doi.org/10.3790/zfke.56.1_2.1c

Basco, R. (2013). The family's effect on family firm performance: A model testing the demographic and essence approaches. *Journal of Family Business Strategy, 4*(1), 42–66. https://doi.org/10.1016/j.jfbs.2012.12.003

Basu, A. (2004). Entrepreneurial aspirations among family business owners: An analysis of ethnic business owners in the UK. *International Journal of Entrepreneurial Behaviour & Research, 10*, 12–33. https://doi.org/10.1108/13552550410521353

Berrone, P., Cruz, C., & Gomez-Mejia, L. R. (2012). Socioemotional wealth in family firms: Theoretical dimensions, assessment approaches, and agenda for future research. *Family Business Review, 25*(3), 258–279. https://doi.org/10.1177/0894486511435355

Bianchi, P. (2002). La rincorsa frenata: L'industria italiana dall'unità nazionale all'unificazione europea. *Il Mulino.*

Brigham, K. H., & Payne, G. T. (2019). Socioemotional wealth (SEW): Questions on construct validity. *Family Business Review, 32*(4), 326–329. https://doi.org/10.1177/0894486519889402

Campopiano, G., & De Massis, A. (2015). Corporate social responsibility reporting: A content analysis in family and non-family firms. *Journal of Business Ethics, 129*(3), 511–534. https://doi.org/10.1007/s10551-014-2174-z

Chua, J. H., Chrisman, J. J., & Sharma, P. (1999). Defining the family business by behavior. *Entrepreneurship Theory and Practice, 23*(4), 19–39. https://doi.org/10.1177/104225879902300402

Chua, J. H., Chrisman, J. J., Steier, L. P., & Rau, S. B. (2012). Sources of heterogeneity in family firms: An introduction. *Entrepreneurship: Theory and Practice, 36*(6), 1103–1113. https://doi.org/10.1111/j.1540-6520.2012.00540.x

Culasso, F., Giacosa, E., Broccardo, L., & Manzi, L. M. (2015). Family Italian listed firms: Comparison in performances and identification of two main configurations. *International Journal of Organizational Analysis, 23*(4), 664–691. https://doi.org/10.1108/IJOA-11-2013-0721

Cyert, R. M., March, J. G., et al. (1963). A behavioral theory of the firm (Vol. 2, 4).

Daspit, J. J., Chrisman, J. J., Ashton, T., & Evangelopoulos, N. (2021). Family firm heterogeneity: A definition, common themes, scholarly progress, and directions forward. *Family Business Review, 34*(3), 296–322. https://doi.org/10.1177/08944865211008350

Davis, J. H., Schoorman, F. D., & Donaldson, L. (1997). Toward a stewardship theory of management. *Academy of Management Review, 22*(1), 20–47. https://doi.org/10.5465/AMR.1997.9707180258

Dodd, S. D., & Dyck, B. (2015). Agency, stewardship, and the universal-family firm: A qualitative historical analysis. *Family Business Review, 28*(4), 312–331. https://doi.org/10.1177/0894486515600860

Donnelley, R. G. (1988). The family business. *Family Business Review, 1*(4), 427–445.

Duran, P., Kammerlander, N., Van Essen, M., & Zellweger, T. (2016). Doing more with less: Innovation input and output in family firms. *Academy of Management Journal, 59*(4), 1224–1264. https://doi.org/10.5465/amj.2014.0424

Eddleston, K. A., & Kellermanns, F. W. (2007). Destructive and productive family relationships: A stewardship theory perspective. *Journal of Business Venturing, 22*(4), 545–565. https://doi.org/10.1016/j.jbusvent.2006.06.004

Eisenhardt, K. M. (1989). Agency theory: An assessment and review. *Academy of Management Review, 14*(1), 57–74. https://doi.org/10.5465/amr.1989.4279003

Gersick, K. E., Davis, J., Hampton, M. M., & Lansberg, I. (1997). Generation to generation: Life cycles of the family business. *Harvard Business School Press.* https://doi.org/10.5860/choice.34-4568

Gómez-Mejía, L. R., Haynes, K. T., Núñez-Nickel, M., Jacobson, K. J. L., & Moyano-Fuentes, J. (2007). Socioemotional wealth and business risks in family-controlled firms: Evidence from Spanish olive oil mills. *Administrative Science Quarterly, 52*(1), 106–137. https://doi.org/10.2189/asqu.52.1.106

Habbershon, T. G., & Williams, M. L. (1999). A resource-based framework for assessing the strategic advantages of family firms. *Family Business Review, 12*(1), 1–25. https://doi.org/10.1111/j.1741-6248.1999.00001.x

Howorth, C., Rose, M., Hamilton, E., & Westhead, P. (2010). Family firm diversity and development: An introduction. *International Small Business Journal, 28*(5), 437–451. https://doi.org/10.1177/0266242610373685

Jensen, M. C., & Meckling, W. H. (1976). Theory of the firm: Managerial behavior, agency costs and ownership structure. *Journal of Financial Economics, 3*(4), 305–360. https://doi.org/10.1016/0304-405X(76)90026-X

Kahneman, D., & Tversky, A. (1979). Prospect theory: An analysis of decision under risk Daniel Kahneman; Amos Tversky. *Econometrica, 47*(2), 263.

Madison, K., Holt, D. T., Kellermanns, F. W., & Ranft, A. L. (2016). Viewing family firm behavior and governance through the lens of agency and stewardship theories. *Family Business Review, 29*(1), 65–93. https://doi.org/10.1177/0894486515594292

Mintzberg, H. (1987). The strategy concept I: Five Ps for strategy. *California Management Review, 30*(1), 11–24. https://doi.org/10.2307/41165263

Neubaum, D. O., Kammerlander, N., & Brigham, K. H. (2019). Capturing family firm heterogeneity: How taxonomies and typologies can help the field move forward. *Family Business Review, 32*(2). https://doi.org/10.1177/0894486519848512

Patuelli, A., Carungu, J., & Lattanzi, N. (2022). Drivers and nuances of sustainable development goals: Transcending corporate social responsibility in family firms. *Journal of Cleaner Production, 373*, 133723. https://doi.org/10.1016/J.JCLEPRO.2022.133723

Porter, M. E. (1985). Technology and competitive advantage. *Journal of Business Strategy, 5*(3), 60–78. https://doi.org/10.1108/eb039075

Poza, E. J. (2013). *Family business*. Cengage Learning.

Schulze, W. S., Lubatkin, M. H., Dino, R. N., & Buchholz, A. K. (2001). Agency relationships in family business. Theory and evidence. *Organizational Science, 2*.

Sharma, P. (2004). An overview of the field of family business studies: Current status and directions for the future. *Family Business Review, 17*(1). https://doi.org/10.1111/j.1741-6248.2004.00001.x

Sharma, P., & Nordqvist, M. (2008). A classification scheme for family firms: From family values to effective governance to firm performance. *Family Values and Value Creation*. https://doi.org/10.1057/9780230594227_5

Simon, H. A. (1955). A behavioral model of rational choice. *Quarterly Journal of Economics, 69*(1), 99–118. https://doi.org/10.2307/1884852

Simon, H. A. (2000). Bounded rationality in social science: Today and tomorrow. *Mind & Society, 1*(1), 25–39. https://doi.org/10.1007/bf02512227

Swab, R. G., Sherlock, C., Markin, E., & Dibrell, C. (2020). "SEW" what do we know and where do we go? A review of socioemotional wealth and a way forward. *Family Business Review, 33*(4), 424–445. https://doi.org/10.1177/0894486520961938

Tagiuri, R., & Davis, J. (1996). Bivalent attributes of the family firm. *Family Business Review, 9*(2), 199–208. https://doi.org/10.1111/j.1741-6248.1996.00199.x

Ward, J. L. (1987). *Keeping the family business healthy: How to plan for continuing growth, profitability, and family leadership*. Palgrave Macmillan US.

Wernerfelt, B. (1984). A resource-based view of the firm. *Strategic Management Journal, 5*(2), 171–180. https://doi.org/10.1002/smj.4250050207

Wortman, M. S. (1994). Theoretical foundations for family-owned business: A conceptual and research-based paradigm. *Family Business Review, 7*(1), 3. https://doi.org/10.1111/j.1741-6248.1994.00003.x

Zahra, S. A., & Sharma, P. (2004). Family business research: A strategic reflection. *Family Business Review, 17*(4), 331–346. https://doi.org/10.1111/j.1741-6248.2004.00022.x

Zellweger, T. M., Eddleston, K. A., & Kellermanns, F. W. (2010). Exploring the concept of familiness: Introducing family firm identity. *Journal of Family Business Strategy, 1*(1), 54–63. https://doi.org/10.1016/j.jfbs.2009.12.003

Chapter 3
The Spatial Dimension of Firm's Economic Activity

3.1 The Different Concepts of Space

Economic activity occurs, grows, and develops in a given space. Firms and economic actors, in general, select their location in the same way as they choose production factors, such as capital, labor, and technology. Additionally, productive resources are distributed unevenly in this space, often concentrated in specific regions or cities. In contrast, they are wholly or partially missing in others. Quantitative and qualitative imbalances in the geographical distribution of resources and economic activities engender additional factor remunerations, different levels of wealth and well-being, and different degrees of control over local development (Pike et al., 2016). Hence, the issue of the allocation of productive resources is more complex than conventionally believed by economists arguing the efficient distribution of factors among various types of production. This is because the spatial dimension of economic activity is also of crucial importance.

Space affects the way an economic system works. It is either a source of economic advantage or disadvantage, depending on the high or low endowment of production factors. It also generates "geographical advantages" such as the ease (or difficulty) of access to an area and the high (or low) endowment of raw materials. Space can also be the source of advantage arising from the cumulative nature of productive processes. In particular, spatial proximity—that is the physical closeness of economic actors (Boschma, 2005)—generates economies that reduce production costs (e.g., the transportation costs of operating in closely concentrated *filières*) and, in more modern terms, transaction costs (e.g., the costs of market transactions due to information gathering). These considerations have led to a move from a static approach to economic activity to a dynamic one in which space arises as an economic resource and an independent production factor that is a generator of advantages for the firms situated within a certain space. That said, it seems necessary to provide a conceptualization of space, because, at first glance, space appears a

S. Amato, A. Patuelli, *Family Firms and Local Roots*, CSR, Sustainability, Ethics & Governance, https://doi.org/10.1007/978-3-031-31793-4_3

fuzzy concept and, therefore, prone to different interpretations with relevant theoretical and methodological implications.

Until the 1970s, spatial thinking oscillated between two poles, namely the absolute and relative concepts of space (Mazúr & Urbánek, 1983; Suwala, 2021). Absolute space originates from the conceptualization of Ptolemy, Copernicus, Galilei, and Descartes and reflects the idea of space as a "container," defined with relative precision by a system of topographical coordinates, where a decoupling of the immobile space area and the mobile physical objects (e.g., persons, firms, and things) is conceivable. Through its independent ontological structure, absolute space is conceived as a superordinate complex of objects, without any pattern of relationships between the objects contained in it (Suwala, 2021), implying, at the same time, passive behavior of space concerning the objects themselves (Mazúr & Urbánek, 1983). Since space exists independently of any objects or relationships, the idea of space as a discrete and autonomous container is possible (Jones, 2009).

In contrast to absolute space, the idea of "relative" space comes to life because objects and/or processes exist and relate to each other. According to this conception, space does not retain its independence but conversely arises from the structure of the relative position of objects to each other (Suwala, 2021). By accentuating the importance of locations, relative positions, and ranges for forming societal and economic realities, space turns into an economic location through an allocation of significance by the observer. The relative conception of space mirrors Newton's view of space in which objects can be interpreted as location of maps of different reference scales because of the relative positions. At the same time, distance/relationships are relative because of changes over time and across space (Jones, 2009). From this view, different territorial units such as states, regions, cities, and neighborhoods emerge as spatial categorizations.

Since the 1970s, the concept of "relational space," also known as the "thinking space relationally" approach (Jones, 2009), has assumed growing relevance in both economic geography and regional studies, becoming the most influential paradigm. The economic actor is no longer the reference point (object) but an active agent (subject) who creates and influences space in the first place. At the same time, "rather than being passive, it (i.e., the space) affects the things it contains, arranging them into a certain spatial structure" (Mazúr & Urbánek, 1983, p. 140). In this concept, space is not only physical but relational, being created by and consisting of a set of relationships—market, power, and cooperative relationships—of economic actors (Capello, 2002). The relational approach understands space as a "social space" or network of relationships (Suwala, 2021) in which economic actors perform not as atomized agents but instead as participants in a flow of actions and interactions with the economic activity that is, therefore, "embedded in concrete, ongoing systems of social relations" (Granovetter, 1985, p. 487). Ultimately, this view regard space as relationally constituted, a product of social relationships (Malecki, 2012; Sunley, 2008).

The fourth and final concept of space is defined "topical," as conceptualized by the Japanese philosopher Nishida, and based on an individually perceptible space that is culturally shaped by geographical substance based on the cognitions, ways of

Table 3.1 An overview of the different concepts of space

Conception of space	Absolute	Relative	Relational	Topical
Visualized model	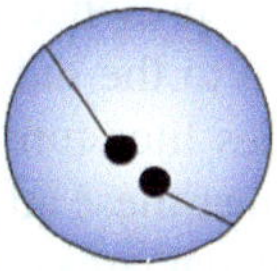	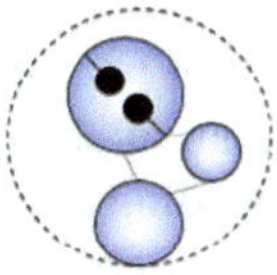		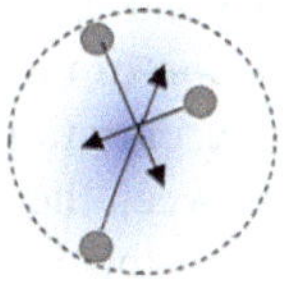
Metaphor	Container	Batch	Network	Field
Term	Space	Location	Place	Landscape
Categories	Points, dots, lines, surfaces, planes	Relative positions, routes, streets, administrative units	Relations, social bonds, social proximity	Landmarks, paths, perception
Relations	No relations	Marginal relations	Mono or polycentric relations	Topocentric relations
Philosophy	Ptolemy	Newton	Leibniz	Nishida
Meaning	No, just abstract and universal	Economic	Social	Cultural

Source*:* From Suwala (2021). Space Concepts, Re-figuration of Spaces and Comparative Research Perspectives from Economic Geography and Regional Economics. *Forum Qualitative Sozialforschung (FQS) /Forum: Qualitative Social Research*, *22*(3), p. 17

thinking, and views of life (in short: experiences) of individuals or groups of individuals. Thus, space receives a cultural meaning through personal and group experiences via space (Suwala, 2021). The result is spaces that are called "cultural landscapes," which are not landscapes in the conventional sense but "mental" landscapes, consisting of strong subjective emotions or normatively imposed images of the geographical substance (e.g., specific arrangements of the buildings, regions, and cities) of individuals (Greffe, 2010). Consequently, topical space transforms space into culturally determined landscapes by perception, interpretation, remembrance, or appropriation (Suwala, 2021).

Table 3.1 shows the distinguishing features and differences among the four conceptions of space.

3.2 The Location Advantages: Marshallian Versus Jacobinian Externalities

The interpretation of space as "relational" restored the concept of external or agglomeration economies as sources of both firm and territorial competitiveness (Capello, 2016). The concentration of economic activity in spatially bounded areas gives rise to advantages for the firms in the form of reduced production and transaction costs,[1] enhanced efficiency of the production factors, and increased innovative capacity. The term "external" means that agglomeration economies are beyond the control of the firm and typically result from the presence and collective action of other firms, thus external to the firm but internal to the industry or urban concentration (Parr, 2002a). The agglomeration economies literature differentiates between the two types of externalities, depending on whether these advantages stem from the location in either specialized or diversified spatial areas. This view of externalities is generally known as "Marshall–Jacobs dichotomy" (Galliano et al., 2015; Van der Panne, 2004).

The first conceptualization of external economies originates from Marshall's theory of industrial districts (1920) with his seminal work *The Principle of Economics*. It was subsequently taken up by Becattini et al. (2009) in Italy.[2] Localization economies, also known as Marshall-Arrow-Romer (MAR) agglomeration economies, are typically related to the degree of industrial specialization in the firm's local area. In particular, Marshall (1920) drew attention to three different sources of localization economies resulting in greater efficiency for the firms concentrated within a specialized and geographically bounded area. The first concerns "labor market pooling," which is access to a pool of labor with specific occupational skills and the related avoidance of shortages or bottlenecks in hiring (Jofre-Monseny et al., 2014). A second source involves the development of a network of dedicated suppliers for the provision of specialized intermediate goods and the availability of a range of specialized services. The third source of localization economies is related to the diffusion of information and knowledge, enabled by the geographical proximity (Boschma, 2005) that, once "created by one firm, may spill-over to other firms" (Van der Panne, 2004, p. 594). Knowledge spillovers are geographically bounded in the spatial context—region and local production system—in which new knowledge is created and subject to the distance-decay effect (Basile et al., 2012). As Marshall (1920) emphasized, knowledge is predominantly industry-specific, and knowledge spillovers arise between firms in the same industry and are characterized by an equivalent technological base.

Unlike Marshall, Jacobs (1969) emphasizes the role of urban space, that is, the city, as the place where agglomeration occurs. In particular, local diversity facilitates access to a qualified and diversified workforce, to a variety of infrastructure and facilities, and, even more importantly, to a complementary knowledge with the

[1] Parr (2002b, p. 152) defines agglomeration economy more broadly as a "decrease in the unit cost of a firm, consequent on the concentration of economic activity at a given location." The traditional conception of agglomeration externalities views these benefits as external economies of scale consisting in decreased average costs for the individual firm resulting from an increase in industry-wide output within a given geographical area. Hence, space becomes a source of *static* efficiency of the firm's production processes.

[2] The *Marshallian industrial district* denotes the existence of a local area characterised by a strong concentration of small and medium enterprises, mostly family owned and managed, each of which is specialized in one or few phases of the production process (Sforzi & Boix, 2015, p. 62).

Table 3.2 Source of static and dynamic urban economies

Spatial dimension Temporal dimension	Urban setting
Static	The city as "cluster" Presence of marked sectoral diversification Network density Reduction of transaction costs
Dynamic	The city as "milieu" Reducers of uncertainty: – Information transcoder – Ex ante coordinator of collective action – Substrate for collective learning

Source: Adapted from Capello (2016). *Regional Economics*, Routledge, p. 215

industry diversification that, contrary to industrial specialization, fosters productivity and innovation (Galliano et al., 2015; Jofre-Monseny et al., 2014). Thus, a diversified local production structure is deemed to increase returns, giving rise to the so-called urbanization economies or "Jacobs externalities."[3] The city is a spatial cluster of productive and residential activities (Parr, 2007). The concentration of a mix of sectors and diversified activities, the density of contacts that develop within them, and easy access to advanced information and knowledge are clear advantages arising from being located in urban settings, positively affecting the productivity of the firms situated therein (Capello, 2016). At the same time, cities can generate "dynamic" economies, thus, becoming the favored location for high-tech companies (Jofre-Monseny et al., 2014) as shown in Table 3.2. Just as much as the *milieu*, characterized by shared values, common codes of behavior, sense of belonging and mutual trust, the city plays a significant role in reducing uncertainty and generating the process of socialization of knowledge and collective learning (Capello, 2016).

Having said that, various approaches exist to measure Marshall and Jacob externalities. The location quotient (LQ) is the most commonly used indicator in the international literature for the evaluation of localization economies (Galliano et al., 2015; Van der Panne, 2004). LQ represents the relationship between a sub-national area's share (i.e., region, province, and municipality) of a particular industry and the national share. This share is, in the majority of cases, measured on employment.[4] It is calculated as the weight of a given sector k in a given geographic area i, considering the total weight of the sector k in the entire territory:

[3]With regard to urbanization economies, which are external to the individual firm and to its industry, these are internal to the urban concentration and cannot therefore be referred to as external economies of scale in the usual Marshallian sense. Rather, it is argued, these may be approached in terms of "economies of scope" (Parr, 2002b).

[4]As an alternative to the number of employees, Rensky (2011) computes the LQ in terms of establishment counts.

$$\mathrm{LQ}_{k,i} = \frac{S_{k,i}}{S_k}$$

An LQ above 1 suggests that sector k is overrepresented in the sub-national area i relative to the nation as a whole, which indicates a relative specialization of the sub-national area.

Conversely, the most commonly used indicator of Jacobs externalities is the Herfindhal index (H) which allows researchers to compare the distribution of the workforces in each zone according to the type of sector classification adopted.[5] The Herfindhal index for an area i with n sectors is expressed as follows:

$$H_i = \sum_{k=1}^{n} (S_{k,i})^2$$

A maximum value equal to 1 of H index indicates that all the employment is concentrated in one sector. Hence, a low value of the index reveals the existence of a diversity of activities capable of generating Jacobinian externalities.

3.3 Proximity, Knowledge Spillovers, and Innovation

The effects of space on economic activity not only result in the improvement of the static efficiency of production processes, as typically manifested in cost reduction but also in firms' innovative capabilities (Parr, 2002b). In this case, location and geographical space become a source of dynamic efficiency (Capello, 2017) or, put differently, "key factors in explaining the determinant of innovation and technological change" (Audretsch & Feldman, 2004, p. 2714). That is because geographical concentration simplifies and encourages the exchange of information and tacit knowledge,[6] face-to-face encounters, the exploitation of technological and scientific knowledge developed by R&D centers, and last but not least, the ready availability of skilled labor and advanced services (Audretsch & Feldman, 1996). The results and the beneficial effects of R&D are not confined to the organization's boundaries but instead "spill-over" into the surrounding environment to the advantage of co-located firms (Breschi & Lissoni, 2010). Hence, such spillovers denote a

[5] The Gini index, which is similar to the Herfindhal index, represents an alternative and largely employed indicator for capturing diversification externalities (Galliano et al., 2015).

[6] A relevant implication of the difference between information and tacit knowledge is that, while the marginal cost of transmitting the former across the geographic space has been rendered invariant by the ICT (Information and Communication Technologies) revolutions, the marginal cost of transmitting the latter is positively associated with spatial distance (Audretsch & Feldman, 2004).

free-of-charge flow of knowledge that is exchanged formally or informally across physically proximate firms (Kesidou et al., 2009).[7]

In explaining the role of space as the determinant of a firm's innovative capacity and territorial innovativeness, the concept of proximity arises as a necessary condition (Morgan, 2004). As Boschma points out (2005, p. 63), the different dimensions of proximity have in common the ability to "reduce uncertainty and solve the problem of coordination and, thus, facilitate interactive learning and innovation." In particular, Capello (2016) identifies the following four complementary dimensions of proximity:

- *Geographical* or *spatial* proximity, the physical distance between firms. By bringing people together closeness facilitates face-to-face contact and, hence, the exchange of codified knowledge. Empirical studies show that knowledge spillovers are fundamentally territorially bounded, as firms near the sources of knowledge perform better than firms located elsewhere (Acs et al., 1994; Audretsch & Feldman, 1996).
- *Social* or *relational* proximity, which relates to the quality and nature of dyadic relationships between actors. Stemming from the embeddedness literature (Granovetter, 1985, 2005), social proximity entails the developing of trust-based and reciprocal social relationships that facilitate the exchange of tacit knowledge and minimize, at the same time, the risk of opportunism (Boschma, 2005).[8] Socially embedded relationships are generally regarded as a prerequisite for interactive learning. This is because, as opposed to trust-based, committed, and durable relationships, relations based on purely market interests dissolve whenever problems among parties arise.
- *Institutional* proximity, taking the form of rules, routines, established practices, and norms regulating the interactions between economic actors (e.g., people, firms, and local institutions). Institutions act as a "glue" for collective actions, influencing the way and the extent to which actions are coordinated. Therefore, institutional proximity: (1) facilitates cooperation and, consequently, the level of knowledge transfer; and (2) assists economic actors in developing organizational forms supporting interactive learning.
- -*Cognitive* proximity, the existence of commonly held knowledge and expertise enables economic actors to communicate, understand, and process what they learn successfully, whereas below a certain threshold firms cannot identify, absorb and exploit new information (Boschma, 2005; Cohen & Levinthal, 1990).

[7]One of the main arguments for the emergence of knowledge spillovers is the existence of public knowledge which is "non-rival" and "non-excludable" in consumption. A good is non-rival, when the consumption by someone does not preclude the opportunity for others to consume it at the same time. A good is non-excludible in the extent to which, once it has been made, it is impossible or extremely difficult preclude the consumption by anyone who has not paid for obtaining it.

[8]Boschma (2005, p. 66) defines social proximity in terms of "socially embedded relations between agents at the micro-level. Relations between actors are socially embedded when they involve trust based on friendship, kinship and experience." The concept of social proximity is strongly related to that of social embeddedness that I shall explore this more thoroughly in Sect. 4.1 of Chap. 4, especially with regard to its spatial implications (i.e., local embeddedness).

Economic geographers, supported mainly by industrial economists, tend to emphasize the importance of mere spatial proximity as a precondition for the diffusion of local, sticky, knowledge among spatially concentrated firms, which affects their innovation capacity (Bathelt et al., 2004; Malmberg & Maskell, 2006). On the other hand, regional economists observe that spatial propinquity is a necessary but not sufficient condition for the exchange of knowledge to take place in a given area (Capello, 2002; Capello & Faggian, 2005). This is because geographical proximity has to be complemented by social proximity encompassing all socio-economic interactions and interpersonal synergies, embedded in informal and more formalized cooperation among local actors, based on trust and a sense of belonging to a culturally homogenous community.[9] Such socio-economic relationships characterize the innovative capability and economic success of specific local areas known as *milieu* innovators, which partly overlap with the traditional industrial districts (Camagni, 1995; Crevoisier, 2009).[10]

That said, social or relational proximity is deemed to generate three types of dynamic advantages. First, collective learning is a dynamic and cumulative process of knowledge creation, diffusion, and appropriation that occurs mainly through interactive mechanisms among local economic actors (Kirat & Lung, 1999). The locution "collective" means that learning occurs in a socialized context with learning taking place outside individual firms but within the local area[11] (Capello, 2002). The second dynamic advantage resides in the reduction of uncertainty associated with the innovation processes. While in large firms, the function of information gathering, the codification of knowledge, and the selection of decision-making routines are generally performed by internal R&D departments, in highly socialized and, therefore, socially embedded local areas such as the *innovative milieu*, these functions are carried out collectively embracing the local area as a whole (Capello, 2016). The third and last dynamic advantage is the reduction of coordination costs across decision-making units. The sharing of common values and similar codes of behavior develops trust, loyalty, and social sanctions that discourage opportunistic

[9] From this perspective, the concept of cultural homogeneity is somewhat overlapping with that of "cultural proximity" consisting in the sharing of same values among local economic actors, which is at the foundation of the high level of cooperation of a given territory (Capello & Faggian, 2005).

[10] Camagni (Camagni, 1995) defines *innovative milieu* as "the set of relationships that occur within a geographical area that bring unity to production system, economic actors, and an industrial culture, that generate a localized dynamic process of collective learning and that act as an uncertainty-reducing mechanism in the innovation process." Examples of *innovative milieu* were found in metropolitan specialized in advanced types of production (e.g., north-eastern part of Milan), in non-metropolitan industrialized areas (e.g., many areas in the Third Italy) old industrial areas (e.g., the Swiss Jura specialized in watch production) and poles of excellence (e.g., Silicon Valley).

[11] Collective learning is the territorial counterpart of learning processes occurring inside the firm. As compared to the "interactive learning," which envisions an explicit decision of cooperate by the local firms, collective learning is related to the spontaneous exchange of knowledge, which occurs through social contact at local level (Capello, 2016).

behavior, thereby reducing the costs of monitoring (Capello, 2016; Kirat & Lung, 1999).

The main contribution of the concept of relational space, whose main conceptualization is the *milieu* innovator theory, is that it explains the channels through which knowledge spillovers occur (Capello & Faggian, 2005). In particular, empirical econometric analysis (e.g., Kesidou et al., 2009; Kesidou & Romijn, 2008) has corroborated the importance of the following mechanisms that contribute to local knowledge diffusion influencing a firm's innovation performance: (1) high labor mobility, consisting in the hiring of workforce endowed with specific information and knowledge relevant for the firm's technological advancement; (2) spin-off ventures by former employees of universities, transnational corporations (TNC) or leading firms within the local area which give rise to the circulation of human-embodied knowledge in the *milieu*; (3) informal interaction, originating from face-to-face contacts, co-presence, and co-location within the same industry and place of local actors.[12] When occurring within clusters of firms or spatially bounded areas (Porter, 2000), the aforementioned social interaction and information exchange is known as "local buzz" or "local broadcasting" and has attracted considerable interest in the investigation of knowledge transfer dynamics, regarding innovation, in particular, of local production systems (e.g., Bathelt et al., 2004; Malmberg & Maskell, 2006).

In addition, since the innovative process is strongly localized, it is influenced by the institutional context in which it takes place (Torre & Rallet, 2005). From this perspective, the concept of "institutional thickness" (Amin & Thrift, 1995) identifies the local conditions supportive of innovative capacity building, hence, regional and local development (Pike et al., 2016).[13] A high level of local interaction provides the basis for the generation of a shared and commonly accepted set of norms, codes, and rules of behaviors thus "creating a particular social atmosphere and relations of trust" (Coulson & Ferrario, 2007, p. 593). Institutional proximity, therefore, is deemed to facilitate "interactive learning," which is a learning process based on cooperation and the exchange of knowledge, which is the key to innovation at local level and, ultimately, for the wider area (Rutten & Boekema, 2012).[14]

---

[12] By drawing on survey data from a software cluster in a developing country, Kesidou and Romijn (2008) identify six types of informal interactions that take place at local level: (1) interactions at exhibitions and conferences; (2) horizontal interaction (i.e., with competitors); (3) backward linkages (i.e., with suppliers); (4) forward linkages (i.e., with distributors and customers); (5) interaction with universities and research institutes; and (6) interaction with support institutes.

[13] These local conditions are attributable to: (1) a strong local institutional presence; (2) high level of interaction between local organizations; (3) a mutual awareness of being involved in a common enterprise; and (4) structures of domination and/or patterns of coalition (Coulson & Ferrario, 2007).

[14] The learning region identifies a socio-economic system able to develop interactive learning internally. In particular, Rutten and Boekema (2012, p. 986) define it as a region in which "regional actors engage in collaboration and coordination for mutual benefit, resulting in a process of regional learning. Regional characteristics affect the degree to which the process of regional learning leads to regional renewal."

Finally, the ability of spatially concentrated firms to innovate is heavily dependent upon their ability to identify, absorb, and capitalize on the information and knowledge present at the local level. This ability, in turn, depends on the presence of a common knowledge base within the industry. Cognitive proximity requires local firms to be endowed with similar knowledge background, common language, and mutual understanding that support local actors in the definition of new technological solutions (Davids & Frenken, 2018). Cognitive proximity further enhances the concept of "absorptive capacity" (Cohen & Levinthal, 1990; Giuliani & Bell, 2005), which involves the ability of a firm to recognize the value of external knowledge and to apply it for innovation. Thus, absorptive capacity highlights a cognitive capacity based on a firm's specific knowledge base that traditionally characterizes a given territory or place (Capello, 2016). The common understanding of technological aspects enabled by cognitive proximity and the other positive externalities stemming from the abovementioned proximity dimensions—reducing the risk of opportunistic behavior, uncertainty, and transaction costs—bolsters knowledge transfer and, in turn, the firm's innovative capabilities.

3.4 Firms in Agglomerated Areas: From Industrial Districts to Business Clusters

Economists and geographers investigating why firms agglomerate in specific locations and benefit from external economies have coined a large *corpus* of neologisms "to capture and represent the spatial form and nature of local business concentrations" (Martin & Sunley, 2003, p. 3). The most popular, igniting massive and ongoing research in recent decades, are the notions of industrial districts and clusters. Both share essential characteristics, such as the analysis of location in global competition and the way that agglomeration of economic activity and the interaction of co-located firms influence economic and innovation performance (Porter & Ketels, 2009). For this reason, the terms industrial districts and cluster are usually used interchangeably, albeit belonging to distinct traditions of study.

The concept of the industrial district can be traced back to Alfred Marshall[15] in England at the turn of the twentieth century. As a result of the long-lasting localization, an industry concentrated in certain localities develops important features, turning from a mere industry localization to a Marshallian Industrial District (MID). These features include:

- The hereditary skills are transmitted across generations, becoming the distinctive feature of the area.

[15] Alfred Marshall (1842–1924) is also the founder of the Cambridge School of Economics and neoclassical economics.

- The division of labor and specialization among firms in the district, which results in plant disintegration but local integration enhancing firm efficiency and productivity.
- A high degree of technological complementarities, and a peculiar combination of competition and cooperation, the so-called "coopetition."
- Finally, an "industrial atmosphere," which furthers the flow of knowledge in the districts (Belussi & Caldari, 2009). According to Marshall, small district firms can compete with the large vertically integrated ones due to the presence of such external economies.

The district model re-emerged strongly in the 1970s with the pioneering studies of Becattini into the competitiveness of the Italian manufacturing SMEs compared to the dominant Fordist production model.[16] Becattini defines an industrial district as a "socio-territorial entity which is characterized by the active presence of people and a population of firms in one naturally and historically bounded area" (Becattini et al., 2009, p. 347). Becattini's view of industrial districts emphasizes the social and institutional forces shaping and regulating firm interaction. Both market and community logics govern the economic activity in the district (Chiarvesio et al., 2010). Firms are indeed embedded in a homogenous setting, where shared social and cultural values, practices, and productive skills give rise to a strong sense of belonging to the local area (Boschma & Lambooy, 2002). Trust-based relationships portray the district social capital that acts both as "glue" for the localized network and "lubricant" for firms' organizational decisions (Bertolini & Giovannetti, 2006). Local institutions play a crucial role in the district by fostering trust and cooperation, accessing additional sources of information, and establishing links outside the district (Belso-Martínez, 2010).

The empirical research on MIDs has mainly focused on their identification[17] (Canello & Pavone, 2016), their evolution in the face of the ongoing globalization and technological change (Guerrieri & Pietrobelli, 2004), and the "district-effect" on firms' outcomes. Indeed, thanks to the growing availability of microdata, the scientific community has managed to capture and estimate the competitive advantages that district localization provides—because of agglomeration economies and the district social environment—compared to firms outside the district. One outcome most assessed by empirical research is the productivity/efficiency and financial performance brought about by localization in MIDs (Becchetti et al., 2007;

[16]Using the local labor market (LLM) areas, the Italian National Institute of Statistics has identified in the ISTAT-Census (2011) 141 industrial districts. They are scattered throughout the country, with a prevalence in the northeast of the country (45 industrial districts). More than 90% of them are specialized in the production typical of Made in Italy, such as mechanical industry (27.0%), textile and clothing (22.7%), furniture (17.0%), and leather and footwear (12.1%).

[17]The Sforzi-ISTAT method was employed in the latest census to map the IDs in Italy. After defining local labor market (LLM) areas, a set of statistical tests based on employment concentration quotients is used to identify: the prevalence of manufacturing activities, the significant presence of SMEs, and high levels of industrial specialization. Such conditions are assumed to be consistent with the presence of an ID.

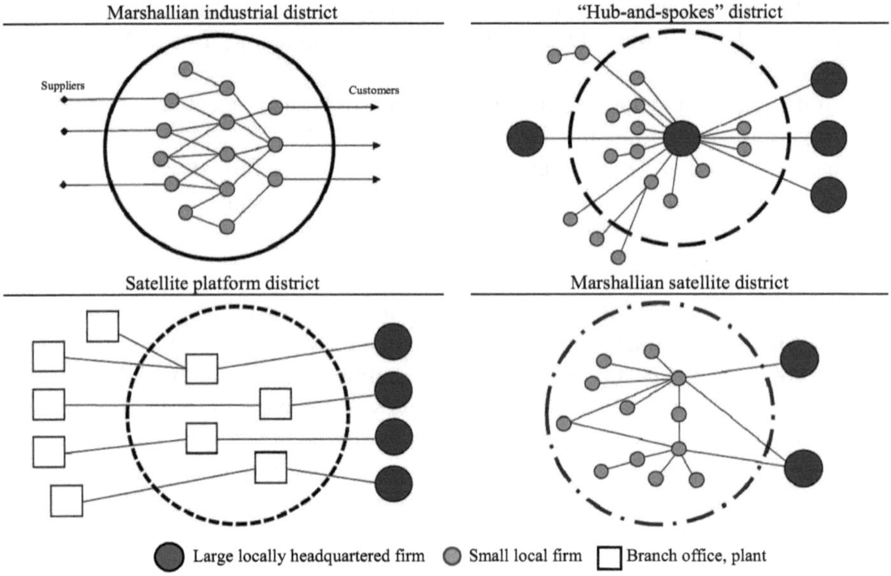

Fig. 3.1 Types of industrial districts. Source: adapted from Markusen (1996) and Coe (2001)

Molina-Morales, 2001). Further evidence shows that interfirm local networks allow district firms to tap into local export spillovers.[18] They consist of a spatially bounded flow of information regarding exporting and the features of foreign markets (Choquette & Meinen, 2015), boosting the export performance of co-located firms. Finally, due to technological spillovers, an "I-district effect" provides district firms with a superior innovation capability over others (Boix & Trullén, 2010).

An interesting categorization of industrial districts is that proposed by Markusen (1996) and Coe (2001), which focuses on three basic classificatory principles: firm size, interfirm relationships, and internal versus external orientations (Fig. 3.1).

The first typology is the traditional *Marshallian* (and *Italianate*) industrial district. This typology portrays a business structure dominated by small and locally-owned firms, with considerable intradistrict trade of buyers and suppliers bound by long-term contracts and informal commitments. The linkages and cooperation with firms outside the district are assumed to be minimal. Firms are embedded in a homogenous institutional setting consisting of shared cultural and social values and a strong sense of belonging.

[18]There are various channels through which local export spillovers occur. Intra-industry linkages among firms operating in the same industry. Labor mobility of workers with market-specific information. The networks of buyer–supplier relationships. And finally, informal interactions, mainly on the occasion of social gatherings. Proximity dimensions in MIDs facilitate the transmission of this type of information (Choquette & Meinen, 2015).

In the *Hub-and-Spoke* type of industrial district, a single or few large key firms (e.g., Boeing in Seattle) act as anchors or hubs to the regional economy, surrounded by smaller firms and suppliers along the spokes of a wheel. The large hub firms also often have substantial links to suppliers, competitors, and customers outside the district and are always in a position to set the terms of long-term cooperation with suppliers.

In the *Satellite Platforms*, the business structure is dominated by a congregation of large, externally owned firms, with headquarters outside the area. Their establishment in the region is often due to policies (e.g., tax breaks) stimulating regional development. As key investment decisions are made out of the ID, tenants must be able to more or less "stand-alone," that is, to be spatially independent of either up- or downstream operations as well as from the agglomeration of other competitors and suppliers in the same area. Cooperation between platform firms tends to be minimal, as is intradistrict trade between buyers and suppliers.[19]

Finally, the *Marshallian satellite* industrial district combines the features of the small-firm network with the external dependency of the satellite platform. In such a configuration, the business structure is dominated by a mass of small and locally-owned firms. As key investment decisions are made externally, there is a high degree of cooperation between local firms to develop the district.

In the 1990s, the cluster theory proposed by Porter sought to explain the advantages of co-location. Although cluster theory also benefitted from the industrial district paradigm, it is broader and more general starting from its definition. Porter defines a cluster as "a geographically proximate group of interconnected companies and associated institutions in a particular field, linked by commonalities and complementarities. The geographic scope of a cluster can be a single city or state or a country or even a network of neighboring countries" (2000, p. 199). Several features differentiate Porter's cluster model from the industrial district *à la* Becattini. While the community of people is the starting point and the social component the key element of the industrial district theory, Porter's point of departure is the analysis of firm's value chain. Regarding the unit of analysis, this is the industrial district for Becattini envisioned as a specialized local area in a particular industry, where a community of people and a number of firms tend to merge. For Porter, the focus shifts to the firm, explaining why the firm's competitive advantage differs according to the location. As to the geographical scope, this is more clearly defined in the case of industrial districts around an area not necessarily administratively and juridically demarcated but chiefly local, with a strong identity component due to natural and historical reasons as well as a productive vocation. Conversely, the cluster approach

[19]When a key anchor tenant in the district is a public or non-profit entity (e.g., a large public university, lab, and military base), the *State-anchored* industrial district does emerge. The local business structure is dominated by the presence of such facilities, hence resembling the satellite platform case. The location choices and economic relationships are determined by political entities rather than by the private sector. Even though facilities can operate with few or minimal connections to the regional economy, some new SMEs may emerge from technological transfer (e.g., via universities) or business services provided by (or spilling over from) the anchor institution.

does not define the geographical scope with clarity, which may span from local to transnational with interconnected firms operating in different countries. What differentiates Porter's cluster model from the Marshallian industrial district is also the aim of the two models. With the industrial district model, Becattini investigated what lay at the foundation of Italy's extraordinary growth during the 1970s, especially in the Northeast of "Belpaese." Instead, the cluster concept developed in the globalization era when production became increasingly fragmented into networks across many and often physically distant locations, and digital and communication technologies had seemingly cancelled out the spatial limits of information transfer (Ortega-Colomer et al., 2016; Porter & Ketels, 2009). However, the cluster model has become the most influential paradigm for European policy-makers aiming to improve firm and regional competitiveness and innovation (European Commission, 2008).[20]

3.5 SMEs in Peripheral Areas

A considerable number of firms are located outside the major agglomerations of socio-economic activity and thus do not benefit from the "location quality" arising from the prevalence of geographically bounded characteristics, such as the local endowment of physical and human resources, localized knowledge and information, the intense local competition, and business opportunities discussed above (Mueller & Jungwirth, 2022). Firms may operate in the so-called "peripheral" areas (or geographical blind spots) characterized by relatively few firms and people, limited resources, poor accessibility, and distance (geographical remoteness) from the "core" economic areas (or geographical hot spots) (Pike et al., 2016). Peripheral areas are far from the core of the knowledge economy, while the low level of clustering and agglomeration hinders the opportunities for interaction with the result that these regions struggle to catch up (Virkkala, 2007). They usually carry on traditional activities with a lower growth capacity (García-Cortijo et al., 2019).

The periphery-core debate essentially revolves mainly around the rural-urban dichotomy. Quantitative criteria such as demography[21] and distance (travel time)

[20] Among the EU cluster initiatives is the European Cluster Collaboration Platform (ECCP), whose ultimate goal is to ease cluster collaboration between clusters in Europe and between cluster members. ECCP reports 2.950 regional industrial clusters across Europe. In 2022, Italy consisted of 86 cluster organizations. For more information, please see https://reporting.clustercollaboration.eu/

[21] Eurostat defines "rural areas" as all areas outside urban clusters. "Urban clusters" are clusters of contiguous grid cells of 1 km^2 with a density of at least 300 inhabitants per km^2 and a minimum population of 5000. On the basis of the share of their population in rural areas, NUTS 3 regions are classified as follows: (1) "Predominantly rural," if the share of the population living in rural areas is higher than 50%; (2) "Intermediate," if the share of the population living in rural areas is between 20% and 50%; (3) "Predominantly urban," when the population living in rural areas is below 20%. The US Census Bureau defines rural areas based on similar population criteria.

from the main welfare services are employed to identify rural areas by both empirical research and policy-makers aiming to reduce territorial marginalization and foster growth and well-being (Pagliacci et al., 2020). However, there are also qualitative "softer" criteria such as rural identity. Rural identity embodies a common ancestry or heritage shared by people who inhabit in a culturally defined place, which is perceived as authentic. Agriculture and other productive activities—such as craftsmanship and local tourism—can become a useful base for building place-sensitive territorial policies (Basile & Cavallo, 2020). The National Strategy for Inner Areas (SNAI)[22] in Italy maps the national territory based on the travel time from the main service centers—that is, municipalities that offer an exhaustive range of secondary schools, at least a first-level DEA (highly specialized) hospital, and at least a "silver-type" railway station—into four areas:

- "Belt" areas, whether the municipality is up to 20 min from the centers
- "Intermediate" areas, from 20 to 40 min
- "Remote" areas, from 40 to 75 min
- "Ultra-remote" areas, over 75 min far

Intermediate, remote, and ultra-remote areas are referred to as "Inner" areas. Such areas cover about 60% of the Italian territory, hosting a population of almost 13,500 million inhabitants, equal to about a quarter of the Italian population divided into over 4000 municipalities as shown in Fig. 3.2 and Table 3.3. These areas have a territorial capital of exceptional value and diversity in terms of natural assets (water resources, agricultural systems, forests, natural landscapes) and cultural resources (archaeological settlements, abbeys, small museums, craft centers), which are largely underused due to the long-term demographic decline going back to the 1950s (Basile & Cavallo, 2020). Besides the geographic isolation, lack of essential services and high-skilled workers, and demographic decline, underdeveloped digital infrastructure usually characterizes rural areas compared to urban ones (Beckmann et al., 2021). In a knowledge-based economy—in other words, today's economy—the digital divide can further marginalize the socio-economic fabric of rural areas, stifling their prospects of economic growth (Morris et al., 2022).

Firms located in peripheral areas have to cope with below-average locational quality. Conventional wisdom suggests that, because of location constraints, these firms have a competitive disadvantage compared to firms located in core areas or agglomerations (Mueller & Jungwirth, 2022; Vaessen & Keeble, 1995). Empirical evidence suggests that peripherally located firms perceive their regions at a disadvantage vis-à-vis centrally located counterparts regarding financial access, physical infrastructure (Amorós et al., 2013), and believe that limited access to skilled labor stifles their growth potential (Gherhes et al., 2021). This adverse effect is also

[22]The SNAI is part of the EU territorial cohesion, included for the first time in the Lisbon Treaty, which seeks to reduce disparities between the levels of development of various regions, focusing on the least developed regions in Europe, mainly rural areas.

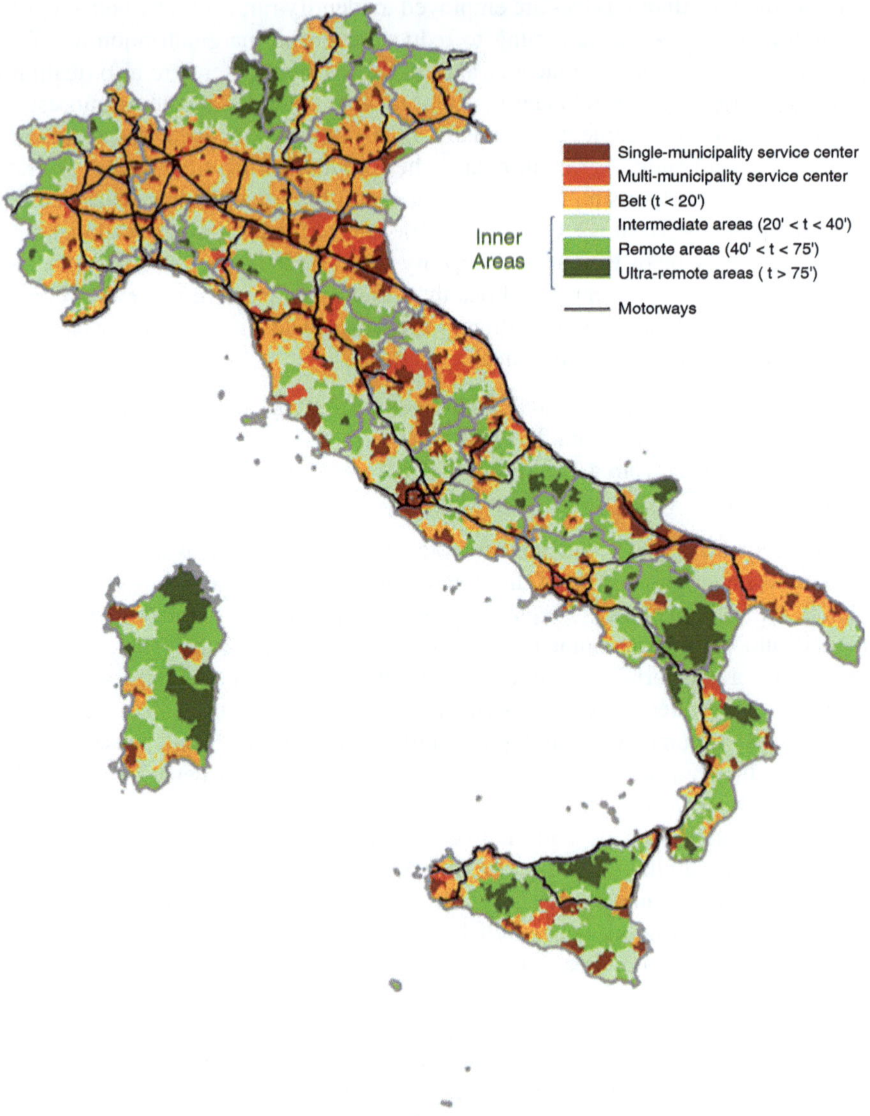

Fig. 3.2 The map of inner areas in Italy. Source: from Locatelli (2016). A Strategy for "Inner Areas" in Italy. X European Mountain Convention - Euromontana

contingent on the firm's size. Microenterprises—that may benefit considerably from closeness to markets, easier access to inputs, and greater networking opportunities with larger firms—are adversely affected by geographical remoteness (Masakure et al., 2009). When it comes to acquiring finance, innovative firms suffer from what is known as "liability of distance." That is to say, they are more likely to have their

Table 3.3 Figures of Italy's inner areas

Classification of municipalities	N.	%	Average elevation	Population	%	km^2	%
Single Municipality Service Center	217	2.7	148	20,983,786	35.3	28,948	9.6
Multi-Municipality Service Center	122	1.5	195	2,986,161	5	8606	2.8
Belt areas	3568	44.1	219	22,135,047	37.2	83,982	27.8
Intermediate areas	2360	29.2	399	8,832,422	14.9	88,187	29.2
Remote areas	1522	18.8	601	3,812,271	6.4	72,829	24.1
Ultra-remote areas	303	3.7	666	684,057	1.2	19,521	6.5
Total	8902	100	358	59,433,744	100	302,073	100

Source: From Locatelli (2016). A Strategy for "Inner Areas" in Italy. X European Mountain Convention—Euromontana. Elaboration on Istat-Census 2011

loan applications rejected than firms located elsewhere (Lee & Brown, 2017). However, physical proximity to education centers and research institutes (García-Cortijo et al., 2019) and cooperative relationships with distant partners (Mueller & Jungwirth, 2022; Virkkala, 2007) are deemed to mitigate the unfavorable conditions of peripheral areas.

Figure 3.3 shows the SWOT analysis for SMEs in peripheral settings, which may represent a source of opportunities for firms located therein. The strong local culture, identity, and social capital make it easier to rely on relational-based and long-term partnerships such as networks and informal cooperation (Pagliacci et al., 2020), counteracting both the inherent weaknesses of SMEs and location disadvantages of rural areas (Beckmann et al., 2021).

3.6 Concluding Remarks

A firm's economic activity is not "spaceless" but rather takes in geographically bounded areas that may become either source of advantage or disadvantage. This chapter has aimed to disentangle the concept of space and its influence on business outcomes. The "relational" view—emphasizing the relational nature of space beside the physical attributes—has become the prominent paradigm in investigating economic activity across spatial settings. Such a paradigm has restored the relevance of externalities arising from either the local specialization (i.e., MAR externalities) or local variety (i.e., Jacobinian externalities), underlying the competitiveness of firms and territories. Spatial and non-spatial proximity dimensions shape the interaction of firms and their ability to benefit from the location in agglomerated areas. Though Marshallian industrial districts and business clusters have dominated the academic and policy debate, many firms are nevertheless located outside agglomerations. The chapter ends with analysis of SMEs in peripheral areas.

	Advantageous	Disadvantageous
	Strengths	**Weaknesses**
Firm perspective	- Access to local social capital - Family and local ownership - Intimate closeness and closeness to local community and customers - Willingness to innovate - Specialized skills - Ability to networking	- Age structure and conservative culture - Reactive and short-term management - Limited innovation input (i.e., R&D expenditures) - Specialized skills limited to niche - Lack/limited resources (e.g. human, financial)
	Opportunities	**Threats**
Spatial perspective	- The rural lifestyle - Tight-knight communities (i.e., social capital) - Natural resources - Unique cultural identity - Authenticity	- Lack of economic growth - Geographical isolation - Demographic decline - Lack of main service centers (i.e., schools, hospitals, and railways) - Poor infrastructures and digital divide - Reduced access to financial services - Resistance against change

Fig. 3.3 SWOT analysis for SMEs in rural areas. Source: adapted from Beckmann et al. (2021), p. 17

As firms are not devoid of connections with their local area, some may be more constrained by the economic activity and social dynamics in that location than others. The following chapter digs deeper into the way people and firms are "anchored" to territories. It does so by disentangling the place attachment of the dominant coalition and local embeddedness of the firm.

References

Acs, Z. J., Audretsch, D. B., & Feldman, M. P. (1994). R&D spillovers and recipient firm size. *The Review of Economics and Statistics, 76*(2), 336–340. https://doi.org/10.2307/2109888

Amin, A., & Thrift, N. (1995). Institutional issues for the European regions: From markets and plans to socioeconomics and powers of association. *Economy and Society, 24*(1), 41–66. https://doi.org/10.1080/03085149500000002

Amorós, J. E., Felzensztein, C., & Gimmon, E. (2013). Entrepreneurial opportunities in peripheral versus core regions in Chile. *Small Business Economics, 40*, 119–139. https://doi.org/10.1007/s11187-011-9349-0

Audretsch, D. B., & Feldman, M. P. (1996). R&D spillovers and the geography of innovation and production. *American Economic Review, 86*(3), 630–640. https://doi.org/10.2307/2118216

Audretsch, D. B., & Feldman, M. P. (2004). Knowledge spillovers and the geography of innovation. In *Handbook of Regional and Urban Economics* (pp. 2713–2739). https://doi.org/10.1016/S1574-0080(04)80018-X

Basile, G., & Cavallo, A. (2020). Rural identity, authenticity, and sustainability in Italian inner areas. *Sustainability, 12*(3), 1272. https://doi.org/10.3390/su12031272

Basile, R., Capello, R., & Caragliu, A. (2012). Technological interdependence and regional growth in Europe: Proximity and synergy in knowledge spillovers. *Papers in Regional Science, 91*(4), 697–722. https://doi.org/10.1111/j.1435-5957.2012.00438.x

Bathelt, H., Malmberg, A., & Maskell, P. (2004). Clusters and knowledge: Local buzz, global pipelines and the process of knowledge creation. *Progress in Human Geography, 28*(1), 31–56. https://doi.org/10.1191/0309132504ph469oa

Becattini, G., Bellandi, M., & De Propris, L. (2009). *A handbook of industrial districts*. Elgar Edward Publishing. https://doi.org/10.4337/9781781007808

Becchetti, L., De Panizza, A., & Oropallo, F. (2007). Role of industrial district externalities in export and value-added performance: Evidence from the population of Italian firms. *Regional Studies, 41*(5), 601–621. https://doi.org/10.1080/00343400701281691

Beckmann, M., Garkisch, M., & Zeyen, A. (2021). Together we are strong? A systematic literature review on how SMEs use relation-based collaboration to operate in rural areas. *Journal of Small Business and Entrepreneurship, 0*(0), 1–37. https://doi.org/10.1080/08276331.2021.1874605

Belso-Martínez, J. A. (2010). International outsourcing and partner location in the Spanish footwear sector: An analysis based in industrial district SMEs. *European Urban and Regional Studies, 17* (1), 65–82. https://doi.org/10.1177/0969776409350789

Belussi, F., & Caldari, K. (2009). At the origin of the industrial district: Alfred Marshall and the Cambridge school. *Cambridge Journal of Economics, 33*(2), 335–355. https://doi.org/10.1093/cje/ben041

Bertolini, P., & Giovannetti, E. (2006). Industrial districts and internationalization: The case of the agri-food industry in Modena. *Italy. Entrepreneurship and Regional Development, 18*(4), 279–304. https://doi.org/10.1080/08985620600613761

Boix, R., & Trullén, J. (2010). Industrial districts, innovation and I-district effect: Territory or industrial specialization? *European Planning Studies, 18*(10), 1707–1729. https://doi.org/10.1080/09654313.2010.504351

Boschma, R. (2005). Proximity and innovation: A critical assessment. *Regional Studies, 39*(1), 61–74. https://doi.org/10.1080/0034340052000320887

Boschma, R., & Lambooy, J. G. (2002). Knowledge, market structure, and economic coordination: Dynamics of industrial districts. *Growth and Change, 33*(2), 291–311. https://doi.org/10.1111/1468-2257.00192

Breschi, S., & Lissoni, F. (2010). Localised knowledge spillovers vs. innovative milieux: Knowledge "tacitness" reconsidered. *Papers in Regional Science, 80*(3), 255–273. https://doi.org/10.1111/j.1435-5597.2001.tb01799.x

Camagni, R. P. (1995). The concept of innovative milieu and its relevance for public policies in European lagging regions. *Papers in Regional Science, 74*(4), 317–340. https://doi.org/10.1111/j.1435-5597.1995.tb00644.x

Canello, J., & Pavone, P. (2016). Mapping the multifaceted patterns of industrial districts: A new empirical procedure with application to Italian data. *Regional Studies, 50*(8), 1374–1387. https://doi.org/10.1080/00343404.2015.1011611

Capello, R. (2002). Spatial and sectoral characteristics of relational capital in innovation activity. *European Planning Studies, 10*(2), 177–200. https://doi.org/10.1080/09654310120114 48

Capello, R. (2016). *Regional economics*. Routledge. https://doi.org/10.4324/9781315720074

Capello, R. (2017). *Seminal studies in regional and urban economics: Contributions from an impressive mind*. Springer. https://doi.org/10.1007/978-3-319-57807-1

Capello, R., & Faggian, A. (2005). Collective learning and relational capital in local innovation processes. *Regional Studies, 39*(1), 75–87. https://doi.org/10.1080/0034340052000320851

Chiarvesio, M., Di Maria, E., & Micelli, S. (2010). Global value chains and open networks: The case of Italian industrial districts. *European Planning Studies, 18*(3), 333–350. https://doi.org/10.1080/09654310903497637

Choquette, E., & Meinen, P. (2015). Export spillovers: Opening the black box. *World Economy, 38*(12), 1912–1946. https://doi.org/10.1111/twec.12225

Coe, N. M. (2001). A hybrid agglomeration? The development of a satellite-marshallian industrial district in Vancouver's film industry. *Urban Studies, 38*(10), 1753–1775. https://doi.org/10.1080/00420980120084840

Cohen, W. M., & Levinthal, D. A. (1990). Absorptive capacity: A new perspective on learning and innovation. *Administrative Science Quarterly, 35*(1), 128–152. https://doi.org/10.1177/0149206310369939

Coulson, A., & Ferrario, C. (2007). "Institutional thickness": Local governance and economic development in Birmingham, England. *International Journal of Urban and Regional Research, 31*(3), 591–615. https://doi.org/10.1111/j.1468-2427.2007.00739.x

Crevoisier, O. (2009). The Innovative milieus approach: Toward a territorialized understanding of the economy? *Economic Geography, 80*(4), 367–379. https://doi.org/10.1111/j.1944-8287.2004.tb00243.x

Davids, M., & Frenken, K. (2018). Proximity, knowledge base and the innovation process: Towards an integrated framework. *Regional Studies, 52*(1), 23–34. https://doi.org/10.1080/00343404.2017.1287349

European Commission. (2008). *The concept of clusters and cluster policies and their role for competitiveness and innovation: Main statistical lessons learned.* Commission Staff Working Document SEC (2008) (Vol. 2637). Retrieved from http://www.ncbi.nlm.nih.gov/pubmed/19097363

Galliano, D., Magrini, M., & Triboulet, P. (2015). Marshall's versus Jacobs' externalities in firm innovation performance: The case of French industry. *Regional Studies, 49*(11), 1840–1858. https://doi.org/10.1080/00343404.2014.950561

García-Cortijo, M. C., Castillo-Valero, J. S., & Carrasco, I. (2019). Innovation in rural Spain. What drives innovation in the rural-peripheral areas of southern Europe? *Journal of Rural Studies, 71*, 114–124. https://doi.org/10.1016/j.jrurstud.2019.02.027

Gherhes, C., Vorley, T., & Brooks, C. (2021). The "additional costs" of being peripheral: Developing a contextual understanding of micro-business growth constraints. *Journal of Small Business and Enterprise Development, 28*(1), 59–84. https://doi.org/10.1108/JSBED-03-2019-0091

Giuliani, E., & Bell, M. (2005). The micro-determinants of meso-level learning and innovation: Evidence from a Chilean wine cluster. *Research Policy, 34*(1), 47–68. https://doi.org/10.1016/j.respol.2004.10.008

Granovetter, M. (1985). Economic action and social structure: The problem of embeddedness. *American Sociology Review, 91*(3), 481–510. https://doi.org/10.1002/9780470755679.ch5

Granovetter, M. (2005). The impact of social structure on economic outcomes social networks and economic outcomes: Core principles. *The Journal of Economic Perspectives, 19*(1), 33–50. Retrieved from https://pubs.aeaweb.org/doi/pdf/10.1257/0895330053147958

Greffe, X. (2010). Urban cultural landscapes: An economic approach. In *EBLA Working Papers*, University of Turin. Retrieved from http://ideas.repec.org/p/uto/eblawp/201001.html

Guerrieri, P., & Pietrobelli, C. (2004). Industrial districts' evolution and technological regimes: Italy and Taiwan. *Technovation, 24*(11), 899–914. https://doi.org/10.1016/S0166-4972(03)00048-8

Jacobs, J. (1969). *The economy of cities*. Random House.

Jofre-Monseny, J., Marín-López, R., & Viladecans-Marsal, E. (2014). The determinants of localization and urbanization economies: Evidence from the location of new firms in Spain. *Journal of Regional Science, 54*(2), 313–337. https://doi.org/10.1111/jors.12076

Jones, M. (2009). Phase space: Geography, relational thinking, and beyond. *Progress in Human Geography, 33*(4), 487–506. https://doi.org/10.1177/0309132508101599

Kesidou, E., & Romijn, H. (2008). Do local knowledge spillovers matter for development? An empirical study of Uruguay's software cluster. *World Development, 36*(10), 2004–2028. https://doi.org/10.1016/j.worlddev.2008.01.003

Kesidou, E., Caniëls, M. C. J., & Romijn, H. A. (2009). Local knowledge spillovers and development: An exploration of the software cluster in Uruguay. *Industry and Innovation, 16*(2), 247–272. https://doi.org/10.1080/13662710902764444

Kirat, T., & Lung, Y. (1999). Innovation and proximity. Territories as loci of collective learning processes. *European Urban and Regional Studies, 6*(1), 27–38. https://doi.org/10.1177/096977649900600103

Lee, N., & Brown, R. (2017). Innovation, SMEs and the liability of distance: The demand and supply of bank funding in UK peripheral regions. *Journal of Economic Geography, 17*(1), 233–260. https://doi.org/10.1093/jeg/lbw011

Malecki, E. J. (2012). Regional social capital: Why it matters. *Regional Studies, 46*(8), 1023–1039. https://doi.org/10.1080/00343404.2011.607806

Malmberg, A., & Maskell, P. (2006). Localized learning revisited. *Growth and Change, 37*(1), 1–18. https://doi.org/10.1111/j.1468-2257.2006.00302.x

Markusen, A. (1996). Sticky places in slippery space: A typology of industrial districts. *Economic Geography, 72*(3), 293–313. https://doi.org/10.2307/144402

Marshall, A. (1920). *Principle of economics*. Palgrave Macmillan.

Martin, R., & Sunley, P. (2003). Deconstructing clusters: Chaotic concept or policy panacea? *Journal of Economic Geography, 3*(1), 5–35. https://doi.org/10.1093/jeg/3.1.5

Masakure, O., Henson, S., & Cranfield, J. (2009). Performance of microenterprises in Ghana: A resource-based view. *Journal of Small Business and Enterprise Development, 16*(3), 466–484. https://doi.org/10.1108/14626000910977170

Mazúr, E., & Urbánek, J. (1983). Space in geography. *GeoJournal, 7*(2), 139–143. https://doi.org/10.1007/BF00185159

Molina-Morales, F. X. (2001). European industrial districts: Influence of geographic concentration on performance of the firm. *Journal of International Management, 7*(4), 277–294. https://doi.org/10.1016/S1075-4253(01)00048-5

Morgan, K. (2004). The exaggerated death of geography: Learning, proximity and territorial innovation systems. *Journal of Economic Geography, 4*(1), 3–21. https://doi.org/10.1093/jeg/4.1.3

Morris, J., Morris, W., & Bowen, R. (2022). Implications of the digital divide on rural SME resilience. *Journal of Rural Studies, 89*, 369–377. https://doi.org/10.1016/j.jrurstud.2022.01.005

Mueller, E. F., & Jungwirth, C. (2022). Are cooperative firms more agile? A contingency perspective on small and medium-sized enterprises in agglomerations and peripheral areas. *Small Business Economics, 58*(1), 281–302. https://doi.org/10.1007/s11187-020-00410-3

Ortega-Colomer, F. J., Molina-Morales, F. X., & de Lucio, I. F. (2016). Discussing the concepts of cluster and industrial district. *Journal of Technology Management and Innovation, 11*(2), 139–147. https://doi.org/10.4067/S0718-27242016000200014

Pagliacci, F., Zavalloni, M., Raggi, M., & Viaggi, D. (2020). Coordination in the agri-food sector: The role of social capital and remoteness in the emergence of Italian network contracts. *Journal of Rural Studies, 77*, 93–104. https://doi.org/10.1016/j.jrurstud.2020.04.036

Parr, J. B. (2002a). Agglomeration economies: Ambiguities and confusions. *Environment and Planning A, 34*(4), 717–731. https://doi.org/10.1068/a34106

Parr, J. B. (2002b). Missing elements in the analysis of agglomeration economies. *International Regional Science Review, 25*(2), 151–168. https://doi.org/10.1177/016001702762481221

Parr, J. B. (2007). Spatial definitions of the city: Four perspectives. *Urban Studies, 44*(2), 381–392. https://doi.org/10.1080/00420980601075059

Pike, A., Rodríguez-Pose, A., & Tomaney, J. (2016). *Local and regional development*. Routledge. https://doi.org/10.4324/9781315767673

Porter, M. E. (2000). Location, competition, and economic development: Local clusters in a global economy. *Economic Development Quarterly, 14*(1), 15–34. https://doi.org/10.1177/089124240001400105

Porter, M., & Ketels, C. (2009). Clusters and industrial districts: Common roots, different perspectives. In *A handbook of industrial districts*. Edward Elgar Publishing. https://doi.org/10.4337/9781781007808.00024

Renski, H. (2011). External economies of localization, urbanization and industrial diversity and new firm survival. *Papers in Regional Science, 90*(3), 473–502. https://doi.org/10.1111/j.1435-5957.2010.00325.x

Rutten, R., & Boekema, F. (2012). From learning region to learning in a socio-spatial context. *Regional Studies, 46*(8), 981–992. https://doi.org/10.1080/00343404.2012.712679

Sforzi, F., & Boix, R. (2015). What about Industrial District(s) in regional science? *Investigaciones Regionales – Journal of Regional Research, 32*, 61–73. Retrieved from https://ebuah.uah.es/dspace/handle/10017/26630

Sunley, P. (2008). Relational economic geography: A partial understanding or a new paradigm? *Economic Geography, 84*(1), 1–26. https://doi.org/10.1111/j.1944-8287.2008.tb00389.x

Suwala, L. (2021). Space concepts, re-figuration of spaces and comparative research – Perspectives from economic geography and regional economics. *Forum Qualitative Sozialforschung (FQS) / Forum: Qualitative Social Research, 22*(3), 1–48. https://doi.org/10.17169/fqs-22.3.3789

Torre, A., & Rallet, A. (2005). Proximity and localization. *Regional Studies, 39*(1), 47–59. https://doi.org/10.1080/0034340052000320842

Vaessen, P., & Keeble, D. (1995). Growth-oriented SMEs in Unfavourable Regional Environments. *Regional Studies, 29*(6), 489–505. https://doi.org/10.1080/00343409512331349133

Van der Panne, G. (2004). Agglomeration externalities: Marshall versus Jacobs. *Journal of Evolutionary Economics, 14*(5), 593–604. https://doi.org/10.1007/s00191-004-0232-x

Virkkala, S. (2007). Innovation and networking in peripheral areas - A case study of emergence and change in rural manufacturing. *European Planning Studies, 15*(4), 511–529. https://doi.org/10.1080/09654310601133948

Chapter 4
Firms in Territories: The Local Roots of Family Firms

4.1 The Concept of Embeddedness[1]

Economic sociology, addressing the issue of economic development and change from a sociological viewpoint, experienced a marked revival in the 1980s (Ritchter, 2015). Economic stagnation and inflation, the Fordism crisis following the emergence of new production regimes (e.g., the industrial districts), and the shift to market-oriented economic policies in developing and former Soviet bloc countries laid the groundwork for the New Economic Sociology (NES) (Beckert, 2007). Besides the actual changes in capitalist economies, the NES is a reaction to the "hegemonic" claim of the orthodox (or neoclassical) economists to exclusively hold the methodological armory for understanding not only the "material" life but also the social one (Guillén et al., 2002). From this perspective, Ingham (1996, p. 551) argues as "orthodox economic theory showed virtually no interest in either social interaction, historically specific social institutions or the systematic or emergent properties of social wholes." Instead, economics was solely concerned with optimizing the behavior of economic agents, within a rational choice framework, in the face of scarcity (Guillén et al., 2002).

The founding manifesto of the NES is Mark Granovetter's (1985) seminal contribution, "Economic Action and Social Structure—The Problem of Embeddedness," inspired by the *Great Transformation* of Karl Polanyi (1957) and centered around the concept of embeddedness of economic behavior. In his seminal paper, Granovetter started by rejecting the *over*socialized and the *under*socialized view of human action, both resulting in a "conception of action and decision carried out by atomized actors" (Granovetter, 1985, p. 485). In the oversocialized view, commonly developed systems of norms and values, which become internalized through socialization, entirely control actor behavior (Beckert, 2007; Wrong,

[1] The Sects. 4.1 and 4.2 are partially based on the doctoral dissertation of Amato, S. (2020). *Family firms and Regional Economics: Current Debate and New Empirical Evidence*, University of Pisa.

S. Amato, A. Patuelli, *Family Firms and Local Roots*, CSR, Sustainability, Ethics & Governance, https://doi.org/10.1007/978-3-031-31793-4_4

1961). In the undersocialized view, in line with classical and neoclassical economics, there is no room for social relations on production, distribution, or consumption, which are treated like friction stunting competitive markets (Beckert, 2007).

Instead, economic actors "do not behave or decide outside a social context. [. . .]. Their attempts at purposive action are instead embedded in concrete, ongoing systems of social relations" (Granovetter, 1985, p. 487). Hence, in the view of Granovetter, to be embedded ("who") is the economic behavior in networks of ongoing and interpersonal (dyadic) relationships ("in what").[2] The actor's behavior and individual choices are exposed to social influences and stem from a flow of interactions and shifting relationships with others (Granovetter, 2005). The social embeddedness of the economy rests on the assumption of economic and non-economic osmosis, with the former linked to, constrained by, or depending on "action or institutions that are non-economic in content, goals or processes" (Granovetter, 2005, p. 35).[3]

In the neoclassical formulation, exchange partners are bound by arm's-length ties: personal relationships are cool, self-interested, and primarily driven by profit-seeking behavior (Guillén et al., 2002). Narrowly economic matters hog the relationships, which take place without reciprocation and non-repeated interactions (i.e., "one-shot" deals) (Uzzi, 1997). On the contrary, following Granovetter's view, embedded ties are imbued with the two main ingredients governing the expectations and behavior of exchange partners. First, *trust*, is broadly defined as a favorable expectation regarding other people's actions and intentions (Möllering, 2001), in the belief that the transaction partner would not act for his/her own self-interest and at another's expense (Uzzi, 1997). Expectations of trust bolster *reciprocity*, the second ingredient of embedded ties, that is the giving of benefits to another in return for benefits received (Molm, 2010). The underlying meaning of reciprocity is that of mutual exchange (Bruni et al., 2008), and no formal devices (e.g., contracts and fines) are used to enforce reciprocation (Uzzi, 1999).[4] Thus, Granovetter's original

---

[2]The meaning of embeddedness envisioned by Granovetter differs essentially from Polanyi's original conceptualization. Granovetter's notion of embeddedness is related to a structuralist approach to economic sociology in which the structural properties of social networks explain economic outcomes. Conversely, Polanyi's view of embeddedness is rooted in institutional analysis (Beckert, 2007). For Polanyi, markets are not networks of structurally fully equivalent producers but "rather fully social institutions, reflecting a complex alchemy of politics, culture, and ideology" (Krippner, 2001, p. 782).

[3]As a concrete application of the embeddedness approach to economic life, Granovetter criticizes Williamson's (1975) arguments around which cases economic activities take place within firm organizational boundaries ("Hierarchies") rather than market processes crossing these boundaries ("Markets"). Bounded rationality and opportunism are claimed to favor transaction internalization. Granovetter observed that transactions of any type are mixed up with social ones, thus rejecting the atomized and anonymous market of neoclassical economics. Trustworthy relationships, repeated personal contacts outside organizational boundaries, expectations on future transactions, and reputational concerns characterize the market (Granovetter, 1985).

[4]The word reciprocity comes from the Latin root meaning *retro-procus*, meaning "going back and forth," that is giving and receiving.

conceptualization of embeddedness is more related to the quality and characteristics of dyadic relationships (i.e., "relational" embeddedness) than to the structure (i.e., "network" embeddedness) itself.

While Granovetter's view is focused on individual choices and actions, the same shift in perspective can be applied to businesses. In fact, "what is true for individuals is also true for organizations" (Kadushin, 2012, p. 68). Indeed, the concept of embeddedness progressed from the individual level of analysis to businesses and thus from personal relationships to inter-organizational relationships of embeddedness. Against this background, Ratajczak-Mrozek (2017) suggests two ways of interpreting inter-organizational embeddedness by unraveling the ambiguity and terminological laxity associated with this shift. The first one, more structural, portrays the types of networks firms are connected to and dependent on. The second, more relational, refers to the qualitative features of such relationships, like the trustworthiness imbued in them, in line with the Granovetterian tradition. Accordingly, inter-organizational embeddedness is the combination of "interdependences" between firms in the network and "adaptation" in the resources and activities with the counterpart fueled by the intensity of the exchanges (Andersson & Forsgren, 1996). By encompassing mutual trust, long-term orientation, and stability, embedded relationships with customers, suppliers, and other economic actors become difficult to substitute, at least in the short term (Ratajczak-Mrozek, 2017).

4.2 Toward a Spatial Understanding of Embedded Ties: The Local Embeddedness of the Firm

In recent decades, the concept of embeddedness has gained growing interest in economic geography (Hess, 2004; Oinas, 1997) and regional studies (Cooke et al., 2005; Lorentzen, 2008). Unlike the original conceptualization, it has been fundamentally conceived in spatial terms. The emphasis is now placed on the social nature of economic phenomena, and their manifestation in territories, that is, spaces socially constructed, culturally marked, and institutionally regulated (Bowen, 2011) where objects are tied together and physical and administrative boundaries can be drawn (Dicken & Malmberg, 2008). Martin (1994, p. 42) observes that "because economic events are necessarily contextual, that is embedded in spatial structure of social relations, our explanation should seek explicitly to incorporate this fact." Hence, embeddedness is an inherently spatial construct (Oinas, 1997).

The contribution of Hess (2004) marked a crucial shift in perspective whereby to be embedded is the firm ("who") in networks and institutional settings ("in what"). Additionally, a spatial scale at the local and regional levels is identified in discontinuity with the traditional view of embeddedness (Granovetter, 2005). Table 4.1 summarizes the perspectives of embeddedness in different academic fields.

Hence, in the conception of embeddedness *à la* Hess (2004), local networks and localized social relationships stand out as the spatial logic of embeddedness. The

Table 4.1 Different views of embeddedness

Academic field	Who?	In What?	Geographical scale
Polany's *Great transformation*	"The economy," systems of exchange	"Society," social and cultural structures	No particular scale, but emphasis on the nation-state
Business systems approach	Firms	Institutions and regulatory frameworks	Nation-state, "home territory"
New economic sociology	Economic behavior, individuals, and firms	Networks of ongoing social (interpersonal) relations	No particular scale
Organization and business studies	Firms, networks	Time, space, social structures, markets, technological systems, political systems, etc.	No particular scale
Economic geography	Firms	Networks and institutional settings	Local/Regional

Source: from Hess, M. (2004). "Spatial relationships"? Towards a reconceptualization of embeddedness. *Progress in Human Geography*, *28*(2), p. 173

geographical scale in which embedded relationships take place is usually considered at the local and regional levels; for three main reasons. First, the relevance of external economies (e.g., knowledge spillovers) stemming from the geographical concentration of economic activity in spatially-bound areas (Parr, 2002). The spatial arrangement and embedded relationships with nearby economic actors affect the way firms behave and the resulting outcomes (Ratajczak-Mrozek, 2017). Second, the institutional "thickness" is associated with a strong local institutional presence, high level of interactions shaped by sticky rules, norms, and conventions, a dominant structure and a common agenda (Zukauskaite et al., 2017). Third, the geographical closeness and a shared identity fostering social interaction, trust building, and reciprocity—in other words, social proximity—among economic actors sharing the same relational space (Boschma, 2005; Capello, 2019). The concept of "locality" embraces exactly the idea of local community as the embodiment of geographical proximity and social proximity, the latter understood in terms of feelings of belonging and similarity (Lähdesmäki et al., 2019).

Just as Granovetter's (1985) view of embeddedness rejects the idea of atomized economic agents, the local embeddedness of the firm rejects the idea of business organizations devoid of connections with the socio-spatial environment they operate in (Oinas, 1997). Local embeddedness instead "considers the extent to which an actor is 'anchored' in particular territories or places. Economic actors become embedded there in the sense that they absorb, and in some cases become constrained by, the economic activities and social dynamics that already exist in those places" (Hess, 2004, p. 177). While such a definition implicitly subsumes the local/regional level as a spatial scale of embeddedness, two main attributes of a firm's local embeddedness arise. First, the *nature* of firm's ties to the immediate surroundings, differentiating between the economic activity strictly speaking, and the non-economic stimulus and processes of change occurring in the local community the firm belongs to. Indeed, both commercial and non-commercial interactions in localized networks frame a firm's existence in a given location (Filippi et al., 2011), with the economic sphere that is deeply intertwined with the social one (Oinas, 1997). Second, the *breadth* of a firm's ties to the immediate surroundings, that is, the variety of local stakeholders the firm interacts with, not limited to the exchange partners (Attig & Brockman, 2017). However, Markusen (1994) and Kalantaridis and Bika (2006) identify a third attribute of local embeddedness, the *depth* of firm's bonds, that is, the degree to which the firm is affected by the localized economic activities and social dynamics.[5] Local embeddedness is, therefore, a multidimensional construct encompassing a broad spectrum of a firm's involvement in a locality (Oinas, 1997).

The dominant approach in the empirical research captures local embeddedness by mainly referring to the economic linkages, thus emphasizing the economic sphere of the firm activity and the depth of such linkages, limited to local exchange partners. The economic or mercantile view of local embeddedness is traceable to the industrial district literature. In this respect, Markusen (1994, p. 483) maintains that "a key feature of the recent debate is whether firms have needs and loyalties which keep them anchored in the region. Central to the affirmative answer to this question is the notion that firms are embedded in local relationships – with competitors and suppliers in particular." Such a view of local embeddedness overlaps to some extent with local economic integration, which refers to the degree to which a firm relies on local resources and carries out its transactions within a delimited geographical area (Courtney et al., 2008). The rationale is that the firm's anchorage to its territory is stronger the more it depends on its immediate surroundings for its sales, employment, and inputs. In contrast, a firm's ties to its home base weaken as it expands further afield. In this perspective, local embeddedness has been computed by detecting whether the majority of customers reside nearby the local firm (Greenberg et al., 2018) or whether the local area represents the firm's primary market (Amato et al., 2021b; Dekker & Hasso, 2016) and the key source of labor force, productive inputs, and information as well (Kalantaridis & Bika, 2006) as shown in Table 4.2. Despite being essentially economic, such measures are intended to capture the latent constraints—and, thus, conditionings for the firm—originating from close social circles carrying expectations, norms, and values (Attig & Brockman, 2017). As such, a firm's sensitiveness toward the social pressures and norms within a given local community increases in line with its dependence on localized resources and capabilities (Dekker & Hasso, 2016).

Distance-based measures are also used to gauge ties to the local area. Among these, the average distance of the firm's subsidiary from its headquarters (Berrone et al., 2010; D'Aurizio & Romano, 2013) and the average distance between the stakeholders and the local firm (Amato et al., 2020). Similarly, the conjecture is that

[5] According to Kalantaridis and Bika (2006), local embeddedness can "be described as the nature, depth, and extent of an entrepreneur's ties into the local environment" (p. 1564).

Table 4.2 Local embeddedness measurement

Dimensions	Percentage rate	
	0	100
% of workers coming from the local area		
% workers coming from the local area		
% of sales to the local area		
Key sources of market information from the local area		
Key sources of process information from the local area		
Key sources of information on finance from the local area		
Degree of local embeddedness	*Low*	*High*

Source: adapted from Kalantaridis, C. & Bika, Z., (2006). Local embeddedness and rural entrepreneurship: case-study evidence from Cumbria, England, *Environment and Planning A: Economy and Space*, *38*(8), p. 1572

a firm's anchorage to the immediate surroundings is higher the closer subsidiaries and stakeholders are to the main office, respectively.

4.3 The Beauty and the Ugliness of Embeddedness

The notion that economic exchange may take place through strong or embedded ties has revived the debate about the positive and negative effects of social relationships on economic life (Granovetter, 1985). The general consensus is that trust-based and reciprocal relationships can "create unique value and motivate exchange partners to share the value for their mutual benefit" (Uzzi, 1997, p. 483). Among the benefits of embedded ties, the reduction—but not the complete elimination—of uncertainty and the risk of opportunistic behavior (Boschma, 2005), which eases the exchange of proprietary and tacit information (Uzzi, 1997). Tacit information is, by nature, more difficult to convey through markets (Boschma, 2005). Conversely, weak ties—typified by distant social interactions and infrequent interactions with acquaintances and strangers—are more effective to transfer novel information and codified knowledge (Granovetter, 1973). Embedded ties enable mutual and flexible troubleshooting (Uzzi, 1997), the mitigation of collaborative tensions in alliances with external parties (Steinmo, 2015),[6] and interactive learning (Boschma, 2005). Embedded ties are not only a source of knowledge and information but also of business opportunities (Jack & Anderson, 2002), thus representing a determinant of innovation, growth, and performance (Ratajczak-Mrozek, 2017). Insofar as such knowledge and information (i.e., knowledge spillovers) and business opportunities are

[6]Extending the analysis to the financial sector, Uzzi (1999) maintains that commercial transactions between lenders and banks that are embedded in social relationships, increase lenders' accessibility to capital and lower the borrowing costs. At the same time, embedded ties add value for the banks by heightening their ability to lower the costs of writing loan costs, to retain clients and to decommodify financial capital.

spatially bounded, that is, freely available in local networks and accessible through informal interactions (Kesidou & Romijn, 2008), embeddedness in local networks allows the firm to better exploit location advantages (Lambooy, 2010). Despite being, in theory, equally accessible to all co-located firms, local embeddedness provides an advantage in harnessing location-specific benefits (Ratajczak-Mrozek, 2017). By facilitating social interaction and, thus, the emergence of trust between actors (Boschma, 2005), spatial proximity is crucial to tap into location advantages (Malmberg & Maskell, 2006).

The research, however, also warns against the risks of over-embeddedness. In fact, the "positive effects of [embeddedness] rise to a threshold, however, after which embeddedness can derail economic performance" (Uzzi, 1997, p. 35). Over-embeddedness identifies an overreliance on a few exchange partners and a large number of redundant ties in which much loyalty is involved (Andersen, 2013). An overload of trust may indeed lead to opportunistic behavior and malfeasance (Granovetter, 1985), especially when social relationships are powered by emotional bonds of friendship and kinship (Uzzi, 1999). Additionally, long-term relationships "may lock members of social networks into established ways of doing things at the expense of their own innovate and learning capacity" (Boschma, 2005, p. 67). Excessively close-knit ties are deemed to restrict the flow of novel information and codified knowledge from outside the network (Uzzi, 1997), thus obstructing internal knowledge heterogeneity (Andersen, 2013) and knowledge creation and accumulation (Ratajczak-Mrozek, 2017). Uzzi (1997) identifies two additional consequences of over-embeddedness. First, a "sclerosis" originating from embedded ties with a network's core actor, which limits the transition to a replacement partner whenever the former vanishes. Second, the loss of competitive advantage, brought by embedded relationships, following the rupture of social ties and the corresponding lack of new embedded ties. Overall, over-embeddedness may stifle a firm's innovation potential (Boschma, 2005) and performance (Ratajczak-Mrozek, 2017). Thus, a proper mix or balance of embedded relationships and arm's length (or market) ties is needed, lowering the transaction costs and preventing insulation, respectively (Boschma, 2005; Uzzi, 1997). From this perspective, when networks are localized, as in the case of business clusters, extra-local linkages (i.e., "network pipelines") are needed to tap into new knowledge (Bathelt et al., 2004), which is "pumped" into the clusters and spreads through local interactions (Malmberg & Maskell, 2006).

Figure 4.1 displays the inverted U-shaped relationships between embeddedness and firm outcomes. The association is positive until a certain threshold, beyond which embeddedness becomes detrimental.

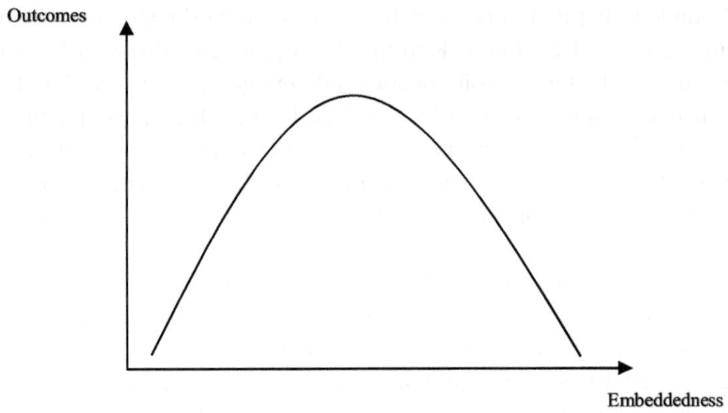

Positive outcomes	Negative outcomes
Uncertainty reduction	Opportunistic behavior and malfeasance
Opportunism reduction	Over reliance
Mutual and flexible adjustment	Limited and redundant information
Collaborative tensions mitigation	Sclerosis
Access to knowledge and information	Insularity
Identification of business opportunities	Limited innovation capability
Improved innovation	Inferior performance
Higher performance	

Source: own elaboration.

Fig. 4.1 Relationship between the degree of embeddedness and outcomes. Source: own elaboration

4.4 The Entrepreneur's Place Attachment

The original conceptualization of local embeddedness—as envisioned by Oinas (1997) and Hess (2004)—assumes the firm as a unit of analysis and the local/regional setting as the spatial logic of embeddedness, respectively. Such a view, goes beyond the idea of "aseptic" firms—numb to the economic and social dynamics occurring in the immediate vicinity—eclipses the place connections of the entrepreneur. Indeed, firms are not impersonal entities but economic actors deeply shaped by the owner–manager running the business. As such, the entrepreneur is the person who ultimately frames the firm's positioning in the socio-spatial context where the economic activity takes place and, therefore, the degree to which the firm itself absorbs and is constrained by the socio-economic events occurring in the local context (Oinas, 1997). Moving from the firm, as organization, to the entrepreneur, as individual, the economic activity occurs in spatial settings "that are produced and maintained through an array of social and cultural mechanisms that ascribe meanings or value to them" (Sampson & Goodrich, 2009, p. 903), that is, places. Thus, places emerge as repositories within which interpersonal, community, and cultural relationships occur (Hidalgo & Hernández, 2001).

Table 4.3 Local embeddedness and place attachment: A comparison

Construct	Local embeddedness	Place attachment
Theoretical base	Sociology/economic geography	Environmental psychology
Unit of analysis	Firm	Individual/groups
Type of connections	Socio-economic	Socio-emotional
Level of analysis	Local/regional	Chiefly local

Source: own elaboration

As a result of long-term interactions and experiences with a particular place, individuals develop a deep sense of connection with the spatial setting; this is known as place attachment in environmental psychology and describes the affective bonds between a person (or group of people) and specific places (Manzo & Perkins, 2006). Specifically, place attachment is defined as the "symbolic relationship formed by people giving culturally shared emotional/affective meanings to a particular space or piece of land that provides the basis for the individual's or group's understanding of, and relation to, the environment" (Sampson & Goodrich, 2009, p. 903). Therefore, as local embeddedness encapsulates the rootedness of the firm, place attachment encapsulates the rootedness of the individual in given spatial contexts people "invest them with meanings, ideas, and sensibilities" (Williams, 2014, p. 76).[7] Table 4.3 depicts the main differences between the concepts.

Place attachment is a multifaceted construct, involving much more than relationships to the biological, topographical, or other physical attributes of a place; it also encompasses the social interactions and cultural traditions (Armstrong & Stedman, 2019). Specifically, Raymond et al. (2010) identify four dimensions making up place attachment. First, *place identity*. This refers to those dimensions of self, such as the blend of feelings about specific physical traits, beliefs, and symbolic connections to places that define who we are. In other words, a place is regarded as a means to distinguish oneself from others, preserve a sense of continuity, and build positive self-esteem and a sense of self-efficacy. Second, *place dependence*. This consists of the functional or goal-directed connections to a setting, which reflects the ability of a place to satisfy needs and provide the appropriate resources and conditions for the desired activities. Third, *social bonding*, which refers to the feelings of belongingness or membership to a group of people, such as friends and family, and the emotional connections based on shared history, interests, and concerns leading to

[7]Williams (2014) identifies four layers of place meaning with a different degree of tangibility: (1) *inherent meaning*, which reflects the material properties that most people would perceive; (2) *instrumental meaning* associated with material features to fulfill desired behavior or economic goals; (3) *socio-cultural meaning*, which is socially or symbolically constructed through language and social interaction; finally, and (4) *identity-expressive meaning*, which emphasizes the subjective and, hence, the innermost recognition of meanings the individual ascribes to places, thus contributing to the construction and affirmation of self.

a "sense of community" (Manzo & Perkins, 2006).[8] Indeed, communities provide the context in which individuals can articulate who they are (Sampson & Goodrich, 2009). Finally, *natural bonding*, reflects the individual emotional connections to some part of the non-human natural environment.[9] The features of the environment bind the individuals to places given that the landscape "does shape many of the ideas we have in our heads, and therefore does have to be elaborated as a socially significant fact" (Sampson & Goodrich, 2009, p. 906).

A common view is that place attachment is a spatially localized phenomenon encompassing beliefs, emotions, and behavioral commitments concerning a localized geographical setting (Lin & Lockwood, 2014). However, place attachment develops with different intensities within various spatial scales (Hidalgo & Hernández, 2001). Some forms of place attachment are chiefly local, taking place in neighborhoods and cities (Lewicka, 2008). The spatial proximity between individuals enabled by the limited size of such settings fosters the temporal continuity of social relationships with and for the place (Banini, 2017). Shared experiences, memories, and practices make places sites of collective significance and common social actions (Hinojosa et al., 2016). This is particularly true in rural settlements where residents tend to have more frequent and direct social interactions, thereby increasing community involvement (Belanche et al., 2021).[10] Although chiefly local, place attachment can be also generalized across a whole region (Brown et al., 2015). Regarding the way in which place attachment develops, being born in a particular place (Sampson & Goodrich, 2009), length of residence (Manzo, 2005), social ties in the place of residence, such as family and friendship connections (Hidalgo & Hernández, 2001), and physical features like the local history and "historical sites creating a sense of continuity with the past" (Lewicka, 2008, p. 211) are associated with the formation of place attachment.[11]

The people-place bond is further "strengthened and reinforced when a person works in a place or with the resources of a place thus becoming the means of the person's or group's economic survival" (Low, 1992, p. 167). Such a bond accounts for the economic dimension of place attachment produced by ownership of or working in a given place (Sampson & Goodrich, 2009). Thus, the process of attachment is the experience of not only living or being in a location but also carrying out, as entrepreneur, an economic activity in the same location (Ren et al., 2021). Entrepreneurship is a socio-economic process grounded in a specific

[8] According to Manzo and Perkins (2006), attachment to the neighborhood is a precondition for developing a sense of community. It can also motivate participation in neighborhood improvement and planning efforts.

[9] Raymond et al. (2010) point out that natural bonding may not be applicable for measuring place attachment in urban settings while being relevant in the case of rural contexts.

[10] According to Belanche et al. (2021), rural communities are portrayed as *Gemeinschaft* places made up of social relationships based on sentiment and reciprocity. On the contrary, urban societies are presented as *Gesellschaft* places where prevail anonymous and impersonal social relationships.

[11] The type of place attachment arising from birth, marrying into a household, and living for an extended time in a given place is defined "genealogical" (Sampson & Goodrich, 2009).

context where the entrepreneur, and by extension, the firm, are also shaped by the immediate surroundings, which provide opportunities and available resources (Welter, 2011), making the survival and growth of the business ventures highly-dependent upon the local context (Siemens, 2019). Thus, a local entrepreneur develops instrumental connections to the place understood in terms of dependence arising from localized resource-based activities. Both aspects of livelihood and restorative experiences (e.g., enjoyment and freedom) may coexist in the same place, mutually reinforcing the entrepreneur's place dependence (Rajala et al., 2020). Place is also where the economic activity occurs, which becomes a component of personal identity whereby the entrepreneur defines him(her)self through the place (Radu-Lefebvre et al., 2021). A blend of past individual experiences related to everyday life and the business makes place a site of meanings, instilling in the entrepreneur certain feelings regarding life or personal purpose (Boley et al., 2021; Ren et al., 2021). Regarding social bonding, places are repositories of personal and shared symbolic meanings expressed through repeated economic and non-economic interactions in the local setting (Belanche et al., 2021). Cognitive elements merge with cultural (e.g., shared cultural values), social (e.g., cooperation attitudes), and economic (e.g., historical productive skills and local specialization) ones, ultimately leading to a sense of togetherness and belonging to the local community, that is "similarity" (Capello, 2019). As a result, the firm may acquire characteristics that make it "fit" into the local environment (Oinas, 1997), whose image is inextricably linked to that of the local area, "this latter sometimes becoming a trademark for all local producers" (Capello, 2019, p. 146). Intimate contacts with the close biophysical world, arising from personal and social memories and experiences, may surge as meaningful local "immaterial" resources as its features (e.g., landscape) are properly communicated, thus inspiring and molding the key value proposition of the venture (Müller & Korsgaard, 2018).

Place attachment is deemed to shape the feelings of the entrepreneur—both as individual and economic actor—about the location and the interplay with the immediate surroundings where the social life and economic activity occur (Jack & Anderson, 2002). As firm boundaries are permeable to external socio-economic dynamics (Oinas, 1997), the place attachment of the entrepreneur cuts across organizational boundaries, and ends up embedding—to some extent—the firm in the local setting. Thus, the place attachment of the entrepreneur is thought to be a latent determinant of the firm's local embeddedness (Lähdesmäki et al., 2019). Spatial proximity and feelings of belonging and similarity imbue with trust and reciprocity the economic exchanges in the locality (Lähdesmäki & Suutari, 2012). As mixing personal and business relationships is typical of local entrepreneurs, embedded ties are not confined to business relationships only, but enmesh with the local community as a whole (Pallares-Barbera et al., 2004). Given the importance of the community as resource "provider" for the firm, mutually supportive relationships are built "that allows each party to achieve their economic and social goals" (Siemens, 2019, p. 669). Group identification, emotional closeness, and a sense of personal obligations of the local entrepreneur bring out the understanding and salience of internal and external stakeholders for their claims (Lähdesmäki et al.,

2019). Finally, the simple fact of coming from and working in the same locality, the rootedness of the entrepreneur impinges, by extension, upon the degree to which the firm is constrained by and dependent on resources and opportunities available in the local area. As the entrepreneur relies on local networks when accessing such resources and opportunities (Rutten et al., 2010), place attachment may restrain the search and opportunity of exploiting extra-local resources. The feelings of belonging to the community, along with the emotional intimacy and the sense of obligation to local economic actors, lead the entrepreneur to use "the resources that are locally available even if these are more expensive to acquire and use than resources acquired through the global market" (Korsgaard et al., 2015, p. 15), thus resulting in a relatively high level of economic integration at the local level.

Besides inspiring the decision to establish a business in the context the individual is bound to (Jack & Anderson, 2002) and influencing the embedding process—that is, the mechanism by which the entrepreneur becomes part of the local economic structure (McKeever et al., 2014)—place attachment may offer the entrepreneur a fulcrum for leveraging tangible and intangible resources (e.g., knowledge and information) and identifying business opportunities in the local *milieu* (Jack & Anderson, 2002). These are available within a localized network of relationships and accessible through embedded ties in professional and social circles (Lambooy, 2010; Uzzi, 1997). Shared rules, norms, values, and place-specific practices, regulate the interactions in the local area (Boschma, 2005), which, in turn, "facilitates contacts, improves bargaining capacity, and attracts and maintains favorable conditions for the firm" (Pallares-Barbera et al., 2004, p. 648). Furthermore, while the fact of belonging to the same social group enables the entrepreneur to rely on the support of the local community (Siemens, 2019), identity to and familiarity with the immediate surroundings is associated with greater perceived self-efficacy, enhancing proactivity and risk-taking (Ren et al., 2021). Thus, local entrepreneurs are in the best position to extract value from the place by identifying, recombining, and codifying[12] local resources (Korsgaard et al., 2015) with a twofold effect at firm and local level, respectively. First, at the firm level, place attachment—which may be empirically captured by the entrepreneur's hometown and firm headquarters co-location—may be source of superior outcomes in terms of innovation (Ren et al., 2021) and financial outcomes (Baù et al., 2019) vis-à-vis non-attached entrepreneurs. Second, at the local level, recombined and codified resources transform places themselves. Utilizing the local potential and qualities of a place to create new products and services revives the place as the site of meaning and felt value for the inhabitants (i.e., "re-valorization" of place), thus fostering the sense of identity with and belonging to the place where one lives and works (Korsgaard et al., 2015).

[12] Codification is a process that makes the resource combinations transferable and known in non-local markets and/or settings. For instance, it may consist of linking the product and the place it comes from, in such a way as to appear meaningful and attractive outside the location (Korsgaard et al., 2015).

Having said that, place attachment can also be a source of disadvantages for the entrepreneur, and, in turn, the firm. Deep connections to the location can indeed incorporate negative and ambivalent feelings (Manzo, 2005),[13] affecting business decision-making (Lähdesmäki & Suutari, 2012). Moreover, place bonds risk getting stuck into inefficiencies or sub-optimality. This is due to norms, habits, and cultural practices prevailing in the local *milieu* (Müller & Korsgaard, 2018) managerial schemes "that have been successful in the past, but which have become redundant over time" (Boschma, 2005, p. 64). Specifically, a "lock-in" effect associated with enduring routines, conservatism, and overreliance on local connections, which obstructs awareness of new market opportunities, technological solutions, and alternative courses of action has been noted (Boschma, 2005). In sum, the risk of the firm getting locked in is greater the more it is emotionally, socially, and economically tied to and culturally permeated by its location.

However, levels of place attachment vary between individuals and entrepreneurs are no exception to the rule (Belanche et al., 2021). Thus, the following section disentangles the local roots of family firms and the influence of the owning family's place connections on the firm's outcomes.

4.5 The Local Roots of Family Firms

While kinship and social bonds with a particular community in a given location foster feelings of belongingness and emotional connections with the location itself (Raymond et al., 2010), the family involvement in the business—as the dominant coalition—lays the foundation for a deep "anchoring" of the members of the owning family and the firm in the place (Basco et al., 2021). In this case, two different but interrelated and overlapping social institutions cohabit in the same location, where family and business affairs enmesh. On the one side, the family as social unit constituted by a group of people sharing legal or genetic bonds whose socialization occurs in space. On the other, the firm as a collective endeavor through which the family earns their livelihood. Thus, place surges as a physical basin—fraught with meanings and emotional engagement—where the owning family lives, socializes, and operates. Thus, family members as individuals and the owning family as a collectivity may develop a distinctive place attachment. This paragraph, therefore, untangles the dimensions of place attachment underlying the family firm's embeddedness in the local context.

Genealogical inheritance and kinship, the co-location of home and workplace, and an intimate and embodied knowledge of the economic activity—generated through the early involvement in the business—bind family members to a particular place (Cheshire et al., 2013). Place becomes a repository for memories of important

[13] Strong affection (*topophilia*) can countervail the aversion (*topophobia*) for particular places, which accounts for the "shadow side" of people–places relationships (Manzo, 2005).

events in both family and firm history, often following interrelated paths. Such memories depend not only on personal experience but also on narrations, cultural transmission, and traditions that sediment in the family members, nourishing the "historical memory" (Hjorth & Dawson, 2016). This historical memory serves to situate family members and the firm historically in a given location, contributing to the construction and affirmation of place identity. Thus, as a social unit involved in the business, the owning family's association with a location becomes an element of individual (the family member), group (the family), and organizational (the firm) distinctiveness (Smith, 2016). Place also provides continuity to the owning family's identity, fostering the sense of positive esteem the owning family gains from being a recognized business player. Finally, by living and working in its home territory, place is deemed to sustain the owning family's belief to carry out the business activity in that place successfully, thus becoming a source of self-efficacy (Hinojosa et al., 2016; Twigger-Ross & Uzzell, 1996).

Family firms develop economic linkages with the place. This dependence on the location is, prima facie, twofold and strongly interconnected. First, for the family, given that doing business in that location is the source of the household's income, which ensures family's livelihood and its social and cultural reproduction over time (Cheshire et al., 2013). Second, for the firm whose economic activity—not unlike other types of firms—is enabled (or constrained) by the existence (absence) of localized resources and place-specific social and cultural amenities (Korsgaard et al., 2015). However, family firms may develop a further and unique goal-directed connection to a setting. Indeed, place represents the physical background where the owning family pursues the enhancement and preservation of the "non-economic utilities" (i.e., socio-emotional wealth) the family derives from its controlling position in the firm (Gómez-Mejía et al., 2007). The pursuit of the main objectives underlying the socioemotional wealth—namely maintaining control and influence over the firm, perpetuating the family dynasty, and sustaining family reputation—occurs in space, thus heightening the functional connections and instrumental meanings of places for family firms (Naldi et al., 2013; Williams, 2014).

To the local entrepreneurs, "places are not simply sites of production and consumption, but areas of meaningful social life" (McKeever et al., 2015, p. 52). This is particularly true for family firms situated in local contexts—whose genealogical inheritance, kinship ties, and homeplace and workplace co-location are intertwined—where family and business boundaries are blurred (Lähdesmäki et al., 2019). Family members' connections to local social networks and the lasting interactions for personal and professional purposes result in a distinctive social bonding of family firms. Social relationships are not only "inherited" from the family as an enduring social unit but maintained and continuously reproduced in the individual and family circle, ending up serving the interests of the firm as well. At the same time, local bonds developed as part of the economic activity merge with preexisting social ties or enlarge actual family members' local networks, thereby enmeshing social and economic life inextricably (Cheshire et al., 2013). Family firms' social bonding is more than a matter of the density of social connections at the local level, which also involves the sentiment regarding the rootedness to the community one lives and works in (Trentelman, 2009), that is, the feelings of belongingness (Raymond et al., 2010). Informal institutions, such as shared values, traditions, and culture, together with local skills and competencies in a given local *milieu*, are prerequisites for the emergence of feelings of belongingness to a community (Capello, 2019). Family firms' historical and pervasive action in the social and productive structure has a twofold effect. On the one hand, family firms play a crucial role in the formation and transmission of informal institutions, which become "crystallized" in the local area (Soleimanof et al., 2018). On the other hand, family firms bring about and nourish the productive skills of a territory, which build a clear economic "vocation" and a local productive specialization, "feeding—in a cumulative and virtuous process—the reinforcement of community loyalty and collective belonging" (Capello, 2019, p. 144).

Shared experiences and memories in the natural environment may result in strong feelings of connectedness with the biophysical context (Raymond et al., 2010). Some characteristics of the natural environment create a sense of continuity with the past, imbuing the natural setting with symbolic meanings that reflect the self-definitions of family members within a particular place (Greider & Garkovich, 1994). When involved in the business, the natural environment means for family members the biophysical background wherein the entrepreneurial dynasty began and reproduced over time (Cheshire et al., 2013). Also because of the peculiarities of the natural environment, place becomes a *locus* of highly recognizable and local-specific products and, therefore, an important site of meaning and identity construction for family members (Amato et al., 2020), informing the corporate image (Balmer & Burghausen, 2015).[14] "More specifically, the consciousness of place and the sense a firm has of belonging to a place can shape corporate heritage identity" (Spielmann et al., 2021, p. 828). Thus, the historical interaction between family members and attributes or characteristics of the natural environment is reinterpreted in terms of distinctiveness, with place that becomes a nexus for the family and organizational uniqueness embodied in the key value proposition (Müller & Korsgaard, 2018).

Taken together, place identity, place dependence, social bonding, and natural bonding account for the individual dimensions binding the family members, that is, to say the people who run the business, to a given location. By embedding the firm in the local *milieu*, the place attachment of the owning family portrays the "local roots" of the firm and, therefore, the intensity with which family firms are anchored, socially and economically, in a particular place. Hence, place attachment is thought to be a latent, time honored, and emotionally built determinant of the local embeddedness of the family firm. As described by Oinas (1997), this local embeddedness takes place as part of an historical process and interplay of both the active involvements of families as entrepreneurs and the passive presences of the same families as social units, in a variety of localized social relationships set, nourished, and constrained by the owning family's place attachment. Finally, just

[14]According to Spielmann et al. (2021), "corporate heritage identities encompass institutional attributes and qualities that meaningfully define an organization's identity" (p. 826).

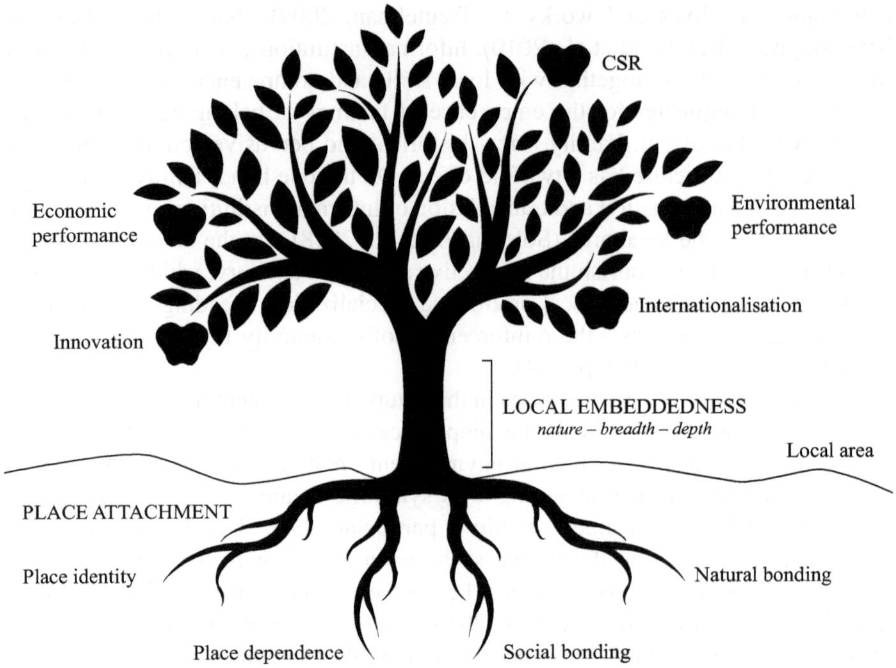

Fig. 4.2 Family firms' local roots. Source: own elaboration

as other roots anchor the plant firmly in the ground, the owning family's place attachment anchors—that is, embeds—the firm in the local area as shown in Fig. 4.2 and described in the following paragraph.

4.6 Family Firms' Local Roots, Embeddedness, and Outcomes

Trust, reciprocity, and exchange cut across family and organizational boundaries (Zahra, 2010), end up shaping commercial relationships and the whole community life the owning family belongs to. Place attachment leads the owning family to closely embed most behavior—including the economic—in localized networks of interpersonal relationships (Lähdesmäki & Suutari, 2012). Therefore, as extension and reflection of the owning family, the firm becomes immersed in the local community and, as such, uniquely bound by the economic activities and social dynamics at local level (Smith, 2016). Feeling part of the same community motivates family firms not only to invest in local contacts (Belanche et al., 2021) but also to maintain an "interest in each other's activities and a shared concern for each other" (McKeever et al., 2015, p. 12). Multiple relationships that family members and a wide array of local stakeholders share beyond the business context increase the "existence and relative importance of stakeholders and their claims from a managerial perspective" (Lähdesmäki et al., 2019, p. 2). Especially at the local level—where the distinction between family and firms becomes more blurred, and personal, family, and firm reputation are often coterminous—the power of local stakeholders and their claims is strengthened (Berrone et al., 2010). As such, family firms feel obliged to meet the expectations of local stakeholders as a way of preserving their reputation (Naldi et al., 2013), heightening their social and economic legitimacy (Lähdesmäki et al., 2019), and maintaining the support of the local community, a necessary requirement for the success of the family firm (Siemens, 2019). Finally, as homeplace and workplace co-location makes family firms inherently spatially "sticky" (Amato et al., 2020, 2021a, 2022b), the feeling of belonging and togetherness with the place and the history of trade with local partners, enmeshed in personal ties, prompt the owning family to rely as much as possible on local resources (Smith, 2016), even when purely economic considerations would suggest otherwise (Korsgaard et al., 2015). Tight local economic linkages nourish a sense of continuity of the owning family as an economic actor traditionally involved in the local economy and committed to the community's well-being (Kalantaridis & Bika, 2006). As a result, family firms display a higher level of local economic integration than their non-family counterparts (Amato et al., 2020). Thus, the owning family's place attachment profoundly influences the nature, extent, and depth—that is, local embeddedness—of the firm's ties to the local *milieu*.

A key issue is related to the various effects of local roots on outcomes, including economic performance, innovation, internationalization, CSR, and also environment as shown in Fig. 4.2. By shaping the interplay uniquely with the immediate surroundings, family firms' local roots impinge upon business decision-making and the acquisition and allocation of resources. The social bonding of family members, which encompasses social and professional local networks, can be mobilized for the benefit of the firm (Uhlaner et al., 2015). The centrality of family members and closure[15] in such networks eases the recognition of (exploration) and access to (exploitation) resources and novel entrepreneurial opportunities (Bird & Wennberg, 2014; Salvato & Melin, 2008), positively influencing efficiency and, thus, economic performance (Baù et al., 2019).

The conflation of spatial and social proximity allows place-attached family members to exchange knowledge, information, and new ideas flowing in the local *milieu* and is crucial for innovation (i.e., knowledge spillovers) (Block & Spiegel, 2013). However, traditions, involving the localized stock of knowledge, competencies, practices, and beliefs pertaining to the past play a crucial role in the innovation

[15]Network centrality is the extent to which family members have ties throughout their networks and thus enjoy a broad span of influence. Network closure refers to the extent to which family members are related to one another, which improves the level of trust between family members and non-family counterparts. Both centrality and closure increase family's "appropriability," that is, the ability of the owning family to leverage interpersonal relationships to identify and access to value resources and business opportunities (Salvato & Melin, 2008).

strategy of family firms. As traditions pass down over time, permeating a given place, family firms leverage past and mostly tacit knowledge about the firm's tradition and that of their territory to develop both product functionalities and meanings (De Massis et al., 2016). The so-called "innovation-through tradition" is based on two main capabilities of family firms: the interiorization of the firm and territory's past knowledge and the reinterpretation of such knowledge by combining it with up-to-date technologies to turn into new products (Magistretti et al., 2020).

Local roots not only shape the type and path of innovation of family firms but also their growth in foreign markets (Baù et al., 2021). Embeddedness in local networks allows family firms to tap easily into a spatially bound flow of information about the practice of exporting and the features of foreign markets (i.e., local export spill-overs), thus facilitating their entry into the export market (Amato et al., 2020). However, the sense of place family members form through long-lasting and every-day interactions (Cheshire et al., 2013) frames their approach toward international-ization. When trading abroad, family firms maintain place authenticity—embodied in and conveyed by their products—directly and uniquely related to the local traditions, history, and cultural heritage of their home territory (Ranfagni et al., 2021). As custodians of place authenticity, family firms communicate the distinctive features of their territory (i.e., territorial identity) externally, with a twofold effect. First, imbuing the products with an intrinsic and enhanced economic value acknowl-edged by foreign customers (Müller & Korsgaard, 2018). Second, nourishing the place consciousness between firms and residents, that is, the "awareness of the value of the territorial common goods as essential elements for the reproduction of individual and collective life, as much as biological and cultural life" (Magnaghi, 2010, p. 133). Such place consciousness also encompasses an economic dimension given that the reproduction of individual and collective life is also reflected in firm's economic activity in a particular place and its expansion in international markets, where the local marries the global (Banini, 2017).

Shared social and cultural values—resulting from repeated socio-economic inter-actions in the same setting (i.e., similarity)—creates a feeling of solidarity with the local community, which brings together private and collective interests (Capello, 2019) and inspires concrete social actions toward the immediate surroundings (Basco et al., 2021). The awareness of being part of the local community comes with raised social expectations toward family firms along with monitoring and sanctioning mechanisms on their behavior (Berrone et al., 2010). Thus, place attachment leads the family owners to engage in philanthropic activities supporting local institutions (Campopiano et al., 2014). In fact, the creation of a foundation, generally bearing the name of the family as a means of coordinating local commu-nity initiatives is quite common (Lähdesmäki & Takala, 2012). Familiarity, emo-tional closeness, and a sense of personal obligation strongly influence the owning family's consideration of the claims of local stakeholders, such as employees during hard times (Amato et al., 2021a). In economic recessions, family firms may feel obliged to honor implicit contracts, for instance, downsizing to a lesser extent than would otherwise be the case (Amato et al., 2020). Employment protection in family firms is stronger the more "anchored" the firm is in the local area (Amato et al., 2020,

Table 4.4 Embedding and disembedding factors of family firms

Dimension	Embedding	Disembedding
Individual/family level	Time/generation	Family conflicts
Firm level	Size	Industry dynamics
Community level	Rural/local production systems	Lack of local reciprocity

Source: own elaboration

2021a, b, c, 2022a, 2023) and higher the (potential) negative consequences for the local community in the event of massive lay-offs (Kim et al., 2020).

Finally, place attachment represents the mechanism through which individuals develop environmental concerns (Armstrong & Stedman, 2019) and motivation for stewardship and actions to care for the environment (Masterson et al., 2017). This is particularly true for family firms, whose investment strategies incorporate the issues, concerns, and expectations of physically and socially proximate stakeholders for the integrity of the local natural environment (Lähdesmäki & Suutari, 2012; Sharma & Sharma, 2011). As regards environmental protection, family firms usually perform better than non-family firms; and the difference increases, the more family firms are rooted in the local *milieu* (Berrone et al., 2010; Dekker & Hasso, 2016). Thus, a strong "spatial loyalty"—arising from and fed by the family's place attachment—drives family firms toward higher sustainability standards vis-à-vis non-family firms (Pallares-Barbera et al., 2004).

However, local embeddedness is not a static construct. Several contingencies, operating at different levels, may influence the family firms' embeddedness in and disembeddedness from the local *milieu* where the owning family and the firm reside as shown in the following paragraph.

4.7 The Embeddedness and Disembeddedness of Family Firms

Several factors may have the opposite effect on local embeddedness, either heightening or weakening anchorage to the local area. Such factors may be played out at different levels—individual/family, firm, and community—as shown in Table 4.4.

Among the embedding factors operating at the individual and family levels is length of residence in a given location. Individuals who have resided longer in a place are more likely to develop meaningful connections with other residents as well as with physical attributes of a place (Jorgensen & Stedman, 2006). In the case of family members, residence, and shared social experiences intertwine with the economic ones (Smith, 2016), strengthening both the functional—with the place providing the resources necessary for the family's livelihood and other interests—and emotional bonds—in terms of psychological investment developed through experiences over time—to the place (Hinojosa et al., 2016). Place connections are not only the result of personal experiences but can be "inherited" as part of the family's historical memory, thus contributing to the formation of a family's place identity (Cheshire et al., 2013). As such, smooth generational transitions in family firms are deemed to cement the owning family's sense of "bondedness," or feelings of belonging, and a sense of "rootedness" to the place (Manzo & Perkins, 2006), framing and nourishing firm's embeddedness to the local *milieu* (Smith, 2016).

Firm size stands out as a critical embedding factor operating at the organizational level. Small firms are inherently territorial, with operations mainly at the local level and heavily reliant on local resources and opportunities (Gherhes et al., 2021). However, the family status may further heighten the intensity with which the firm absorbs, and in some cases, becomes constrained by the economic activities and social dynamics occurring in the place (Kalantaridis & Bika, 2006). Especially in the case of small family firms, the distinction between the family and the firm may become blurred, which makes the firm extremely permeable to economic events affecting the area (Pallares-Barbera et al., 2004). Direct personal connections of family members, built up and maintained over time in social and business gatherings, are mobilized to deploy critical local inputs, making small family firms highly-dependent upon the immediate surroundings for their growth (Basco et al., 2021). Due to the lack of organizational layers, "social monitoring of family owners is strengthened, and the likelihood of enforcing social sanctions increase" (Berrone et al., 2010, p. 91). As such, the location has a notable effect on the decision-making of small family firms and their conception of corporate social responsibility (Lähdesmäki & Suutari, 2012).

Particular contexts, conflating a sense of place, geographical, and social proximity, may favor the spontaneous embedding of family firms. Among these, rural areas and local production systems, such as the industrial districts. Rural dwellers tend to have more frequent social interactions than urban ones, which increases group identification, emotional affinity, and community involvement (Belanche et al., 2021). In such contexts, trust-based and reciprocal ties within and across families help overcome the limitations of rural environments (Steiner & Atterton, 2015). Take the case for instance of farmers, their inheritance, homeplace and workplace co-location, and iterative business practices closely bind farming families to rural settlements (Cheshire et al., 2013). Empirical evidence shows the tendency of family firms in rural areas to be more closely integrated into the local community (Steiner & Atterton, 2015), as local embeddedness enables them to outperform non-family counterparts (Baù et al., 2019). In industrial districts, a spatial concentration of firms coexists with a community of people, which is characterized by a "relatively homogeneous system of values and views" (Becattini, 1990, p. 39). A feeling of belonging and similarity—based on shared social values, culture, and common production competences—tie family firms to industrial districts (Cucculelli & Storai, 2015). As valuable tacit knowledge is transmitted across generations, socially proximate relationships between family firms and local agents facilitate the exchange of knowledge and information, interactive learning, and a proper balance between competition and cooperation (Amato et al., 2021c). Thus, the owning family's attachment to the local community and the firm's embeddedness in the local production network, allow such firms to extract more value from district localization (Cucculelli & Storai, 2015; Naldi et al., 2013).

Among the disembedding factors operating at the individual and family level are the conflicts within the owning family, which may involve the family members of the same generation (e.g., siblings) or between generations (e.g., parent-offspring) (Bettinelli et al., 2022). Conflicts can disrupt family cohesion as "an individual's sense of belonging to a particular family and his or her feelings of morale associated with membership in the family" (Bollen & Hoyle, 1990, p. 482). Besides the adverse effects on the firm (Bettinelli et al., 2022), lack of cohesion and family conflicts may weaken the individual–family bonds to the territory. Negative experiences due to the family feud permeate family members' social as well as economic life. In such cases, by upsetting the family firm's cohesion, the place may acquire ambivalent meanings for family members (Smith, 2016) and lead them to forego entering the firm, and follow different paths away from home, thus constituting a rupture in the spatial continuity between the owning family and a given location (Amato et al., 2020; Smith, 2016). As the sense of belonging to the owning family and emotional bonds perceived by the family members weaken, the cooling of family relationships may spill over into the organizational domain, affecting the interaction with local agents (Salvato & Melin, 2008). Thus, conflicts and lack of cohesion may endanger the emotional, spatial, and social continuity of the owning family in the place.

Some industries, such as food and wine,[16] are by nature locally embedded. Production occurs in a given biophysical space whose characteristics—soil, climate, and sunlight—foster growth and give the natural products their distinctive character (*terroir*) (Müller & Korsgaard, 2018). Instead, for some industries, local embeddedness results from a complex set of emotional, social, and economic reasons that prompt the entrepreneur to "anchor" the firm in a given location. Therefore, changing economic conditions may suggest relocating all or part of the productive activity elsewhere, severing the firm's economic dependence on a given territory (Di Mauro et al., 2018). Operational and labor cost reduction are typically associated with offshoring decisions (Mudambi & Venzin, 2010). Family firms operating in specific manufacturing industries are no exception, whereby relocation uproots the firm from its home territory. Despite being motivated primarily by non-financial objectives (Gómez-Mejía et al., 2007), family firms operating in particular industries cannot disregard the need for minimum profitability to keep the business afloat, and offshoring could become an option. Another important factor for uprooting the firm from the locality, is the lack of reciprocity.

Localities arise from trust-based and reciprocal social relationships, ignited and nourished by geographical closeness. By holding local actors together, reciprocity "can be considered as indispensable in generating and sustaining productive social exchange" (Becker, 1986, p. 132). In the firm context, reciprocity accounts for the mutual expectation of quid pro quo between local firms and local agents, as

[16]The local roots of family firms in the wine sector will be explored in an empirical qualitative study in the Chap. 6.

consumers and suppliers (Park & Campbell, 2017; Uzzi, 1997). As the local community fulfils the firm's expectations in the form of purchases, loyalty, and promotion (Park & Campbell, 2017), the local firm strongly commit to the welfare and development of the local community (Müller & Korsgaard, 2018). When reciprocity is missing, for instance, the local community does not know about or is not interested in the operations of the local firm (Lähdesmäki & Suutari, 2012). Likewise, the firm is not particularly committed to the area and unwilling to invest in the development of the local community, embracing a "fortress enterprise" mentality in which it dissociates itself totally from any responsibility for its immediate surroundings (Spence, 1999). In the case of family firms, the deadweight loss resulting from the lack of reciprocity would be particularly high, for two main reasons. First, for the family firm itself, given the "value" of territorial ties underpinning their competitive advantage, in particular, contexts would be weakened (Baù et al., 2019; Cucculelli & Storai, 2015). Second, the local community may not benefit from family firms' potential success and pro-social behavior to the local economic sustainability and social well-being (Kim et al., 2020; Shrivastava & Kennelly, 2013). Indeed, without reciprocity, as family firms would be much less committed to the local community, place-relevant decisions such as downsizing, local supply, and relocation, among others, would be easier to make (Amato et al., 2021a, b, c; Lähdesmäki & Suutari, 2012).

Apart from the embedding and uprooting factors described above, too tight bonds are associated with a "lock-in" effect, resulting in organizational inertia, path dependency, and core rigidity (De Massis et al., 2016). Such a lock-in results from a double-layered over-embeddedness involving the relationships within family members and between the owning family and the local area. At family level, as the overload of trust among family members may give rise to opportunistic behavior (Schulze et al., 2001), long-term ties may trap the family firm into established ways of doing things. Shared cognitive schema, created through the time spent under the family's influence (Arregle et al., 2007), may also obscure the prospect of new knowledge, technologies, or market possibilities (Calabrò et al., 2019). When the relationships with the locality are accounted for, the socio-spatial continuity of family firms may be a source of three main adverse effects. First, the embeddedness ties connecting family firms to the local network may reduce the flow of new information, thus compounding the inherent rigidity. At local level, the risk of network "ossification," increases as the number of local firms within the embedded loop grows (Uzzi, 1997) and the degree of openness toward extra-local networks declines (Bathelt et al., 2004). Second, too much institutional proximity—that is, a set of common habits, established routines, and shared values assimilated and reproduced by the owning family over time—implies a lack of awareness of alternative courses of action and impedes the required institutional readjustment (Boschma, 2005; Soleimanof et al., 2018). Finally, a family's strong feeling of belonging to the local *milieu* can come into conflict with the firm's economic imperatives, as the place attachment forces the owning family to favor local interests even when financial reasons would suggest otherwise (Amato et al., 2021a, b, c).

4.8 Concluding Remarks

Embeddedness has become the main paradigm in investigating firms in their socio-spatial environments. Unlike its original conceptualization, embeddedness is now understood in spatial terms, occurring in local networks of social relationships. "Local" refers to a characteristic of a particular area that conflates geographical and social proximity in terms of feelings of belonging and similarity. Local embeddedness is the process through which the firm becomes part of the local structure, enabling it to draw upon local resources and business opportunities. At the same time, being "anchored" in the local area, local embeddedness means that the firm is also constrained by the economic activities and social dynamics already existing therein. However, to fully understand the influence of the location on firm decision-making, it is necessary to look at the deepest, almost hidden, layer of a firm's local embeddedness, which accounts for the personal ties binding the entrepreneur to the local context where the firm operates. To this end, the chapter has disentangled the place attachment of the entrepreneur, that is, the socio-emotional connections binding individuals to a spatial setting replete with meanings and value. When working in the same spatial setting where the entrepreneur was born or has lived for a considerable time, place involves a complex process of the symbolic and social meanings, providing the basis for the understanding of, and relation to, the entrepreneur and the local environment. As shown in the chapter, it is the entrepreneur's place attachment that ends up, ultimately, embedding the firm in the immediate surroundings. However, particular types of firms are regarded as being particularly embedded in the local *milieu*. Anchorage of family firms is produced through a multifaceted historical process of "embedding," which involves a continuous interaction between specific cognitive, cultural, social, institutional, and economic characteristics of the firm's home territory. The chapter has shown that location is not only where the firm is located, but also the physical basin where the owning family lives and evolves over time both as a social entity, participating in the biological and socio-cultural reproduction of the society, as well as an economic actor, shaping the economic course of a territory. In this way, business affairs mingle with family ones, framed in and molded by the same location. Even in the case of family firms, exploring the firm's local embeddedness requires an understanding of what uniquely binds the owning family to the firm's home territory. Their place attachment acts as the latent driver of the firm's local embeddedness, that is, the "local roots" deeply entangling and engaging the firm with a given location. Thus, sticky families result in sticky firms. By uncovering the dimensions of a family firm's place attachment, this chapter has brought together the main empirical evidence on the micro-territorial foundations of family firms. Only by looking at the owning family's socio-emotional and economic connections to the place, that is, place attachment, is it possible to really grasp the interplay between family firms and territory and the distinctive influence of location on family firms' behavior. Nevertheless, as pointed out, too tight-place connections may have ambivalent effects on family firms and the risks associated with over-embeddedness call for an adequate balance between rootedness and openness.

References

Amato, S., Basco, R., Gómez-Ansón, S., & Lattanzi, N. (2020). Family-managed firms and employment growth during an economic downturn: Does their location matter? *Baltic Journal of Management, 15*(4), 607–630. https://doi.org/10.1108/BJM-07-2019-0260

Amato, S., Backman, M., & Peltonen, J. (2021a). Are family firms more locally embedded than non-family firms? Evidence from the Finnish context. In R. Basco, R. Stough, & L. Suwala (Eds.), *Family business and regional development*. Routledge. https://doi.org/10.4324/9780429058097

Amato, S., Basco, R., Backman, M., & Lattanzi, N. (2021b). Family-managed firms and local export spillovers: Evidence from Spanish manufacturing firms. *European Planning Studies, 29*(3), 469–492. https://doi.org/10.1080/09654313.2020.1743238

Amato, S., Patuelli, A., & Lattanzi, N. (2021c). Developing digital innovation in family firms: Evidence from Italian industrial districts. In R. In Basco, R. Stough, & L. Suwala (Eds.), *Family business and regional development*. Routledge. https://doi.org/10.4324/9780429058097

Amato, S., Basco, R., & Lattanzi, N. (2022a). Contextualizing employment outcomes in family business research: Current findings and future research avenues. *Management Review Quarterly, 72*(2), 531–604. https://doi.org/10.1007/s11301-021-00226-9

Amato, S., Ricotta, F., & Basco, R. (2022b). Family-managed firms, external sources of knowledge and innovation. *Industry and Innovation, 29*(6), 701–733. https://doi.org/10.1080/13662716.2021.1976623

Amato, S., Patuelli, A., Basco, R., & Lattanzi, N. (2023). Family firms amidst the global financial crisis: A territorial embeddedness perspective on downsizing. *Journal of Business Ethics, 183*(1), 213–236. https://doi.org/10.1007/s10551-021-04930-0

Andersen, K. V. (2013). The problem of embeddedness revisited: Collaboration and market types. *Research Policy, 42*(1), 139–148. https://doi.org/10.1016/j.respol.2012.05.005

Andersson, U., & Forsgren, M. (1996). Subsidiary embeddedness and control in the multinational corporation. *International Business Review, 5*(5), 487–508. https://doi.org/10.1016/0969-5931(96)00023-6

Armstrong, A., & Stedman, R. C. (2019). Understanding local environmental concern: The importance of place. *Rural Sociology, 84*(1), 93–122. https://doi.org/10.1111/ruso.12215

Arregle, J.-L., Hitt, M. A., Sirmon, D. G., & Very, P. (2007). The development of organizational social capital: Attributes of family firms. *Journal of Management Studies, 44*(1), 73–95. https://doi.org/10.1111/j.1467-6486.2007.00665.x

Attig, N., & Brockman, P. (2017). The local roots of corporate social responsibility. *Journal of Business Ethics, 142*(3), 479–496. https://doi.org/10.1007/s10551-015-2757-3

Balmer, J. M. T., & Burghausen, M. (2015). Explicating corporate heritage, corporate heritage brands and organisational heritage. *Journal of Brand Management, 22*(5), 364–384. https://doi.org/10.1057/bm.2015.26

Banini, T. (2017). Proposing a theoretical framework for local territorial identities: Concepts, questions and pitfalls. *Territorial Identity and Development, 2*(2), 16–23. https://doi.org/10.23740/tid220172

Basco, R., Stough, R., & Suwala, L. (2021). *Family business and regional development*. Routledge. https://doi.org/10.4324/9780429058097

Bathelt, H., Malmberg, A., & Maskell, P. (2004). Clusters and knowledge: Local buzz, global pipelines and the process of knowledge creation. *Progress in Human Geography, 28*(1), 31–56. https://doi.org/10.1191/0309132504ph469oa

Baù, M., Block, J., Discua Cruz, A., & Naldi, L. (2021). Bridging locality and internationalization–A research agenda on the sustainable development of family firms. *Entrepreneurship and Regional Development, 33*(7–8), 477–492. https://doi.org/10.1080/08985626.2021.1925846

Baù, M., Chirico, F., Pittino, D., Backman, M., & Klaesson, J. (2019). Roots to grow: Family firms and local embeddedness in rural and urban contexts. *Entrepreneurship Theory and Practice, 43* (2), 360–385. https://doi.org/10.1177/1042258718796089

Becattini, G. (1990). The Marshallian industrial district as a socio-economic notion. In F. Pyke, G. Becattini, & W. Sengenberger (Eds.), *Industrial district and inter-firm co-operation in Italy*. International Institute for Labour Studies (ILO). https://doi.org/10.4000/rei.6507

Becker, L. C. (1986). *Reciprocity*. Routledge Revivals. https://doi.org/10.4324/9781315780719

Beckert, J. (2007). *The great transformation of embeddedness: Karl Polanyi and the new economic sociology*. Colonia. https://doi.org/10.2139/ssrn.2465810

Belanche, D., Casaló, L. V., & Rubio, M. Á. (2021). Local place identity: A comparison between residents of rural and urban communities. *Journal of Rural Studies, 82*, 242–252. https://doi.org/10.1016/j.jrurstud.2021.01.003

Berrone, P., Cruz, C., Gomez-Mejia, L. R., & Larraza-Kintana, M. (2010). Socioemotional wealth and corporate responses to institutional pressures: Do family-controlled firms pollute less? *Administrative Science Quarterly, 55*(1), 82–113. https://doi.org/10.2307/27856089

Bettinelli, C., Mismetti, M., De Massis, A., & Del Bosco, B. (2022). A review of conflict and cohesion in social relationships in family firms. *Entrepreneurship: Theory and Practice, 46*(3), 539–577. https://doi.org/10.1177/10422587211000339

Bird, M., & Wennberg, K. (2014). Regional influences on the prevalence of family versus non-family start-ups. *Journal of Business Venturing, 29*(3), 421–436. https://doi.org/10.1016/j.jbusvent.2013.06.004

Block, J. H., & Spiegel, F. (2013). Family firm density and regional innovation output: An exploratory analysis. *Journal of Family Business Strategy, 4*(4), 270–280. https://doi.org/10.1016/j.jfbs.2013.10.003

Boley, B. B., Strzelecka, M., Yeager, E. P., Ribeiro, M. A., Aleshinloye, K. D., Woosnam, K. M., & Mimbs, B. P. (2021). Measuring place attachment with the Abbreviated Place Attachment Scale (APAS). *Journal of Environmental Psychology, 74*, 101577. https://doi.org/10.1016/j.jenvp.2021.101577

Bollen, K. A., & Hoyle, R. H. (1990). Perceived cohesion: A conceptual and empirical exandnation. *Social Forces, 69*(2), 479–504. https://doi.org/10.2307/2579670

Boschma, R. (2005). Proximity and innovation: A critical assessment. *Regional Studies, 39*(1), 61–74. https://doi.org/10.1080/0034340052000320887

Bowen, S. (2011). The importance of place: Re-territorialising embeddedness. *Sociologia Ruralis, 51*(4), 325–348. https://doi.org/10.1111/j.1467-9523.2011.00543.x

Brown, G., Raymond, C. M., & Corcoran, J. (2015). Mapping and measuring place attachment. *Applied Geography, 57*, 42–53. https://doi.org/10.1016/j.apgeog.2014.12.011

Bruni, L., Gilli, M., & Pelligra, V. (2008). Reciprocity: Theory and facts. *International Review of Economics, 55*(1–2), 1–11. https://doi.org/10.1007/s12232-008-0042-9

Calabrò, A., Vecchiarini, M., Gast, J., Campopiano, G., De Massis, A., & Kraus, S. (2019). Innovation in family firms: A systematic literature review and guidance for future research. *International Journal of Management Reviews, 21*(3), 317–355. https://doi.org/10.1111/ijmr.12192

Campopiano, G., De Massis, A., & Chirico, F. (2014). Firm philanthropy in small- and medium-sized family firms: The effects of family involvement in ownership and management. *Family Business Review, 27*(3), 244–258. https://doi.org/10.1177/0894486514538450

Capello, R. (2019). Interpreting and understanding territorial identity. *Regional Science Policy and Practice, 11*(1), 141–158. https://doi.org/10.1111/rsp3.12166

Cheshire, L., Meurk, C., & Woods, M. (2013). Decoupling farm, farming and place: Recombinant attachments of globally engaged family farmers. *Journal of Rural Studies, 30*, 64–74. https://doi.org/10.1016/j.jrurstud.2012.11.005

Cooke, P., Clifton, N., & Oleaga, M. (2005). Social capital, firm embeddedness and regional development. *Regional Studies, 39*(8), 1065–1077. https://doi.org/10.1080/00343400500328065

Courtney, P., Lépicier, D., & Schmitt, B. (2008). Spatial patterns of production linkages in the context of Europe's small towns: How are rural firms linked to the local economy? *Regional Studies, 42*(3), 355–374. https://doi.org/10.1080/00343400701291542

Cucculelli, M., & Storai, D. (2015). Family firms and industrial districts: Evidence from the Italian manufacturing industry. *Journal of Family Business Strategy, 6*(4), 234–246. https://doi.org/10.1016/j.jfbs.2015.07.002

D'Aurizio, L., & Romano, L. (2013). *Family firms and the great recession: Out of sight, out of mind?* (No. 905). Temi di discussione (Working Papers). https://doi.org/10.1162/JEEA.2008.6.6.1109

De Massis, A., Frattini, F., Kotlar, J., Petruzzelli, A. M., & Wright, M. (2016). Innovation through tradition: Lessons from innovative family businesses and directions for future research. *Academy of Management Perspectives, 30*(1), 93–116. https://doi.org/10.5465/amp.2015.0017

Dekker, J., & Hasso, T. (2016). Environmental performance focus in private family firms: The role of social embeddedness. *Journal of Business Ethics, 136*(2), 293–309. https://doi.org/10.1007/s10551-014-2516-x

Di Mauro, C., Fratocchi, L., Orzes, G., & Sartor, M. (2018). Offshoring and backshoring: A multiple case study analysis. *Journal of Purchasing and Supply Management, 24*(2), 108–134. https://doi.org/10.1016/j.pursup.2017.07.003

Dicken, P., & Malmberg, A. (2008). Firms in territories: A relational perspective firms. *Economic Geography, 77*(4), 345–363.

Filippi, M., Frey, O., & Torre, A. (2011). The modalities of territorial embeddedness of French cooperative groups. *Territorial Governance*, 43–63. https://doi.org/10.1007/978-3-7908-2422-3_3

Gherhes, C., Vorley, T., & Brooks, C. (2021). The "additional costs" of being peripheral: Developing a contextual understanding of micro-business growth constraints. *Journal of Small Business and Enterprise Development, 28*(1), 59–84. https://doi.org/10.1108/JSBED-03-2019-0091

Gómez-Mejía, L. R., Takács Haynes, K., Núñez-Nickel, M., & Jacobson, K. J. L. (2007). Socioemotional wealth and business risks in family-controlled firms: Evidence from Spanish olive oil mills. *Administrative Science Quarterly, 52*(1), 106–137. https://doi.org/10.2189/asqu.52.1.106

Granovetter, M. (1973). The strength of weak ties. *American Journal of Sociology, 78*(6), 1360–1380. https://www.jstor.org/stable/2776392

Granovetter, M. (1985). Economic action and social structure: The problem of embeddedness. *American Sociology Review, 91*(3), 481–510. https://doi.org/10.1002/9780470755679.ch5

Granovetter, M. (2005). The impact of social structure on economic outcomes social networks and economic outcomes: Core principles. *The Journal of Economic Perspectives, 19*(1), 33–50. Retrieved from https://pubs.aeaweb.org/doi/pdf/10.1257/0895330053147958

Greenberg, Z., Farja, Y., & Gimmon, E. (2018). Embeddedness and growth of small businesses in rural regions. *Journal of Rural Studies, 62*, 174–182. https://doi.org/10.1016/j.jrurstud.2018.07.016

Greider, T., & Garkovich, L. (1994). Landscapes: The social construction of nature and the environment. *Rural Sociology, 59*(1), 1–24. https://doi.org/10.1111/j.1549-0831.1994.tb00519.x

Guillén, M. F., Collins, R., England, P., & Meyer, M. (2002). *The new economic sociology: Developments in an emerging field.* Russell Sage Foundation. https://www.jstor.org/stable/10.7758/9781610442602

Hess, M. (2004). "Spatial" relationships? Towards a reconceptualization of embeddedness. *Progress in Human Geography, 28*(2), 165–186. https://doi.org/10.1191/0309132504ph479oa

Hidalgo, M. C., & Hernández, B. (2001). Place attachment: Conceptual and empirical questions. *Journal of Environmental Psychology, 21*(3), 273–281. https://doi.org/10.1006/jevp.2001.0221

Hinojosa, L., Lambin, E. F., Mzoughi, N., & Napoléone, C. (2016). Place attachment as a factor of mountain farming permanence: A survey in the French southern Alps. *Ecological Economics, 130*, 308–315. https://doi.org/10.1016/j.ecolecon.2016.08.004

Hjorth, D., & Dawson, A. (2016). The burden of history in the family business organization. *Organization Studies, 37*(8), 1089–1111. https://doi.org/10.1177/0170840615613375

Ingham, G. (1996). Review essay. The "New Economic Sociology". *Work, Employment and Society, 10*(3), 549–564. https://www.jstor.org/stable/23746650

Jack, S. L., & Anderson, A. R. (2002). The effects of embeddedness on the entrepreneurial process. *Journal of Business Venturing, 17*(5), 467–487. https://doi.org/10.1016/S0883-9026(01)00076-3

Jorgensen, B. S., & Stedman, R. C. (2006). A comparative analysis of predictors of sense of place dimensions: Attachment to, dependence on, and identification with lakeshore properties. *Journal of Environmental Management, 79*(3), 316–327. https://doi.org/10.1016/j.jenvman.2005.08.003

Kadushin, C. (2012). *Understanding social networks. Theories, comncepts, and findings*. Oxford University Press. Inc.. Retrieved from https://www.ptonline.com/articles/how-to-get-better-mfi-results

Kalantaridis, C., & Bika, Z. (2006). Local embeddedness and rural entrepreneurship: Case-study evidence from Cumbria, England. *Environment and Planning A, 38*(8), 1561–1579. https://doi.org/10.1068/a3834

Kesidou, E., & Romijn, H. (2008). Do local knowledge spillovers matter for development? An empirical study of Uruguay's software cluster. *World Development, 36*(10), 2004–2028. https://doi.org/10.1016/j.worlddev.2008.01.003

Kim, K., Haider, Z. A., Wu, Z., & Dou, J. (2020). Corporate social performance of family firms: A place-based perspective in the context of layoffs. *Journal of Business Ethics, 167*, 235–252. https://doi.org/10.1007/s10551-019-04152-5

Korsgaard, S., Müller, S., & Tanvig, H. W. (2015). Rural entrepreneurship or entrepreneurship in the rural – between place and space. *International Journal of Entrepreneurial Behavior & Research, 21*(1), 5–26. https://doi.org/10.1108/IJEBR-11-2013-0205

Krippner, G. (2001). The elusive market: Embeddedness and the paradigm of economic sociology. *Theory and Society, 30*(6), 775–810. https://www.jstor.org/stable/658117

Lähdesmäki, M., & Suutari, T. (2012). Keeping at arm's length or searching for social proximity? Corporate social responsibility as a reciprocal process between small businesses and the local community. *Journal of Business Ethics, 108*(4), 481–493. https://doi.org/10.1007/s10551-011-1104-6

Lähdesmäki, M., & Takala, T. (2012). Altruism in business - An empirical study of philanthropy in the small business context. *Social Responsibility Journal, 8*(3), 373–388. https://doi.org/10.1108/17471111211247947

Lähdesmäki, M., Siltaoja, M., & Spence, L. J. (2019). Stakeholder salience for small businesses: A social proximity perspective. *Journal of Business Ethics, 158*, 373–385. https://doi.org/10.1007/s10551-017-3707-z

Lambooy, J. G. (2010). Knowledge transfers, spillovers and actors: The role of context and social capital. *European Planning Studies, 18*(6), 873–891. https://doi.org/10.1080/09654311003701407

Lewicka, M. (2008). Place attachment, place identity, and place memory: Restoring the forgotten city past. *Journal of Environmental Psychology, 28*(3), 209–231. https://doi.org/10.1016/j.jenvp.2008.02.001

Lin, C. C., & Lockwood, M. (2014). Forms and sources of place attachment: Evidence from two protected areas. *Geoforum, 53*, 74–81. https://doi.org/10.1016/j.geoforum.2014.02.008

Lorentzen, A. (2008). Knowledge networks in local and global space. *Entrepreneurship and Regional Development, 20*(6), 533–545. https://doi.org/10.1080/08985620802462124

Low, S. M. (1992). Symbolic ties that bind. Place attachment in the plaza. In I. Altman & S. M. Low (Eds.), *Place attachment*. Springer. https://doi.org/10.1007/978-1-4684-8753-4_8

Magistretti, S., Dell'Era, C., Frattini, F., & Messeni Petruzzelli, A. (2020). Innovation through tradition in design-intensive family firms. *Journal of Knowledge Management, 24*(4), 823–839. https://doi.org/10.1108/JKM-07-2019-0399

Magnaghi, A. (2010). *Il Progetto locale. Verso la coscienza di luogo*. Bollati Boringheri.

Malmberg, A., & Maskell, P. (2006). Localized learning revisited. *Growth and Change, 37*(1), 1–18. https://doi.org/10.1111/j.1468-2257.2006.00302.x

Manzo, L. C. (2005). For better or worse: Exploring multiple dimensions of place meaning. *Journal of Environmental Psychology, 25*(1), 67–86. https://doi.org/10.1016/j.jenvp.2005.01.002

Manzo, L. C., & Perkins, D. D. (2006). Finding common ground: The importance of place attachment to community participation and planning. *Journal of Planning Literature, 20*(4), 335–350. https://doi.org/10.1177/0885412205286160

Markusen, A. (1994). Studying regions by studying firms. *Professional Geographer, 46*(4), 477–490. https://doi.org/10.1111/j.0033-0124.1994.00477.x

Martin, R. (1994). Economic theory and human geography. In D. Gregory, R. Martin, & G. Smith (Eds.), *Human geography: Society, space and social science*. The MacMillan Press LTD. https://doi.org/10.1007/978-1-349-23638-1

Masterson, V. A., Stedman, R. C., Enqvist, J., Tengö, M., Giusti, M., Wahl, D., & Svedin, U. (2017). The contribution of sense of place to social-ecological systems research: A review and research agenda. *Ecology and Society, 22*(1). https://doi.org/10.5751/ES-08872-220149

McKeever, E., Anderson, A., & Jack, S. (2014). Entrepreneurship and mutuality: Social capital in processes and practices. *Entrepreneurship and Regional Development, 26*(5–6), 453–477. https://doi.org/10.1080/08985626.2014.939536

McKeever, E., Jack, S., & Anderson, A. (2015). Embedded entrepreneurship in the creative re-construction of place. *Journal of Business Venturing, 30*(1), 50–65. https://doi.org/10.1016/j.jbusvent.2014.07.002

Möllering, G. (2001). The nature of trust: From Georg Simmel to a theory of expectation, interpretation and suspension. *Sociology, 35*(2), 403–420. https://doi.org/10.1017/S0038038501000190

Molm, L. D. (2010). The structure of reciprocity. *Social Psychology Quarterly, 73*(2), 119–131. https://doi.org/10.1177/0190272510369079

Mudambi, R., & Venzin, M. (2010). The strategic nexus of offshoring and outsourcing decisions. *Journal of Management Studies, 47*(8), 1510–1533. https://doi.org/10.1111/j.1467-6486.2010.00947.x

Müller, S., & Korsgaard, S. (2018). Resources and bridging: The role of spatial context in rural entrepreneurship. *Entrepreneurship and Regional Development, 30*(1–2), 224–255. https://doi.org/10.1080/08985626.2017.1402092

Naldi, L., Cennamo, C., Corbetta, G., & Gomez-Mejia, L. (2013). Preserving socioemotional wealth in family firms: Asset or liability? The moderating role of business context. *Entrepreneurship: Theory and Practice, 37*(6), 1341–1360. https://doi.org/10.1111/etap.12069

Oinas, P. (1997). On the socio-spatial embeddedness of business firms. *Erdkunde, 51*(1), 23–32. https://doi.org/10.3112/erdkunde.1997.01.03

Pallares-Barbera, M., Tulla, A. F., & Vera, A. (2004). Spatial loyalty and territorial embeddedness in the multi-sector clustering of the Berguedà region in Catalonia (Spain). *Geoforum, 35*(5), 635–649. https://doi.org/10.1016/j.geoforum.2004.03.004

Park, J., & Campbell, J. M. (2017). U.S. SMEs' corporate citizenship: Collectivism, market orientation, and reciprocity. *Journal of Small Business and Entrepreneurship, 29*(2), 120–139. https://doi.org/10.1080/08276331.2016.1256930

Parr, J. B. (2002). Agglomeration economies: Ambiguities and confusions. *Environment and Planning A, 34*(4), 717–731. https://doi.org/10.1068/a34106

Polanyi, K. (1957). *The great transformation: The political and economic origins of our time*. Beacon Press.

Radu-Lefebvre, M., Lefebvre, V., Crosina, E., & Hytti, U. (2021). Entrepreneurial identity: A review and research agenda. *Entrepreneurship: Theory and Practice, 45*(6), 1550–1590. https://doi.org/10.1177/10422587211013795

Rajala, K., Sorice, M. G., & Thomas, V. A. (2020). The meaning(s) of place: Identifying the structure of sense of place across a social–ecological landscape. *People and Nature, 2*(3), 718–733. https://doi.org/10.1002/pan3.10112

Ranfagni, S., Runfola, A., & Sarti, D. (2021). Family firms between territory and internationalization: An authenticity based perspective. *Entrepreneurship and Regional Development, 33*(7–8), 555–579. https://doi.org/10.1080/08985626.2021.1925850

Ratajczak-Mrozek, M. (2017). *Network embeddedness: Examining the effect on business performance and internationalization*. Palgrave Macmillan. https://doi.org/10.1007/978-3-319-56511-8

Raymond, C. M., Brown, G., & Weber, D. (2010). The measurement of place attachment: Personal, community, and environmental connections. *Journal of Environmental Psychology, 30*(4), 422–434. https://doi.org/10.1016/j.jenvp.2010.08.002

Ren, S., Cheng, Y., Hu, Y., & Yin, C. (2021). Feeling right at home: Hometown CEOs and firm innovation. *Journal of Corporate Finance, 66*, 101815. https://doi.org/10.1016/j.jcorpfin.2020.101815

Ritchter, R. (2015). New economic sociology and new institutional economics. In *Essays on new institutional economics* (pp. 51–75). Springer. https://doi.org/10.1007/978-3-319-14154-1_3

Rutten, R., Westlund, H., & Boekema, F. (2010). The spatial dimension of social capital. *European Planning Studies, 18*(6), 863–871. https://doi.org/10.1080/09654311003701381

Salvato, C., & Melin, L. (2008). Creating value across generations in family-controlled businesses: The role of family social capital. *Family Business Review, 21*(3), 259–276. https://doi.org/10.1111/j.1741-6248.2008.00127.x

Sampson, K. A., & Goodrich, C. G. (2009). Making place: Identity construction and community formation through "Sense of Place" in Westland, New Zealand. *Society and Natural Resources, 22*, 901–915. https://doi.org/10.1080/08941920802178172

Schulze, W. S., Lubatkin, M. H., Dino, R. N., & Buchholtz, A. K. (2001). Agency relationships in family firms: Theory and evidence. *Organization Science, 12*(2), 99–116. https://doi.org/10.1287/orsc.12.2.99.10114

Sharma, P., & Sharma, S. (2011). Drivers of proactive environmental strategy in family firms. *Business Ethics Quarterly, 21*(2), 309–334. https://doi.org/10.5840/beq201121218

Shrivastava, P., & Kennelly, J. J. (2013). Sustainability and place-based enterprise. *Organization and Environment, 26*(1), 83–101. https://doi.org/10.1177/1086026612475068

Siemens, L. (2019). Strengthening and sustaining a community through reciprocal support between local businesses and the community. *Journal of Enterprising Communities, 13*(5), 668–680. https://doi.org/10.1108/JEC-09-2018-0060

Smith, C. (2016). Environmental jolts: Understanding how family firms respond and why. *Family Business Review, 29*(4), 401–423. https://doi.org/10.1177/0894486516673906

Soleimanof, S., Rutherford, M. W., & Webb, J. W. (2018). The intersection of family firms and institutional contexts: A review and agenda for future research. *Family Business Review, 31*(1), 32–53. https://doi.org/10.1177/0894486517736446

Spence, L. J. (1999). Does size matter? The state of the art in small business ethics. *Business Ethics: A European Review, 8*(3), 163–174. https://doi.org/10.1111/1467-8608.00144

Spielmann, N., Discua Cruz, A., Tyler, B. B., & Beukel, K. (2021). Place as a nexus for corporate heritage identity: An international study of family-owned wineries. *Journal of Business Research, 129*(February 2017), 826–837. https://doi.org/10.1016/j.jbusres.2019.05.024

Steiner, A., & Atterton, J. (2015). Exploring the contribution of rural enterprises to local resilience. *Journal of Rural Studies, 40*, 30–45. https://doi.org/10.1016/j.jrurstud.2015.05.004

Steinmo, M. (2015). Collaboration for innovation: A case study on how social capital mitigates collaborative challenges in university–industry research alliances. *Industry and Innovation, 22*(7), 597–624. https://doi.org/10.1080/13662716.2015.1105127

Trentelman, C. K. (2009). Place attachment and community attachment: A primer grounded in the lived experience of a community sociologist. *Society and Natural Resources, 22*(3), 191–210. https://doi.org/10.1080/08941920802191712

Twigger-Ross, C. L., & Uzzell, D. L. (1996). Place and identity process. *Journal of Environmental Psychology, 16*, 205–220. https://doi.org/10.1006/jevp.1996.0017

Uhlaner, L. M., Matser, I. A., Berent-Braun, M. M., & Flören, R. H. (2015). Linking bonding and bridging ownership social capital in private firms: Moderating effects of ownership–management overlap and family firm identity. *Family Business Review, 28*(3), 260–277. https://doi.org/10.1177/0894486515568974

Uzzi, B. (1997). Social structure and competition in interfirm networks: The paradox of embeddedness. *Administrative Science Quartertly, 42*(1), 35–67. https://doi.org/10.2307/2393808

Uzzi, B. (1999). Embeddedness in the making of financial capital: How social relations and networks benefit firms seeking financing. *American Sociological Review, 64*(4), 481–505. https://doi.org/10.2307/2657252

Welter, F. (2011). Contextualizing entrepreneurship—Conceptual challenges and ways forward. *Entrepreneurship: Theory and Practice, 35*(1), 165–184. https://doi.org/10.1111/j.1540-6520.2010.00427.x

Williams, D. R. (2014). Making sense of "place": Reflections on pluralism and positionality in place research. *Landscape and Urban Planning, 131*, 74–82. https://doi.org/10.1016/j.landurbplan.2014.08.002

Williamson, O. E. (1975). *Markets and hierarchies: Analysis and antitrust implications*. The Free Press.

Wrong, D. H. (1961). The oversocialized conception of man in modern sociology. *American Sociological Review, 26*(2), 183–193. https://doi.org/10.2307/2089854

Zahra, S. A. (2010). Harvesting family firms' organizational social capital: A relational perspective. *Journal of Management Studies, 47*(2), 345–366. https://doi.org/10.1111/j.1467-6486.2009.00894.x

Zukauskaite, E., Trippl, M., & Plechero, M. (2017). Institutional thickness revisited. *Economic Geography, 93*(4), 325–345. https://doi.org/10.1080/00130095.2017.1331703

Chapter 5
Family Firms, Corporate Social Responsibility, and Place-Based Enterprises

5.1 Introduction

What does it mean for a business to be "responsible"? To whom and for what actions should companies be responsible? These are just a few questions based on the academic debate on CSR (Moir, 2001). How does the family dimension affect a family firm's responsible behaviors? What impact do local roots have? What happens to a firm's engagement in CSR when these two aspects—local roots and the family nature—are combined? This latter issue is fascinating to scholars but underexplored in practice (Baù et al., 2021). To answer, this chapter uses a novel integration of three research streams, connecting family firms, local roots, and CSR.

First, this chapter will provide an excursus of the main definitions associated with CSR, then deepen the theoretical approaches used to explain why companies engage in CSR, namely stakeholder theory, social contract theory, and legitimacy theory. It will then disentangle how the family dimension can impact a firm's CSR engagement. Rather than comparing family versus non-family firms' approaches to CSR, the chapter will discuss why family firms could show peculiar social and environmentally responsible behaviors. While Chap. 4 has already described the concept of local roots for firms and family firms in detail, this chapter will discuss a specific perspective of this relationship, namely the effects that local roots can have on firms' responsible behaviors. Last, building on Shrivastava & Kennelly (2013), the chapter will present the notion of "place-based family enterprise," proposing an integrated approach to explain how and why family firms with strong connections to their local territory could show a very high engagement in CSR.

S. Amato, A. Patuelli, *Family Firms and Local Roots*, CSR, Sustainability, Ethics & Governance, https://doi.org/10.1007/978-3-031-31793-4_5

5.2 Corporate Social Responsibility

The world of CSR is highly multifaceted. CSR is a multidimensional concept, and it has been variously defined in the last 70 years. Today, CSR is associated with many topics, including Corporate Citizenship, Sustainability, Corporate Environmental Management, and others (Matten & Moon, 2004). The term has been discussed in the academic debate, and the world of businesspeople debates its meaning and operationalization. The term also entered the political debate and has been approached from many perspectives, including philosophical, biological, psychological, sociological, and economic ones (Mintzberg, 1983). By nature, CSR as a concept and its practical implications change depending on many factors, including the historical period and social expectations (Latapí Agudelo et al., 2019), the managerial worldviews and perceptions (Pedersen, 2009), the industry a firm belongs to (Patuelli et al., 2021) and many others. As expectations about the social and environmental aspects change depending on time and space, what constitutes CSR in practice cannot be univocally defined.

However, the CSR literature has made many attempts to conceptualize and uniquely define CSR in the last 70 years.[1] The term first appeared in the business and management literature in the 1950s (Mariani et al., 2021). It referred to questioning which obligations businesspeople should have to society (Bowen, 1953). The 1960s was a time of significant change, marked by the growth of a protest culture that asked for more civil rights and was against the war. Consequently, the CSR concept attracted interest and endorsement in the following decades, with contributions from eminent scholars of the time (Frederick in 1960 and Davis in 1960, as cited in Latapí Agudelo et al., 2019). Later, CSR was broadened and further defined as all the company's responsibilities to society, including the economic, legal, ethical, and discretionary dimensions (Carroll, 1979). The 1980s were times of further global acknowledgment of environmental and social issues. Indeed, relevant international events took place, including the publication of "Our common future," which posed the definition of sustainable development.[2] The 1990s brought two critical contributions to the debate and operationalization of CSR. First, Carroll (1991) developed the "Pyramid of Corporate Social Responsibility," thus conceptualizing CSR as composed of four dimensions: economic, legal, ethical, and philanthropic. Meanwhile, today well-known triple bottom line principle has come to life. Differently from Carrol, Elkington

---

[1] This chapter briefly depicts some definitions and time evolutions of CSR concepts. It is not aimed to provide a detailed excursus of the development of the CSR concepts and definitions over time, although the theme is fascinating. To this extent, please consult, among others, Moir (2001) and Windsor (2001) for a thorough discussion of the changes in CSR in the academic debate; and Latapí Agudelo et al. (2019) for a review of both academic pieces and public international events that have shaped the evolution of CSR.

[2] Sustainable development is intended as "the development that meets the needs of the present without compromising the ability of future generations to meet their own needs" (WCED, 1987). Later contributions from the United Nations continued to specify and refine sustainable development components (Tsalis et al., 2020).

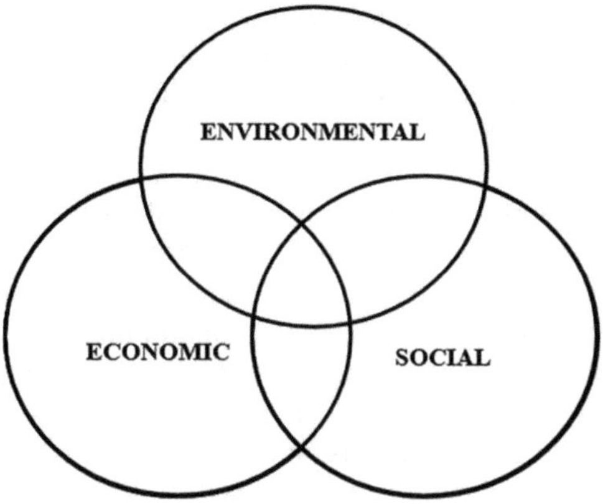

Fig. 5.1 The three dimensions of CSR (Source: Own elaboration, adapted from Barbier (1987) and Elkington (1998))

(1998) conceptualized the responsibilities of businesses as environmental, social, and economic (Fig. 5.1).

These are consistent with the three systems (or perspectives) combined in the sustainability and sustainable development literature,[3] which considers three dimensions humans should pursue (Barbier, 1987; Purvis et al., 2019).

The development of quality certifications for companies' processes, internationally developed and recognized, increased the relevance of CSR, supporting businesses to implement it in practice (Latapí Agudelo et al., 2019). Indeed, from the 1980s–1990s, the International Organization for Standardization (ISO)[4] issued voluntary standards that can be used internationally to establish quality systems in companies. Some certifications are aimed at protecting the environment, such as EMAS and UNI EN ISO 14001, or involve relations with social partners, for example, AS 8000.

Additionally, the establishment in 2015 of the Sustainable Development Goals (SDGs), global objectives that the United Nations set for all humanity, represent a reinforcement of the importance of CSR within businesses. Apart from being addressed to all society members, firms are considered critical players in achieving global goals (Scheyvens et al., 2016). The goals promote action in crucial areas for people and the entire planet while balancing the three aspects of sustainable development (economic, social, and environmental). As such, they are coherent with the CSR dimensions (Elkington, 1998).[5]

[3] Although sustainability and sustainable development are concepts somehow related to CSR, it is outside the aim of this chapter to discuss them in detail.

[4] In 1947, the ISO was settled, and it is now the largest organization for standardization in the world. The standards published by ISO are voluntary: companies are not obliged to transpose them unless this is imposed by national legislation. For further information, please see www.iso.org

[5] The SDGs are 17 in number. They address challenges that affect every human being on the planet: goal 1 "No poverty," goal 2 "Zero hunger," goal 3 "Good health and well-being," goal 4 "Quality

Today, a generally recognized approach defines CSR "as actions that appear to further some social good, beyond the interests of the firm and that which is required by law. This definition underscores that, to us, CSR means going beyond obeying the law" (McWilliams & Siegel, 2001). It is also intended as a general umbrella concept for business operations directed toward society, including charitable giving, volunteer work, environmental initiatives, and moral business conduct (Freeman & Dmytriyev, 2017). The European Union acknowledges that companies' decisions greatly influence how people live, not simply in terms of the goods and services they provide, the employment they provide, or the opportunities they open up, but also in terms of the workplace, human rights, health, the environment, innovation, education, and training. It broadly defines CSR as the "responsibility of enterprises for their impact on society," recognizing its multifaceted nature (European Commission, 2011). In sum, CSR includes initiatives businesses do to improve society and the environment locally and internationally.

However, this definition responds only partially to our introductory question: what does it mean for a business to be responsible? Why would a company decide to act responsibly? Indeed, apart from agreeing (or not agreeing) on a definition, CSR could be communicated, implemented, and reported in many different ways depending on the business and its context. There is no one-side-fit-all approach for CSR among firms (van Marrewijk & Werre, 2003).

A primary research stream[6] in the CSR literature investigates the factors that bring a firm to engage in CSR actions (Attig & Brockman, 2017). This chapter engages with and contributes to this stream of research, with a specific interest in discussing how CSR varies in various organizational contexts and under particular circumstances (Mariani et al., 2021). First and foremost, before entering the intersections between the family business and the CSR domains, it is essential to understand the prevalent theoretical approaches[7] that explain why companies engage with CSR, namely, stakeholder, social contract, and legitimacy theory (Moir, 2001). The three approaches described below should be seen as distinct and overlapping, mutually enhancing perspectives on the same phenomenon (Gray et al., 1995).

education," goal 5 "Gender equality," goal 6 "Clear water and sanitation," goal 7 "Affordable and clean energy," goal 8 "Decent work and economic growth," goal 9 "Industry, innovation and infrastructure," goal 10 "Reduced inequalities," goal 11 "Sustainable cities and communities," goal 12 "Responsible consumption and production," goal 13 "Climate action," goal 14 "Life below water," goal 15 "Life on land," goal 16 "Peace, justice, and strong institutions," goal 17 "Partnership for the goals." The goals can be grouped into the social dimension (goals 1–5, 10, 16, and 17), the economic (goals 7–9, 11, and 12), and the environmental one (goals 6, 13–15) (D'Adamo et al., 2021).

[6]CSR has generated a significant body of knowledge in academic research (Attig & Brockman, 2017). The other primary research stream investigates the relationship between corporate social responsibility and financial results. However, discussing this literature section is outside this chapter's aims.

[7]Indeed, many theories and approaches contribute to explaining why firms engage in responsible initiatives. As the objectives of this chapter are to disentangle the relationships between CSR, family businesses and their local roots, this part will be selective on the concepts presented, focusing on the basic ideas explaining the main drivers of CSR.

Freeman first proposed the stakeholder approach in his study, published in 1984. It claims that firms engage in CSR because they have duties to a variety of stakeholders in addition to shareholders. Stakeholder theory focuses on the local society rather than the global picture. Indeed, it is centered upon those actors within the business' reach, which include the community where the business functions and its surroundings (Freeman & Dmytriyev, 2017). The key stakeholders are often the firm's workers, clients, communities, suppliers, and funders; however, the mix of stakeholders may vary based on the industry and business model of the organization. Each of these stakeholders is equally significant to the business, and executives must discover means of directing various interests in the same direction (Freeman & Dmytriyev, 2017). Incorporating such expectations into operations or communication becomes crucial for businesses (Castelo et al., 2007). In sum, firms behave consistently with stakeholders' expectations, developing long-term relationships with them (Freeman, 2015).

Coming from the business ethics field, the basic notion in social contract theory is that society is made up of implicit contracts (Donaldson & Dunfee, 2002), as if businesses and individuals within society were tied by contracts (Hsieh, 2015). It integrates a macrosocial contract with several microsocial contracts unique to each community. The first comprises hyper norms that represent universal principles everyone should adhere to. The microsocial contracts are based on sets of moral guidelines that are pertinent to the members of the specific community. Communities can be formal or informal, including businesses, departments, professional organizations, and industries (Jahn & Brühl, 2016). Social contracts, as morality, are not absolutes. They are conditional to specific communities. The concepts of what is acceptable and what is not may vary depending on the situation, and economic actors should acknowledge the (implicit) social contract occurring in their community. As social contracts change, businesses will face different challenges too. For example, 50 years ago, enterprises were primarily expected to concentrate on producing goods and services at competitive costs; now, businesses are held accountable for several concerns concerning equality and life quality (Donaldson & Dunfee, 2002). Under this perspective, companies engaging in responsible activities are considered to serve society as a whole (Hsieh, 2015).

According to the legitimacy theory (Brown & Deegan, 1998), businesses should act following societal norms and values. These are not constant; they change across time and space. Although the first empirical attempts did not confirm this approach (Guthrie & Parker, 1989), further inquiry proved legitimacy as a reason why firms disclose more about CSR than others (Lanis & Richardson, 2013). Legitimacy theory holds that organizations should behave following the laws and standards of the society where they operate. If a firm cannot work as expected, the business will be negatively impacted in the long term. Community expectations are not believed to be static but rather fluctuate with time, necessitating the need for organizations to be sensitive to their operating environment. By adopting this viewpoint, an organization might lose its legitimacy even though its behaviors have not altered from those previously regarded as appropriate (Deegan et al., 2002).

Despite the many findings and theoretical approaches, more research on why companies engage in CSR is needed, especially systems that combine different levels of analysis and theoretical perspectives. In particular, we need explanations that combine the micro-level with the meso- and macro-levels, as well as theoretical approaches coming from different disciplines, with combinations of multiple theories also possible to explain the CSR phenomenon (Frynas & Yamahaki, 2016). The following section will discuss the interrelationships between the fields of CSR and a specific type of organization, the objective of this book: the family business.

5.3 CSR in Family Firms

A significant portion of the scholarly discussion over the past two decades has focused on the motivations and practices that influence CSR and how CSR varies in organizational contexts (Mariani et al., 2021). As previously described,[8] family enterprises are a peculiar kind of organization. Although with mixed findings, the literature has generally empirically discovered that family firms engage more in CSR activities (Campopiano & de Massis, 2015; Lamb & Butler, 2016; Venturelli et al., 2021). However, rather than comparing family and non-family firms, it is far more crucial to analyze the antecedents that are more likely to determine family firms' approaches to CSR (Bergamaschi & Randerson, 2016; Izzo & Ciaburri, 2018). The question would be how the family and its unique interaction with the business affect CSR (Ernst et al., 2022a).

SEW theory explains the higher concern in CSR. SEW theory, which refers to the non-financial components of family owners' "affective endowments," suggests that family firms are frequently motivated by and committed to the maintenance of their SEW. Family businesses consider gains or losses in SEW as their main point of reference when making choices (Berrone et al., 2012). According to this logic, a family business is, on some occasions, more willing to face financial hardships than non-family businesses, along with favoring other non-financial objectives, such as CSR (Breton-Miller & Miller, 2016; Gómez-Mejía et al., 2007). However, depending on the relevance that different family firms attribute to distinctive SEW dimensions, family firms can be different in their engagement with CSR (Diéguez-Soto et al., 2021).

The family nature of the business influences firms' engagement both in CSR activities and mentions on the firms' websites (Venturelli et al., 2021), as well as firms' environmental disclosure, meaning that the family nature brings firms to be more transparent about their responsible actions (Terlaak et al., 2018). To mention a few examples of what this means, the family dimension was found to play a crucial role in the decision to invest in methods to lessen their environmental impact

[8] Please see Chap. 2, "Defining and Understanding the Family Firm" for a clear picture of what a family firm is and how it differs from other organizations.

(Bammens & Hünermund, 2020). Indeed, family values, also coming from the previous generations, are essential both to develop CSR initiatives and for family firms to engage with global challenges[9] (Patuelli et al., 2022). However, a competing perspective on SEW and CSR commitment contends that family enterprises may use CSR investments to pursue self-oriented profits rather than to advance the "greater good" (Zientara, 2017).

Family businesses do choose to participate in CSR for various reasons. Breton-Miller and Miller (2016) identify four reasons why family businesses act in an ethical, socially, and ecologically responsible manner: (1) family values, beliefs, parenting methods, and education (i.e., growing up in difficult circumstances encourages more awareness of societal issues); (2) aspects of governance, such as ownership, the structure of the board, and the participation of family members, can affect how responsibly a company conducts itself; (3) the structure of the organization (i.e., some firm-level elements, such as size and strategy, may facilitate sustainable behavior); (4) and the environment in which the business is situated (i.e., some environments tend to support sustainable practices owing to the institutional background, values, spatial and social proximity to the local community, or other variables). Supporting the latter viewpoint, family businesses are more likely to express great care for their home region than non-family businesses (Amato et al., 2023; Basco, 2015; Mariani et al., 2021).

Indeed, the motivations that drive family firms to act responsibly toward their territories and societies require further investigation (Bergamaschi & Randerson, 2016). Although this need is felt among family business and CSR scholars (Fehre & Weber, 2019; Randerson, 2022), the topic still has much potential to mature, and the results so far could be more consistent (Mariani et al., 2021). This chapter will focus on this latter perspective in the fifth paragraph. As anticipated in the introduction, the objective of this chapter is to propose an integrated view of CSR in family firms, considering the effects that the local roots of the family firm could have. However, before presenting this view, it is necessary to take another step back and explore the relationships between firms, local roots, and CSR.

5.4 Local Roots as Boosters of Firms' Responsible Actions

Human beings and firms can be active participants in preserving their local areas, sustaining the life of the ecosystems and, consequently, individuals and businesses themselves (Walck, 1996). Depending on multiple aspects, including ownership, governance, the sector of the activities, and how operations are spread in the

[9] A global initiative aimed at incentivising family firms to embed sustainability in their strategy is the Family Business Sustainability Pledge. Developed from a partnership between the United Nations and the global family business community. The partnership produced a pledge that family businesses committing to the SDGs can sign and indicators for family firm reporting. The Family Business Sustainability Pledge is available at: https://fbsd.unctad.org/pledge/

territories, firms can have different nuances of attachments to where they are settled.[10] This attachment may manifest in different approaches to protecting and nurturing the place and its people. Scholars have widely discussed if, why, and how a firm is willing to care and act responsibly for the territory and the community where it is rooted, combining different theoretical approaches and developing novel ones.

Indeed, the place can be critical in developing a responsibility logic within businesses (Hermelingmeier et al., 2022). On the one hand, firms embedded in a local context are aware of local needs and expectations and contribute to them (Blombäck & Wigren, 2009). Their engagement and identification with the place can become critical assets for firms and for supporting a local area, determining its recovery and growth (Pallares-Barbera et al., 2004). On the other hand, the behaviors of different actors (individuals or organizations) in a circumscribed place can influence local firms' behaviors. Local firms tend to be more proactive regarding CSR in communities where residents are used to pro-social behaviors. In practice, the unique characteristics of the social dimension in terms of philanthropic actions in the place create a higher engagement for firms in CSR activities (Attig & Brockman, 2017). Similarly, when the place where firms are embedded values sustainability, this can stimulate firms to adopt sustainability practices (Sharafizad et al., 2022). When firms are embedded in a community of other firms actively interested in environmental engagement, they benefit from other organizations' knowledge and spillovers, translating into a stimulus to act environmentally responsibly. Eventually, local firms stimulate each other's responsible actions, thus shaping an ecosystem of firms rooted in a region and engaged in environmentally accountable acts (DeBoer et al., 2017).

Another explanation of locally embedded firms' more profound concern for the local area is found in the stakeholder salience literature. Stakeholder salience is defined as "the degree to which managers give priority to competing stakeholder claims" (Mitchell et al., 1997, p. 854). Developing from stakeholder theory (Freeman, 1984), this approach aims to explain why firms prioritize the needs of some stakeholders compared to others. A firm's perceptions of its social ties to a particular actor can significantly influence whether the actor and its arguments should be prioritized. Thus, social closeness affects how firms perceive stakeholder power, urgency, and legitimacy (Lähdesmäki et al., 2019). Small business owners and managers typically emphasize community claims and concerns because they believe them to be meaningful and valid, regardless of how much power they believe the community has over their company (Park & Campbell, 2018). Local stakeholders' claims might be felt as closer, and firms might prioritize these compared to national ones, which appear remote (Ernst et al., 2022b). However, social proximity does not always translate into good relationships, as it can also result in negative feelings toward stakeholders (Siltaoja & Lähdesmäki, 2015).

---

[10]While the academic literature on firms and places has already been discussed in Chaps. 3 and 4, this part will refer to some of the concepts already mentioned and focus on local roots' effects on CSR.

In 2013, the novel concept of the place-based enterprise was developed, which encloses the ideas abovementioned. The concept defines a firm deeply rooted in its local territory that, in return, would show a strong orientation toward preserving it with environmentally and socially respectful actions. The place-based enterprise has specific characteristics (Shrivastava & Kennelly, 2013), namely:

- Local ownership and control: such businesses tend to invest their capital in the long term.
- Production operations that are dependent on location for specific, exclusive, and unique resources, with the firm's identity becoming closely tied to location.
- Relationships between the business and the place that are complex and integrated one with the other, with places that generate businesses and businesses that create places.
- A high awareness that the place is a complex nexus of meaning and goes beyond being a simple location, region, or landscape.

Place-based enterprises are more anchored to their local places than other firms and, thus, are more likely to engage in CSR actions. They are interdependent with the place they are settled in. Indeed, these firms can balance the three dimensions of CSR (Elkington, 1998) and recognize that the well-being of the local territory and society is intrinsically essential for them and is functional to reach their organizational goals (Shrivastava & Kennelly, 2013).

However, the intersection between firms, place, and sustainability is still underexplored in academic research and business education (Larty, 2021). Specifically, a promising research path lies in the intersection between family firms, place-based enterprises, and CSR. Family firms are a peculiar kind of business that share some characteristics with place-based enterprises (Shrivastava & Kennelly, 2013). Indeed, there are some overlaps between the two research streams discussed in this and the previous paragraph. Despite the overlaps, there is space to maintain that when a business is simultaneously place-based and of a family nature, a unique synergy arises, acting as an incredible spontaneous force for responsible actions toward the territory and the local community. The following paragraph will expand on this idea, proposing the novel concept of place-based family enterprise.

5.5 The Place-Based Family Enterprise

The previous paragraphs discussed two separate (sometimes overlapping) literature streams concerning firms' CSR engagement. On the one hand, family businesses are susceptible to local demands to behave in an environmentally responsible and place-sensitive manner. This is true, especially for those firms with operations where the family resides and cares over the legacy they leave for future generations. On the other hand, businesses embedded in the local environment (regardless of their family or non-family nature) are, too, more sensitive to their stakeholder's claims and more concerned about the local territory and social community.

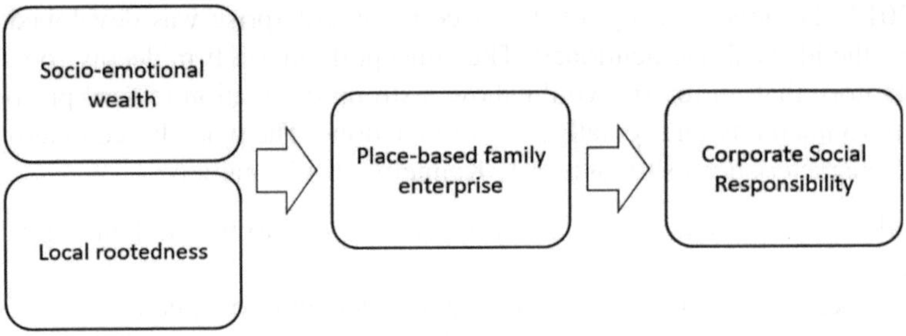

Fig. 5.2 A conceptual model of the place-based family enterprise. Own elaboration

Combining these two streams of literature allows room for a unique kind of enterprise to rise. Specifically, when a firm is of a family nature and embedded in the local area, a unique synergy arises as a force for good for the local area and community. This organization could be conceptualized as a place-based family enterprise, which benefits both from the family dimensions, as depicted in SEW theory (Berrone et al., 2012), and the rootedness to the territory (Shrivastava & Kennelly, 2013). The idea of a place-based family enterprise is a firm that responds to the place-based enterprise definition (Shrivastava & Kennelly, 2013) and the family firm one, as described by Chua et al. (1999), combining both the demographic approach and the essence one.

Such a firm would show care for its local territory and the community that arises from its family nature, bringing stronger connections to the social dimension and higher respect for the stakeholders. It would also show more significant concerns to the territory and local community arising from the robust linkages resulting from the place-based dimension. The two theories' linkages with the territory and community are recurrent elements. However, although there are some overlaps, a conjunction of the two theories brings forward a novel explanation that could help understand specific behaviors of family firms rooted in a local area, i.e., family place-based enterprises (Fig. 5.2).

Some empirical research has already highlighted the intense synergy arising when these two elements (the family and the local roots) are combined. Specifically, comparing different combinations of family and non-family firms, embedded and non-embedded in the place, Amato et al. (2023) found that family firms with strong connections to the place care more about their employees and are particularly concerned about them in crisis times. This tendency is much higher for family firms territorially embedded in the area than all the other categories. Taking a similar but slightly different perspective, Kim et al. (2020) conceptualize that family firms are intrinsically more rooted in a place than non-family firms, with effects on their social performance. They empirically test this proposition, arguing that family firms have a lower tendency to lay off.

Such relationships between firms and the locality appear even more strongly in specific places and industries for historical reasons and traditions. In Italy[11] and France, for example, artisans are strongly interdependent with their place, and their businesses and products are firmly attached to the region or even the locality where they are settled. This is true, for example, in the wine[12] and brewery sector, in the cheese industry and in many other industries whose products are somehow the result of local resources and are intermingled with local culture, history, and traditions (Shrivastava & Kennelly, 2013).

While the higher engagement in CSR aspects has been explained by combining different theoretical approaches, we maintain that such behavior results from the combination of the family nature and the feeling of being rooted in a place. In a nutshell, it is a result of the strong bonds with the community and the territory arising from the nature of the place-based family enterprise.

While research on the two streams of literature (how family firms and local roots impact CSR separately) is well-developed, the two joint research streams deserve more attention. This chapter provides a theoretical background to explore the family and place dimensions and their combined impact on firms' responsible actions. Future research should empirically test under what conditions the synergy of the two aspects becomes a force for engagement in CSR. Indeed, such investigations should provide practical implications to support firms, local communities, and policy-makers. First, firms could learn to exploit their origins and attachment to the territory to act more responsibly and communicate externally. They would learn how to channel their intrinsic force for good into well-planned CSR actions. Second, local communities could benefit from firms that know how to leverage their intangible resources, with advantages for preserving the local territory and caring for social aspects. Last, policy-makers should be able to support firms and the local community, giving the tools for family firms to preserve their family nature of the firms among generations and local rootedness. Indeed, if policy-makers can provide a fertile ground for firms to be economically sustainable long-term, both firms, individuals, and local communities would benefit.

The next chapter ("Unveiling the Origins of Local Roots: A Case Study in the Chianti Classico Wine Cluster") will provide empirical evidence on how the local roots of individuals, the family, and the family firm are interrelated and how a concern for the local area spontaneously arises.

---

[11] In Italy, trademarks connected to the recognition of the place of production and the practices of that location legally protect the food and drink sectors. Some examples are "indicazione geografica tipica" (IGT, meaning Typical Geographical Indication), "denominaziome di origine controllata" (DOC, meaning Denomination of Controlled Origin), "denominaziome di origine controllata e garantita" (DOCG, meaning Denomination of Controlled and Guaranteed Origin), and "denominazione di origine protetta" (DOP, meaning Denomination of Protected Origin) (Pant, 2016). These terms will be mentioned again in Chap. 7, "Unveiling the origins of local roots: a case study in the Chianti Classico wine cluster."

[12] Chapter 7, will focus on this industry, presenting the case of a small family business in Tuscany with strong bonds to the local area and an interest to preserve it.

References

Amato, S., Patuelli, A., Basco, R., & Lattanzi, N. (2023). Family firms amidst the global financial crisis: A territorial embeddedness perspective on downsizing. *Journal of Business Ethics., 183*, 213–236. https://doi.org/10.1007/s10551-021-04930-0

Attig, N., & Brockman, P. (2017). The local roots of corporate social responsibility. *Journal of Business Ethics, 142*(3), 479–496. https://doi.org/10.1007/s10551-015-2757-3

Bammens, Y., & Hünermund, P. (2020). Nonfinancial considerations in eco-innovation decisions: The role of family ownership and reputation concerns. *Journal of Product Innovation Management, 37*(5), 431–453. https://doi.org/10.1111/jpim.12550

Barbier, E. B. (1987). The concept of sustainable economic development. *Environmental Conservation, 14*(2), 101–110. https://doi.org/10.1017/S0376892900011449

Basco, R. (2015). Family business and regional development—A theoretical model of regional familiness. *Journal of Family Business Strategy, 6*(4), 259–271. https://doi.org/10.1016/J.JFBS.2015.04.004

Baù, M., Block, J., Discua Cruz, A., & Naldi, L. (2021). Bridging locality and internationalization–a research agenda on the sustainable development of family firms. *Entrepreneurship and Regional Development, 33*(7–8), 477–492. https://doi.org/10.1080/08985626.2021.1925846

Bergamaschi, M., & Randerson, K. (2016). The futures of family businesses and the development of corporate social responsibility. *Futures, 75*, 54–65. https://doi.org/10.1016/J.FUTURES.2015.10.006

Berrone, P., Cruz, C., & Gomez-Mejia, L. R. (2012). Socioemotional wealth in family firms: Theoretical dimensions, assessment approaches, and agenda for future research. *Family Business Review, 25*(3), 258–279. https://doi.org/10.1177/0894486511435355

Blombäck, A., & Wigren, C. (2009). Challenging the importance of size as determinant for CSR activities. *Management of Environmental Quality: An International Journal, 20*(3), 255–270. https://doi.org/10.1108/14777830910950658

Bowen, H. R. (1953). *Social responsibilities of the businessman*. University of Iowa Press.

Le Breton-Miller, I., & Miller, D. (2016). Family firms and practices of sustainability: A contingency view. *Journal of Family Business Strategy, 7*(1), 26–33. https://doi.org/10.1016/j.jfbs.2015.09.001

Brown, N., & Deegan, C. (1998). The public disclosure of environmental performance information—A dual test of media agenda setting theory and legitimacy theory. *Accounting and Business Research, 29*(1), 21–41.

Campopiano, G., & de Massis, A. (2015). Corporate social responsibility reporting: A content analysis in family and non-family firms. *Journal of Business Ethics, 129*(3), 511–534. https://doi.org/10.1007/s10551-014-2174-z

Carroll, A. B. (1979). A three-dimensional conceptual model of corporate performance. *Academy of Management Review, 4*(4), 497–505.

Carroll, A. B. (1991). The pyramid of corporate social responsibility: Toward the moral management of organizational stakeholders. *Business Horizons, 34*(4), 39–48. https://doi.org/10.1016/0007-6813(91)90005-G

Castelo, M., Lúcia, B., & Rodrigues, L. (2007). Positioning stakeholder theory within the debate on corporate social responsibility. *EJBO - Electronic Journal of Business Ethics and Organization Studies, 12*(1), 5–15. https://jyx.jyu.fi/handle/123456789/25388.

Chua, J. H., Chrisman, J. J., & Sharma, P. (1999). Defining the family business by behavior. *Entrepreneurship Theory and Practice, 23*(4), 19–39. https://doi.org/10.1177/104225879902300402

D'Adamo, I., Gastaldi, M., Imbriani, C., & Morone, P. (2021). Assessing regional performance for the sustainable development goals in Italy. *Scientific Reports, 11*(1), 24117. https://doi.org/10.1038/S41598-021-03635-8

Davis, K. (1960). Can business afford to ignore social responsibilities? *California Management Review, 23–29*, 70–76. https://doi.org/10.2307/41166246

DeBoer, J., Panwar, R., & Rivera, J. (2017). Toward a place-based understanding of business sustainability: The role of green competitors and green locales in firms' voluntary environmental engagement. *Business Strategy and the Environment, 26*(7), 940–955. https://doi.org/10.1002/BSE.1957

Deegan, C., Rankin, M., & Tobin, J. (2002). An examination of the corporate social and environmental disclosures of BHP from 1983-1997: A test of legitimacy theory. *Accounting, Auditing & Accountability Journal, 15*(3), 312–343. https://doi.org/10.1108/09513570210435861/FULL/PDF

Diéguez-Soto, J., Campos-Valenzuela, M., Callejón-Gil, Á. M., & Aldeanueva-Fernández, I. (2021). Family firm heterogeneity on CSR approach: A socio-emotional (SEW) perspective. *BRQ Business Research Quarterly.*, 234094442110638. https://doi.org/10.1177/23409444211063889

Donaldson, T., & Dunfee, T. W. (2002). Ties that bind in business ethics: Social contracts and why they matter. *Journal of Banking & Finance, 26*(9), 1853–1865. https://doi.org/10.1016/S0378-4266(02)00195-4

Elkington, J. (1998). Partnerships from cannibals with forks: The triple bottom line of 21st-century business. *Environmental Quality Management, 8*(1), 37–51. https://doi.org/10.1002/TQEM.3310080106

Ernst, R. A., Gerken, M., Hack, A., & Hülsbeck, M. (2022a). Family firms as agents of sustainable development: A normative perspective. *Technological Forecasting and Social Change, 174*, 121135. https://doi.org/10.1016/j.techfore.2021.121135

Ernst, R. A., Gerken, M., Hack, A., & Hülsbeck, M. (2022b). SMES' reluctance to embrace corporate sustainability: The effect of stakeholder pressure on self-determination and the role of social proximity. *Journal of Cleaner Production, 335*, 130273. https://doi.org/10.1016/J.JCLEPRO.2021.130273

European Commission. (2011). *A renewed EU strategy 2011–14 for corporate social responsibility.*

Fehre, K., & Weber, F. (2019). Why some are more equal: Family firm heterogeneity and the effect on management's attention to CSR. *Business Ethics: A European Review, 28*(3), 321–334. https://doi.org/10.1111/BEER.12225

Frederick, W. C. (1960). The growing concern over business responsibility, *2*(4), 54–61. https://doi.org/10.2307/41165405

Freeman, R. E. (1984). *Strategic management: A stakeholder approach.* Pitman Publishing.

Freeman, R. E. (2015). Stakeholder theory. *Wiley Encyclopedia of Management*, 1–6.

Freeman, R. E., & Dmytriyev, S. (2017). Corporate social responsibility and stakeholder theory: Learning from each other. *Symphonya. Emerging Issues in Management, 2*(1), 7–15. https://doi.org/10.4468/2017.1.02FREEMAN.DMYTRIYEV

Frynas, J. G., & Yamahaki, C. (2016). Corporate social responsibility: Review and roadmap of theoretical perspectives. *Business Ethics, 25*(3), 258–285. https://doi.org/10.1111/beer.12115

Gómez-Mejía, L. R., Haynes, K. T., Núñez-Nickel, M., Jacobson, K. J. L., & Moyano-Fuentes, J. (2007). Socioemotional wealth and business risks in family-controlled firms: Evidence from Spanish olive oil mills. *Administrative Science Quarterly, 52*(1), 106. https://doi.org/10.2189/asqu.52.1.106

Gray, R., Kouhy, R., & Lavers, S. (1995). Corporate social and environmental reporting a review of the literature and a longitudinal study of UK disclosure. *Accounting, Auditing & Accountability Journal, 8*(2), 47–77. https://doi.org/10.1108/09513579510146996/FULL/XML

Guthrie, J., & Parker, L. D. (1989). Corporate social reporting: A rebuttal of legitimacy theory. *Accounting and Business Research, 19*(76), 343–352.

Hermelingmeier, V., Augenstein, K., & Palzkill, A. (2022). The role of place in shaping responsibility logics: Revisiting the relation between place and business sustainability. *Business Strategy and the Environment,* 1–13. https://doi.org/10.1002/BSE.3289

Hsieh, N. H. (2015). The social contract model of corporate purpose and responsibility. *Business Ethics Quarterly, 25*(4), 433–460. https://doi.org/10.1017/BEQ.2016.1

Izzo, M. F., & Ciaburri, M. (2018). Why do they do that? Motives and dimensions of family firms' CSR engagement. *Social Responsibility Journal, 14*(3), 633–650. https://doi.org/10.1108/SRJ-08-2017-0148

Jahn, J., & Brühl, R. (2016). How Friedman's view on individual freedom relates to stakeholder theory and social contract theory. *Journal of Business Ethics, 153*(1), 41–52. https://doi.org/10.1007/S10551-016-3353-X

Kim, K., Haider, Z. A., Wu, Z., & Dou, J. (2020). Corporate social performance of family firms: A place-based perspective in the context of layoffs. *Journal of Business Ethics, 167*(2), 235–252. https://doi.org/10.1007/S10551-019-04152-5/TABLES/11

Lähdesmäki, M., Siltaoja, M., & Spence, L. J. (2019). Stakeholder salience for small businesses: A social proximity perspective. *Journal of Business Ethics, 158*(2), 373–385. https://doi.org/10.1007/S10551-017-3707-Z/FIGURES/1

Lamb, N. H., & Butler, F. C. (2016). The influence of family firms and institutional owners on corporate social responsibility performance, *57*(7), 1374–1406. https://doi.org/10.1177/0007650316648443

Lanis, R., & Richardson, G. (2013). Corporate social responsibility and tax aggressiveness: A test of legitimacy theory. *Accounting, Auditing and Accountability Journal, 26*(1), 75–100. https://doi.org/10.1108/09513571311285621/FULL/PDF

Larty, J. (2021). Towards a framework for integrating place-based approaches in entrepreneurship education. *Industry and Higher Education, 35*(4), 312–324. https://doi.org/10.1177/09504222211021531

Latapí Agudelo, M. A., Jóhannsdóttir, L., & Davídsdóttir, B. (2019). A literature review of the history and evolution of corporate social responsibility. *International Journal of Corporate Social Responsibility, 4*(1), 1–23. https://doi.org/10.1186/s40991-018-0039-y

Mariani, M. M., Al-Sultan, K., & de Massis, A. (2021). Corporate social responsibility in family firms: A systematic literature review, 1. https://doi.org/10.1080/00472778.2021.1955122

Matten, D., & Moon, J. (2004). Corporate social responsibility. *Journal of Business Ethics 2004 54: 4, 54*(4), 323–337. https://doi.org/10.1007/S10551-004-1822-0

McWilliams, A., & Siegel, D. (2001). Corporate social responsibility: A theory of the firm perspective. *Academy of Management Review, 26*(1), 117–127. https://doi.org/10.5465/AMR.2001.4011987

Mintzberg, H. (1983). The case for corporate social responsibility. *Journal of Business Strategy, 4*(2), 3–15. https://doi.org/10.1108/EB039015/FULL/PDF

Mitchell, R. K., Agle, B. R., & Wood, D. J. (1997). Toward a theory of stakeholder identification and salience: Defining the principle of who and what really counts, *22*(4), 853–886. https://doi.org/10.5465/AMR.1997.9711022105

Moir, L. (2001). What do we mean by corporate social responsibility? *Corporate Governance: The International Journal of Business in Society, 1*(2), 16–22. https://doi.org/10.1108/EUM0000000005486/FULL/PDF

Pallares-Barbera, M., Tulla, A. F., & Vera, A. (2004). Spatial loyalty and territorial embeddedness in the multi-sector clustering of the Berguedà region in Catalonia (Spain). *Geoforum, 35*(5), 635–649. https://doi.org/10.1016/J.GEOFORUM.2004.03.004

Pant, D. R. (2016). Management consulting in times of austerity: Sustainability & the business-place-community nexus in Italy. In *Handbook of anthropology in business* (pp. 223–233). Routledge.

Park, J., & Campbell, J. M. (2018). U.S. small business's philanthropic contribution to local community: Stakeholder salience and social identity perspectives, *30*(3), 317–342. https://doi.org/10.1080/10495142.2018.1452823

Patuelli, A., Caldarelli, G., Lattanzi, N., & Saracco, F. (2021). Firms' challenges and social responsibilities during Covid-19: A Twitter analysis. *PLoS One, 16*(7), e0254748. https://doi.org/10.1371/JOURNAL.PONE.0254748

Patuelli, A., Carungu, J., & Lattanzi, N. (2022). Drivers and nuances of sustainable development goals: Transcending corporate social responsibility in family firms. *Journal of Cleaner Production, 373*, 133723. https://doi.org/10.1016/J.JCLEPRO.2022.133723

Pedersen, E. R. (2009). Modelling CSR: How managers understand the responsibilities of business towards society. *Journal of Business Ethics, 91*(2), 155–166. https://doi.org/10.1007/S10551-009-0078-0

Purvis, B., Mao, Y., & Robinson, D. (2019). Three pillars of sustainability: In search of conceptual origins. *Sustainability Science, 14*(3), 681–695. https://doi.org/10.1007/S11625-018-0627-5/FIGURES/1

Randerson, K. (2022). Conceptualizing family business social responsibility. *Technological Forecasting and Social Change, 174*, 121225. https://doi.org/10.1016/J.TECHFORE.2021.121225

Scheyvens, R., Banks, G., & Hughes, E. (2016). The private sector and the SDGs: The need to move beyond 'business as usual. *Sustainable Development, 24*(6), 371–382.

Sharafizad, J., Redmond, J., & Parker, C. (2022). The influence of local embeddedness on the economic, social, and environmental sustainability practices of regional small firms. *Entrepreneurship and Regional Development, 34*(1–2), 57–81. https://doi.org/10.1080/08985626.2021.2024889

Shrivastava, P., & Kennelly, J. J. (2013). Sustainability and place-based enterprise. *Organization and Environment, 26*(1), 83–101. https://doi.org/10.1177/1086026612475068

Siltaoja, M., & Lähdesmäki, M. (2015). From rationality to emotionally embedded relations: Envy as a signal of power in stakeholder relations. *Journal of Business Ethics, 128*(4), 837–850. https://doi.org/10.1007/s10551-013-1987-5

Terlaak, A., Kim, S., & Roh, T. (2018). Not good, not bad: The effect of family control on environmental performance disclosure by business group firms. *Journal of Business Ethics, 153*(4), 977–996. https://doi.org/10.1007/s10551-018-3911-5

Tsalis, T. A., Malamateniou, K. E., Koulouriotis, D., & Nikolaou, I. E. (2020). New challenges for corporate sustainability reporting: United Nations' 2030 agenda for sustainable development and the sustainable development goals. *Corporate Social Responsibility and Environmental Management, 27*(4), 1617–1629. https://doi.org/10.1002/CSR.1910

van Marrewijk, M., & Werre, M. (2003). Multiple levels of corporate sustainability. *Journal of Business Ethics, 44*(2), 107–119. https://doi.org/10.1023/A:1023383229086

Venturelli, A., Principale, S., Ligorio, L., & Cosma, S. (2021). Walking the talk in family firms. An empirical investigation of CSR communication and practices. *Corporate Social Responsibility and Environmental Management, 28*(1), 497–510. https://doi.org/10.1002/CSR.2064

Walck, C. L. (1996). Organizations as places: A metaphor for change. *Journal of Organizational Change Management, 9*(6), 26–40. https://doi.org/10.1108/09534819610150503/FULL/PDF

WCED. (1987). Our common future (The Brundtland report). In *Medicine and War* (Vol. 4).

Windsor, D. (2001). The future of corporate social responsibility. *The International Journal of Organizational Analysis, 9*(3), 225–256. https://doi.org/10.1108/EB028934

Zientara, P. (2017). Socioemotional wealth and corporate social responsibility: A critical analysis. *Journal of Business Ethics, 144*, 185–199. https://doi.org/10.1007/S10551-015-2848-1

Chapter 6
Unveiling the Origins of Local Roots: A Case Study in the Chianti Classico Wine Cluster

6.1 Purpose and Research Question[1]

Existing research in the family business has traditionally focused on investigating the family and business interplay (Basco, 2013). More recently, academics turned their interest to the bonds family firms develop with the territory where they are located. Some empirical papers investigate the influence of local settings on family firms' decision-making (Amato et al., 2023). Understanding family firms' role in the individuals and the families' place attachment has important real-world implications. In a nutshell, place attachment[2] describes an affective bond or connection between a person (or group of people) and specific places (Hidalgo & Hernández, 2001). It largely determines people's actions within places: "how they treat them, whether they protect or neglect, improve or destroy them, and whether they choose to sacrifice them for some perceived benefit" (de Wit, 2013, p. 122).

Empirical papers exploring which role firms play in the development of the individuals and the family's bonds toward the locality are a minority. In other words, an in-depth understanding of the relationships between the individuals, the family, the (family) firm, and the place is currently missing. In particular, family firms are a peculiar type of firm worth investigating under the place attachment lenses. This is because family firms are intrinsically "spatial," more responsive to the geographical distance and spatial unevenness in the availability of resources and business opportunities than non-family firms (Amato et al., 2021). At the same time, they are intrinsically "territorial," with business activities occurring mainly at the

[1]A preliminary work-in-progress version of this study was presented at the International Family Enterprise Research Academy (IFERA) held in Santander (Spain) on June 21–24, 2022, and at the Interdisciplinary European Conference on Entrepreneurship Research (IECER) held in Maastricht (The Netherlands) on October 26–28, 2022.

[2]Please find a detailed analysis of place attachment and local embeddedness in Chap. 4 ("Firms in Territories: the Local Roots of Family Firms"). As the concepts at the foundation of this chapter were already thoroughly described in Chap. 4, this study will mainly focus on the empirical side.

S. Amato, A. Patuelli, *Family Firms and Local Roots*, CSR, Sustainability, Ethics & Governance, https://doi.org/10.1007/978-3-031-31793-4_6

local level, and with the owning family and the firm sharing the same relational space (Kalantaridis & Bika, 2006). The interactions of family firms with their immediate surroundings—which are framed in socially proximate relationships—affect firms' decisions, for example, their attitudes toward social responsibility (Amato et al., 2023) and the advantages they gain from co-location (Cucculelli & Storai, 2015). While conceptual papers (Basco, 2015) and anecdotal evidence reveal the influence of place attachment on family firms' behavior (Smith, 2016), empirical qualitative research is currently missing.

Thus, this research aims to answer the following question: *How does the family business influence the individual and family's place attachment*?

Also, building on Chap. 5 ("Family Firms, Corporate Social Responsibility, and Place-Based Enterprises"), the study will investigate the role that local roots play in the family firms' Corporate Social Responsibility (CSR) approaches. As previously discussed, family firms share some characteristics of place-based enterprises (Shrivastava & Kennelly, 2013). More specifically, when the family nature and the rootedness in a place combine, this becomes an additional force for family firms to engage in CSR.

This chapter develops a case study (Yin, 2018), which is a suitable method to understand the "why" and "how" of phenomena. Thus, it bases on document analysis, a field visit, and semi-structured interviews with a family firm operating in the wine sector and based in Tuscany (Italy), "Il Campino" (which means "the small land"). By linking environmental psychology and regional studies, this study contributes to the debate on the micro-territorial foundation of the family firm phenomenon. It brings practical implications, which can be helpful for firms, policy-makers, and business schools. Most importantly, the chapter shows how a family firm's local roots originate and develop over time and the impact these relationships have on the firm's and families' responsible initiatives toward the territory.

This chapter develops as follows. First, it describes the study's territory and outlines the methodology. After this, it presents the results, describing the firm and providing extracts of the interviews. Last, the chapter will present the discussion and concluding remarks.

6.2 Methodology

6.2.1 The Research Approach

This research is based on interpretivism (Abdallah et al., 2011; Bluhm et al., 2011), aiming to capture insights from organizational phenomena rather than generalizable theory. It also assumes that the individuals who create organizational realities are "knowledgeable agents"; that is, people in organizations understand what they are attempting to do and can explain their thoughts, intentions, and actions. Although this approach has been used by a minority of studies in the family business field compared to the positivistic approach, it has the potential to capture the variety of aspects and dynamics within family firms (Leppäaho et al., 2015). In line with the interpretivism framework, we adopt the case study approach, which is indicated to understand the "why" and "how" of phenomena (Yin, 2018).

Specifically, a case study-based qualitative technique is appropriate in this setting for several reasons. First, it enables us to examine a current event in its native environment (Yin, 2018). Second, by documenting their ideas and experiences, the interviewees are given a "voice" (Bluhm et al., 2011). Third, family firms are a unique context for qualitative case study research. Given the complexities of the relationships between individuals, families, and family businesses, the case study is an excellent method to unravel phenomena and unaddressed research questions (de Massis & Kotlar, 2014). The advantage of using a single case study is that it enables a greater understanding of the business, family, and individual dimensions. As the study's findings align with its methodology and reflect the firm's realities, they cannot be generalized to the greater family business community. Thus, this research aims at sharing lessons learned rather than generalizations (Buchanan & Denyer, 2013).

6.2.2 The Research Setting: Chianti Classico in Tuscany, Italy

Family firms operating in the wine sector were selected for three reasons. First, the wine sector is particularly suitable to the aim of this research (Bélis-Bergouignan et al., 2011), as wineries and places are intrinsically linked (Spielmann et al., 2021). Thus, wineries develop strong economic, social, and emotional connections with the local territory (Rocchi & Gabbai, 2013). Second, most wineries primarily operate in their region (Bélis-Bergouignan et al., 2011). Third, the wine sector has a high presence of family businesses, which are a typical form of business in the sector (Spielmann et al., 2021). Firms located in Italy were selected for two main reasons. First, Italy is a proper context for studying family firms, as more than 85% of companies are family firms, generating 70% of total employment (AIDAF, 2018). Second, the Italian wine industry is a century-old sector characterized by family wineries (Conz et al., 2020). It is the world's largest wine producer in terms of volume (Ufficio Studi Mediobanca, 2018). Among the Italian regions, Tuscany is one of Italy's leading wine regions in terms of export. After Piedmont and Veneto, Tuscany produces the third-highest volume of DOCG (Denomination of Controlled and Guaranteed Origin) and DOC (Denomination of Controlled Origin). Tuscany has 11 DOCG and 41 DOC designations with an international reputation for producing high-quality wine. Moreover, Tuscany is one of the areas in the world where wine has a long heritage and history—the region is characterized by many wine-related activities, which are rich in historical value (Conz et al., 2020).

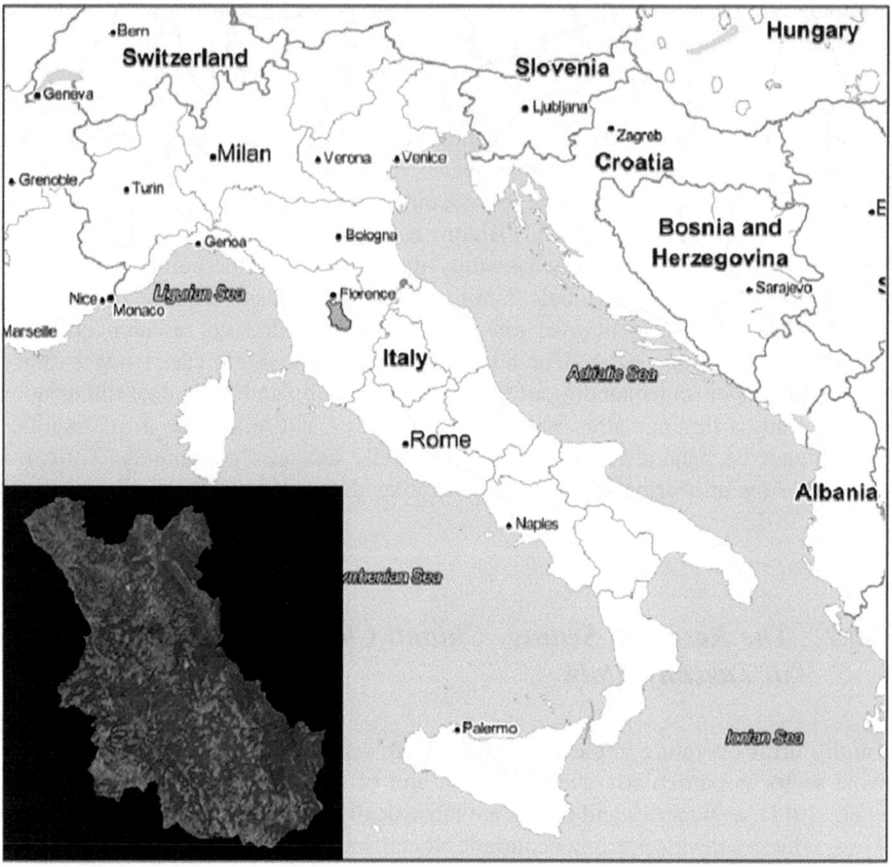

Fig. 6.1 Map highlighting the Chianti Classico area (Source: Sottini et al., 2019, p. 132)

Chianti is one of the most well-known geographic names worldwide, tracing its history back to the fourteenth century (Scozzafava et al., 2018). All over the globe, Chianti wine is exported, and each year, hundreds of thousands of people visit this region. Its physical area (about 88,000 acres) is divided between the municipalities of Florence and Siena. It includes the oldest region for producing Chianti wine, which accounts for 80% of the territory and is known as Chianti Classico (Brunori & Rossi, 2007). Between Florence and Siena, the Chianti Classico region is a territory made of gentle hills, covering more than 70,000 hectares (see Fig. 6.1). Seven thousand two hundred hectares of vines designated for the Chianti Classico label cover it. Although the vineyard only occupies 15% of the total area in this region, viticulture serves as the primary component of the local landscape and the whole local socioeconomic identity (Sottini et al., 2019).

Table 6.1 Overview of the interviews conducted

Interviewee	Generation	Length
Owner	7th	65 min
Owner's wife	7th	29 min
Grandson	9th	35 min

Own elaboration

6.2.3 Data Collection and Analysis

All the businesses belonging to the Consorzio Chianti Classico were contacted. Consorzio Chianti Classico[3] is the oldest winemakers association in Italy, consisting of 515 associates whose territory is shared by the provinces of Firenze and Siena.[4] We first contacted the businesses in December 2021. Thirteen businesses replied. We held introductory meetings with them by phone or videoconferencing (using Google Meet) to verify they met the needs of this study and confirm the firms' availability to participate in our research. Specifically, following the essence approach (Chua et al., 1999), we checked that the business was identified as a family business.[5] At the same time, we asked additional questions related to the succession, the number of generations involved in the business, and the coincidence between the firm's and the family's territory. We selected firms that met the criteria for being a family firm, i.e., they identify as a family firm, have family ownership, and have family members involved in the governance and/or management (Basco, 2015). Also, the firms confirmed their willingness to proceed with the study. Among the selected firms, one seemed particularly suitable for the analysis: it was a family firm governed by the seventh generation, with more than two centuries-long history, and strong territorial roots. Additionally, three family members were willing to participate in our interviews. We conducted in-depth, face-to-face semi-structured interviews at the family firm's location. Before starting the interviews, we had a field visit to the firm—the owner showed us the firm and historical documents and artifacts. While we did not record the first part of the field visit, we could record the last 15 min. Then, we proceeded to interview each family member separately (Table 6.1).

Each interview was made of open-ended questions, following the same topic guide built on combining the existing family business studies and place attachment literature. The interview questions covered the following main areas: (1) the history

[3]Please find more about Consorzio Chianti Classico at: www.chianticlassico.com

[4]Although Alessia Patuelli wrote this chapter, the data was collected with Stefano Amato.

[5]Please note the definition we refer to identify a business as a family business: "a business governed and/or managed with the intention to shape and/or pursue the vision of the business held by a dominant coalition controlled by members of the same family or a small number of families in a manner that is potentially sustainable across generations of the family or families" (Chua et al., 1999, p. 25). Please consult Chap. 1 ("Defining and Understanding the Family Firm") for a detailed discussion about the definitional dilemma in family firms.

Table 6.2 Data sources

Data gathering (multiple sources to allow for triangulation)	*Documentary evidence* Two leaflets about the firm's history *Online data* The firm's website Google searches using the firm's name *Three in-person semi-structured interviews* Average length: 43 min *Field visit* Notes and pictures taken during the visit 15-min recording of the visit

of the family business and the characteristics of the area; (2) the individual and the family's attachment to the territory; and (3) the firm's attachment to the territory.

Each interview was conducted in the participants' and researchers' native language (i.e., Italian). All interviews were recorded with the interviewees' written consent. All interviewees agreed to be recorded. Interviews were then transcribed word by word. Only relevant extracts were translated into English for research purposes. Overall, the data we collected comprises interviews, archival data, notes and pictures taken during the field visit, the firm's website, and Internet articles about the family firm (Table 6.2).

We analyzed the data using an open coding approach (Yin, 2018) to discover similar patterns and compare them to previous research (Miles & Huberman, 1994).

6.3 Results

Il Campino is owned and managed by one family, the seventh generation. It is the smallest firm in the Chianti Classico Consortium, producing only 15.50 quintals of wine annually. Formally, the business was founded in 1969, after the end of sharecropping.[6] In reality, the business is much older, with the first documents going back to 1814 when the first generation started to run the business in Monsanto (a small village in the Chianti Classico area). The owning family is still currently living and working at Monsanto. The business is a micro-enterprise, with only two

[6] Sharecropping was a type of agricultural contract whereby the sharecropper (head of a farmhouse family) agreed to cultivate the lands of one owner. The owner and the sharecropper agreed to divide in half, or slightly different shares, the products and profits deriving from the farm itself. In 1964, a ban was introduced in Italy on entering new sharecropping contracts. Also, under certain conditions, previously stipulated sharecropping contracts were converted into leases (Treccani, www.treccani.it). The advantages and disadvantages of sharecropping have long been debated. To learn more about the evolution of agriculture in Italy and the debate on sharecropping, with some insights on family businesses, please consult, among others, Patuelli (1992).

Fig. 6.2 A model of place attachment's origins, development, and relationships with CSR. Own elaboration

persons working permanently, the owner and his wife, who are now in their 80s. Their children and grandchildren occasionally help with the business, too.

The analysis of the interviews highlighted that place attachment originated with the previous generations, who were born and lived in the local area for two centuries. It was then transferred to the current generations and translated into feelings and actions to support the local territory. Figure 6.2 depicts this process. The related findings will be explained in the remainder of this paragraph.

6.3.1 Previous Generations' Place Attachment

Place attachment originates from previous generations who lived in the territory and used to run the business. This is clear both in the owner's and his wife's words. Although the owner's wife's parents used to work in a different land, her words highlight that her parents were firmly attached to their territory.

> Even my family . . . even my parents, they are dead now, they were born here, they were very attached. (Owner's wife)

Work and family economic sustainability reasons are prevalent when it comes to why the previous generations lived and worked in the Chianti Classico territory. The owner's ancestors used to move around only in the local area, which was the most productive. The first written traces about the business go back to the first family firm's written and preserved documents in 1814.

> They never went out of Chianti Classico. Always, every change they made, they were always in the Chianti Classico territory, from one land to another, but always in the Chianti Classico. (Owner)

A series of motives add to the original reasons why the current families are firmly attached to the territory. They trace back to the owner and his wife's youth. First, traditionally, before the 1950s, the land was a means of economic sustainability and provided food for the whole family.

> It all came from the farm, from the land, then there was the livestock, the vegetable garden, there were many things, there were the chickens, to support the family. (Owner)

However, many social factors add to economic sustainability as motives for the strong relationships with the territory. First, the owners felt strong bonds to their territory, as they were born there and always lived there (like the previous generations). The love for the surroundings also added to personal reasons and the birth sentiment.

> I am passionate about where I was born. For me, the birthplace has a feeling. (Owner)

Second, the two owners had solid bonds with their families; they would never go far from them and wanted to live nearby. As their parents and grandparents lived in the same territory, this intense attachment to the family contributed to the decision to stay in the same place, even at the times when the end of sharecropping and the general move to cities pushed people to leave the countryside and move to the nearby cities to get a job.[7]

> I was very attached to the family, my father, my mother, really attached to the family. I never wanted to go, separate. (Owner)

The relationships between the individuals, the family, and the previous generations in the attachment to the territory are evident in the owner's words. The previous generations' bonds to the territory contribute to his feeling attached to the place. At that time, these strong relationships between individuals and the family were mirrored in the business dimension, with children that used to help their families care for their farming business.

> These are the farms where my family has been, where my family has toured. [. . .] We have always been, always lived in this range. (Owner)

Third, the ties with the other families living in the local territory were robust, meaning the families had strong relationships with each other. These relationships are gone in current times. Life focused on the local territory, also due to the shortage of means to travel to other cities. Social events took place primarily within walking distance of local people. Thus, geographical proximity strengthened social relationships within the territory.

> Our fraction had many people, now there are fewer. Back then, we used to meet, always here, we used to celebrate, one time and another. It is this, this bounded us here, too. (Owner)

Families also used to help each other to carry out their work. Especially in the harvest seasons, families went to help other families doing their harvesting. This led to reinforcing the bonds not only between different families but also between family firms, although the interviewees did not feel the distinction. However, they described relationships focused on the business dimension, i.e., concerning harvesting.

> If one family finished earlier while another still had to do its harvesting, the first one would help that family. Both in the grape harvest and the harvest of the wheat, we helped each other in everything. (Owner's wife)

---

[7] In Europe, Italy is considered a "latecomer" in industrialization (Bianchi, 2013). To learn more about industrialization in Italy, please also see (Gomellini & Toniolo, 2017).

When the owner's father died, he took over his father's business, as the previous generations did before him. In this case, it was not for economic reasons, as the field did not provide economic support for the whole family alone, and the owner and his wife had to take other jobs. However, they were passionate about working in the field, passionate about the landscape and felt togetherness and belonging to the territory; thus, they continued the wine business.

6.3.2 Current Place Attachment

Nowadays, the lifestyle has changed compared to the owner and his wife's youth in the 1940s and 1950s. The relationships with other families living in the territory are not as strong as they were once, and the use of helping each other families during harvest time has now ended. People have many chances to move around with public and private transport, while the local territory is losing the families that traditionally lived there and the essential shops. The family itself has changed. Today, the owner and his wife are in their 80s; they have children and grandchildren. The grandchild we interviewed was born in another town, but he decided to live in Monsanto, next to his grandparents and the family business. Family members have different jobs and do not economically depend on the family firm as it was in the past. However, place attachment is still felt at the individual, family, and firm levels.

From an individual dimension, within younger generations, place attachment mostly comes out of the love for the landscape and time spent there during childhood.

> We are immersed in this splendor; for me, it is marvelous. (Grandson)

From the family perspective, family members are still attached to each other and regularly organize events and celebrations in Monsanto, where the original family and the family firm are based. These events are social, intending to bring the whole family together. They contribute to keeping families and family members attached to the territory.

> Sunday lunches were never missing, all together. There was no shortage of celebrating personal events, or annual ones together. (Grandson)

Still, the family firm plays a central role in keeping the families attached to the territory. It keeps different families—within the same family—around the family firm's territory.

> Even though he [the grandson] was born in Colle, the business is here. Even though he does another job, this is anyway a bond. My daughter built her house here. My grandchildren are here. They group where there is something the old ones had built. (Owner)

The family firm is also another motive that keeps family members together. All the interviewees agreed that the relationships between the family and the business are vital. Plus, the business has and is still helping reinforce the individuals' and families' place attachment. Without the business, the families would still be attached to the place. However, the presence of the business makes these relationships stronger.

> It certainly helped and continues to help in having moments to be together. Because there are activities to do, which fortunately oblige you to find time to get together. (Grandson)

The three dimensions (the individual, the family, and the family firm) appear to interact with each other in the relationships with the territory. They are evident in the owner's willingness to continue the business, despite being in his 80s.

> They always ask me: why do you still continue? This is my passion, why don't I have to continue? These are the farms where my family has been, where my family has gone around. (Owner)

The younger generation is still firmly attached to the territory and living in Monsanto. Our young interviewee sees himself in the distant future as living in Monsanto. Interestingly, this attachment and long-term perspective does not come from having limited means to travel. However, it truly comes out from a feeling of loving and being attached to the territory.

> I love, I love Monsanto. And I love being there, and I would hope to grow old here, but now I do not have any constraint. (Grandson)

6.3.3 CSR Toward the Territory

All the interviewees highlighted aspects relating to CSR initiatives. In a nutshell, the attachment to the territory seems to reflect in activities oriented toward protecting the environment. In our interviews, this aspect appeared before the end of sharecropping, with collaborations between families and family firms said to be essential to preserve the local territory.

> The territory was always maintained with this collaboration. (Owner)

In recent times, these vital links to the territory have turned into being actively protective toward it. The family was proactive in defending the original landscape from changing and constructing buildings. The owner and his wife actively argued with the local municipality, maintaining that the territory had to be preserved the way it was.

> We fought for our territory, even when they began to build, we were against having to destroy... this was a beautiful hill, with beautiful olive trees. (Owner's wife)

Eventually, the younger generation also highlights that they would try to preserve the local territory, which is essential both from an ecological perspective and an effective one, comprising both the personal and family dimension.

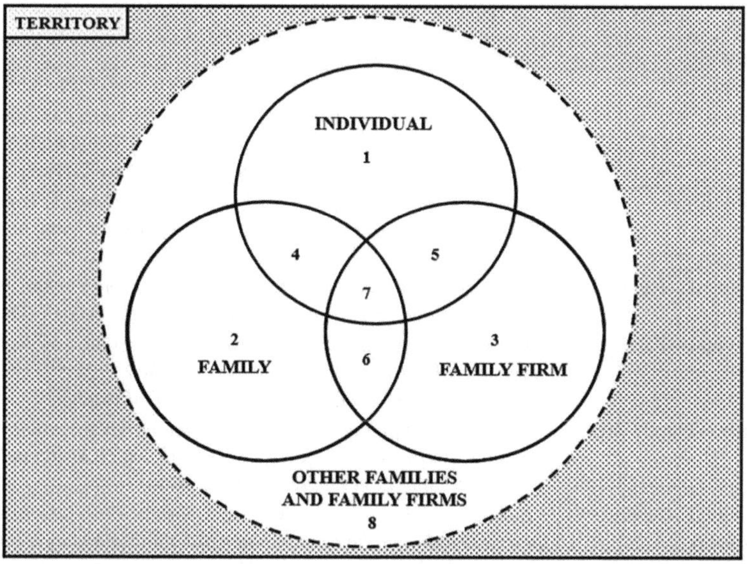

Fig. 6.3 The relationships between the individual, the family, and the family firm with the territory. Own elaboration, inspired by the three-circle model (Please read Chap. 1 ("Defining and Understanding the Family Firm") for more details of the three-circle model. Although the visual approach is similar to the one developed by Tagiuri and Davis (1996), please note that in this figure the circles have different meanings compared to the original model)

6.4 Discussion: The Family Firm as a Facilitator of individual's and Families' Place Attachment

Throughout the different historical periods, the family firm has been a facilitator of the individuals' and families' attachment to the place. While the precise motives have changed throughout the years, the three dimensions (individual, family, and family firm) have always had unique bonds to the territory. This research highlights that the interactions between the three dimensions reinforce each dimension's place attachment. Another dimension external to the family and family firm reinforces the links with the territory: the other families and family firms located there. However, this dimension only served in the last century and is not as strong nowadays. Although this is not a dimension experienced by the younger generations, the interaction with other families and family firms in the local territory, based on reciprocity (Lähdesmäki & Suutari, 2012), once helped reinforce the individuals' and family's place attachment. Please find a model of these relationships in Fig. 6.3 and captions from each dimension in Table 6.3.

In this model, the family firm interacts and strengthens the individuals' and families' place attachment. Without the family firm, individuals and families would still be attached to the local territory. However, the family firm reinforces these links, making them stronger, ultimately translating into the willingness to

Table 6.3 Captions from the interviews

# Dimension	Caption (example)
1 (Individual)	"*I have always been here; I feel that this is mine*" (Owner's wife)
2 (Family)	"*My grandfather was born, [...] he was also born here at Monsanto. My grandfather's father [...] they brought him here to Monsanto [...]. And they have always been here*" (Owner's wife)
3 (Family firm)	"*The bond is so strong, there is an extremely important correlation. They are really inseparable, that is, I do not even know how...*" (Grandson)
4 (Individual—Family)	"*I was very attached to the family, my father, my mother, really attached to the family. I never wanted to go, separate*" (Owner)
5 (Individual—Family firm)	"*You have to care for the field, like having a child, you know, you have to look after everything*" (Owner's wife) "*I am fond of the land, to work in the field*" (Owner)
6 (Family—Family firm)	"*It certainly helped and continues to help in having moments to be together. Because there are activities to do, which fortunately oblige you to find time to get together*" (Grandson)
7 (Individual—Family—Family firm)	"*Even though he [the grandson] was born in Colle, the business is here. Even though he does another job, this is anyway a bond. My daughter built her house here. My grandchildren are here. They group where there is something the old ones had built*" (Owner)
8 (Other families and family firms)	"*We helped each other. One the family went to help another family. That is, every family when there was the olive harvest, the wheat beating, it was the family itself that moved. We went to help*" (Owner)

Own elaboration

protect the local environment when it seems in danger (Amato et al., 2023; Armstrong & Stedman, 2019).

Apart from the family firm's facilitator role, which answers this study's research question, the collected evidence highlights the contributions and interactions of the identified dimensions to place attachment. On the individual level (dimension no. 1), the interviewees assert their sense of belonging and togetherness to the local territory, which comes from personal reasons (including birth and love for the landscape). On the family level (dimension no. 2), the interviewees narrated their families' attachment to the territory. These dimensions are consistent with previous literature on individuals' place attachment, with residence length, social ties, and physical features associated with place attachment (Lewicka, 2008). The interviewees also describe the family firm (dimension no. 3) as being attached (literally, "inseparable") to the territory.

Place attachment also arises from the crossing of different dimensions. Intersecting the individual and the family sphere (dimension no. 4) to place attachment, we see that our interviewee's strong connection with his own family contributes to the decision to stay in the territory and appears intermingled with the willingness to stay together with his family. These two circles interact, and a stronger attachment to the territory arises. The same happens concerning the interactions between the other circles. In dimension no. 5, the individual and family firm circles interact in a sense that the individual passion for working in the field and this work contribute to preserving solid roots in the territory. In dimension no. 6, we see the interaction between the family and the family firm's circles. Today, the family firm is still a means to keep the families together, as the families reunite to help harvest. The interviewees confirmed that this contributed to keeping the families bound to the local place. Dimension no. 7 shows the intersection between the three circles, namely the individual, the family, and the family firm. In this dimension, we see that all the circles combine, reinforcing each other's attachment to the territory. The family firm creates an attraction point where the younger generations are attracted (and where the old ones had always lived). Family reunions happen in the same place, thus fostering individual attachment. Last, the model depicts the impact of other families and family firms in dimension no. 8. The dashed line in this circle symbolizes that this dimension is not as strong as the other ones today. However, in the past (till the end of sharecropping), it fostered the interviewees' sense of attachment to the place.

6.5 Concluding Remarks

This chapter aimed to investigate family firms' role in the individuals' and the families' place attachment by developing a single case study of a family firm operating in the wine sector in the Chianti Classico territory. Findings show that the individual, the family, and the family firm dimensions are all intrinsically linked with each other and the territory. Place attachment arises in the single dimensions and, most importantly, in their interactions. More specifically, results show the family firm's role in fostering individuals' and families' attachment to the territory, adding to existing bonds to the place. In this sense, the family firm strengthens the individual's and family's attachment to the place. Eventually, the case shows that a family firm with a solid attachment to the local territory tends to be spontaneously oriented toward responsible actions supporting the place (Amato et al., 2023; Armstrong & Stedman, 2019; Kim et al., 2020). The business of this study might be considered an example of a place-based family enterprise, i.e., a family firm with strong links to their local place that show a high propension toward CSR activities.[8] Thus, the case study confirms that place and social relationships indeed play a role in the actors' feelings of responsibility (Attig & Brockman, 2017; Hermelingmeier et al., 2022). Social proximity strengthens the relationships between the actors living in a territory, with benefits for them and the place itself (Lähdesmäki et al., 2019).

[8] Please see Chap. 5 ("Family Firms, Corporate Social Responsibility and Place-Based Enterprises") for a detailed discussion of place-based enterprises (Shrivastava & Kennelly, 2013) and the novel concept of place-based family enterprise.

The chapter makes several contributions that will be helpful for the academic community, firms, policy-makers, and business schools. For the former, our results fill a gap highlighted in the literature, enriching the existing knowledge on family firms and localities (Basco, 2015). The chapter sheds light on the underlying mechanisms and reasons why family firms are more attached to the place than non-family firms. For family firms, the research can be beneficial for understanding how place attachment originates, develops, and is maintained through time. Such an understanding could help design strategies to increase young family members' sense of attachment to the territory and the family business. This chapter suggests that the three dimensions (individual, family, and family firm) are all inextricably linked and reinforce one another in the relationship to the territory. Thus, the older generation could use these findings to involve the younger ones in the family and firm activities to foster their attachment to the local place.

The study may inform local, regional, and national policy-makers about how local roots originate and develop within family firms and how this translates into responsible actions. Policy-makers could use such knowledge to enhance the sustainable development of local territories in different ways (Horlings, 2015). First, as the family firms' place attachment reinforces the families and family members' place attachment, policy-makers could design specific support systems for family firms to help them be economically sustainable. This, in turn, would strengthen the families and family members' attachment to the local territory and reduce the phenomenon of disembedding (Haunschild, 2004). Second, policy-makers could understand and design specific incentives or support mechanisms for family firms to protect their territory. As family firms attached to the local place naturally tend to defend it, national and regional policy-makers could work with family firms and local governments to protect the environment. Moreover, if more than one family firm in a local area is spontaneously defending the territory, this would start a chain process, nudging other family firms to behave responsibly toward the environment (DeBoer et al., 2017).

Finally, this chapter could be helpful for business schools to develop novel courses on entrepreneurship, family business, and place, as the latter needs to be included in university programs (Larty, 2021). A holistic, sustainable management education that integrates relevant interdisciplinary perspectives would be beneficial (Kolb et al., 2017).

References

Abdallah, C., Denis, J. L., & Langley, A. (2011). Having your cake and eating it too: Discourses of transcendence and their role in organizational change dynamics. *Journal of Organizational Change Management, 24*(3), 333–348. https://doi.org/10.1108/09534811111132730/FULL/PDF

AIDAF. (2018). *Dieci anni di capitalismo familiare*. X osservatorio AUB.

Amato, S., Backman, M., & Peltonen, J. (2021). Are family firms more locally embedded than non-family firms? Findings from the finnish context. *Family Business and Regional Development, 140–156*. https://doi.org/10.4324/9780429058097-11

Amato, S., Patuelli, A., Basco, R., & Lattanzi, N. (2023). Family firms amidst the global financial crisis: A territorial embeddedness perspective on downsizing. *Journal of Business Ethics, 183*, 213. https://doi.org/10.1007/s10551-021-04930-0

Armstrong, A., & Stedman, R. C. (2019). Understanding local environmental concern: The importance of place. *Rural Sociology, 84*(1), 93–122. https://doi.org/10.1111/RUSO.12215

Attig, N., & Brockman, P. (2017). The local roots of corporate social responsibility. *Journal of Business Ethics, 142*(3), 479–496. https://doi.org/10.1007/s10551-015-2757-3

Basco, R. (2013). The family's effect on family firm performance: A model testing the demographic and essence approaches. *Journal of Family Business Strategy, 4*(1), 42–66. https://doi.org/10.1016/j.jfbs.2012.12.003

Basco, R. (2015). Family business and regional development—A theoretical model of regional familiness. *Journal of Family Business Strategy, 6*(4), 259–271. https://doi.org/10.1016/J.JFBS.2015.04.004

Bélis-Bergouignan, M.-C., Bélis-Bergouignan, & Marie-Claude. (2011). *Bordeaux wines: An archetypal Terroir Cluster?* https://EconPapers.repec.org/RePEc:hal:journl:hal-00652869

Bianchi, P. (2013). *La rincorsa frenata: l'industria italiana dall'unità alla crisi globale.* Il mulino. https://www.libreriauniversitaria.it/rincorsa-frenata-industria-italiana-unita/libro/9788815245380

Bluhm, D. J., Harman, W., Lee, T. W., & Mitchell, T. R. (2011). Qualitative research in management: A decade of Progress. *Journal of Management Studies, 48*(8), 1866–1891. https://doi.org/10.1111/J.1467-6486.2010.00972.X

Brunori, G., & Rossi, A. (2007). Differentiating countryside: Social representations and governance patterns in rural areas with high social density: The case of Chianti, Italy. *Journal of Rural Studies, 23*(2), 183–205. https://doi.org/10.1016/J.JRURSTUD.2006.10.001

Buchanan, D. A., & Denyer, D. (2013). Researching tomorrow's crisis: Methodological innovations and wider implications. *International Journal of Management Reviews, 15*(2), 205–224. https://doi.org/10.1111/IJMR.12002

Chua, J. H., Chrisman, J. J., & Sharma, P. (1999). Defining the family business by behavior. *Entrepreneurship Theory and Practice, 23*(4), 19–39. https://doi.org/10.1177/104225879902300402

Conz, E., Lamb, P. W., & de Massis, A. (2020). Practicing resilience in family firms: An investigation through phenomenography. *Journal of Family Business Strategy, 11*(2), 100355. https://doi.org/10.1016/j.jfbs.2020.100355

Cucculelli, M., & Storai, D. (2015). Family firms and industrial districts: Evidence from the Italian manufacturing industry. *Journal of Family Business Strategy, 6*(4), 234–246. https://doi.org/10.1016/J.JFBS.2015.07.002

de Massis, A., & Kotlar, J. (2014). The case study method in family business research: Guidelines for qualitative scholarship. *Journal of Family Business Strategy, 5*(1), 15–29. https://doi.org/10.1016/J.JFBS.2014.01.007

de Wit, C. W. (2013). Interviewing for sense of place, *30*(1), 120–144. https://doi.org/10.1080/08873631.2012.745979

DeBoer, J., Panwar, R., & Rivera, J. (2017). Toward a place-based understanding of business sustainability: The role of green competitors and green locales in firms' voluntary environmental engagement. *Business Strategy and the Environment, 26*(7), 940–955. https://doi.org/10.1002/BSE.1957

Gomellini, M., & Toniolo, G. (2017). The industrialization of Italy, 1861–1971. *The Spread of Modern Industry to the Periphery since, 1871*, 115–141. https://doi.org/10.1093/ACPROF:OSO/9780198753643.003.0006

Haunschild, A. (2004). Contingent work: The problem of disembeddedness and economic reembeddedness. *Management Revue, 15*(1), 74–88. http://www.jstor.org/stable/41783451

Hermelingmeier, V., Augenstein, K., & Palzkill, A. (2022). The role of place in shaping responsibility logics: Revisiting the relation between place and business sustainability. *Business Strategy and the Environment.* https://doi.org/10.1002/BSE.3289

Hidalgo, M. C., & Hernández, B. (2001). Place attachment: Conceptual and empirical questions. *Journal of Environmental Psychology, 21*(3), 273–281. https://doi.org/10.1006/JEVP.2001.0221

Horlings, L. G. (2015). Values in place; a value-oriented approach toward sustainable place-shaping. *Regional Studies, Regional Science, 2*(1), 257–274. https://doi.org/10.1080/21681376.2015.1014062

Kalantaridis, C., & Bika, Z. (2006). Local embeddedness and rural entrepreneurship: Case-study evidence from Cumbria, England. *Environment and Planning A, 38*(8), 1561–1579. https://doi.org/10.1068/A3834

Kim, K., Haider, Z. A., Wu, Z., & Dou, J. (2020). Corporate social performance of family firms: A place-based perspective in the context of layoffs. *Journal of Business Ethics, 167*(2), 235–252. https://doi.org/10.1007/S10551-019-04152-5/TABLES/11

Kolb, M., Fröhlich, L., & Schmidpeter, R. (2017). Implementing sustainability as the new normal: Responsible management education – From a private business school's perspective. *The International Journal of Management Education, 15*(2), 280–292. https://doi.org/10.1016/J.IJME.2017.03.009

Lähdesmäki, M., Siltaoja, M., & Spence, L. J. (2019). Stakeholder salience for small businesses: A social proximity perspective. *Journal of Business Ethics, 158*(2), 373–385. https://doi.org/10.1007/S10551-017-3707-Z/FIGURES/1

Lähdesmäki, M., & Suutari, T. (2012). Keeping at arm's length or searching for social proximity? Corporate social responsibility as a reciprocal process between small businesses and the local community. *Journal of Business Ethics, 108*(4), 481–493. https://doi.org/10.1007/S10551-011-1104-6

Larty, J. (2021). Towards a framework for integrating place-based approaches in entrepreneurship education. *Industry and Higher Education, 35*(4), 312–324. https://doi.org/10.1177/09504222211021531

Leppäaho, T., Plakoyiannaki, E., & Dimitratos, P. (2015). The case study in family business, *29*(2), 159–173. https://doi.org/10.1177/0894486515614157

Lewicka, M. (2008). Place attachment, place identity, and place memory: Restoring the forgotten city past. *Journal of Environmental Psychology, 28*(3), 209–231. https://doi.org/10.1016/J.JENVP.2008.02.001

Miles, M. B., & Huberman, A. M. (1994). *Qualitative data analysis: An expanded sourcebook.* Sage.

Patuelli, V. (1992). *Le trasformazioni dell'agricoltura. Scritti 1950–1988.* Edizioni Agricole.

Rocchi, B., & Gabbai, M. (2013). Territorial identity as a competitive advantage in wine marketing: A case study. *Journal of Wine Research, 24*(4), 291–310. https://doi.org/10.1080/09571264.2013.837382

Scozzafava, G., Gerini, F., Dominici, A., Contini, C., & Casini, L. (2018). Reach for the stars: The impact on consumer preferences of introducing a new top-tier typology into a PDO wine. *Wine Economics and Policy, 7*(2), 140–152. https://doi.org/10.1016/J.WEP.2018.09.001

Shrivastava, P., & Kennelly, J. J. (2013). Sustainability and place-based enterprise. *Organization and Environment, 26*(1), 83–101. https://doi.org/10.1177/1086026612475068

Smith, C. (2016). Environmental jolts: Understanding how family firms respond and why. *Family Business Review, 29*(4), 401–423. https://doi.org/10.1177/0894486516673906

Sottini, V. A., Barbierato, E., Bernetti, I., Capecchi, I., Fabbrizzi, S., & Menghini, S. (2019). Winescape perception and big data analysis: An assessment through social media photographs in the Chianti Classico region. *Wine Economics and Policy, 8*(2), 127–140. https://doi.org/10.1016/J.WEP.2019.07.001

Spielmann, N., Discua Cruz, A., Tyler, B. B., & Beukel, K. (2021). Place as a nexus for corporate heritage identity: An international study of family-owned wineries. *Journal of Business Research, 129*, 826–837. https://doi.org/10.1016/J.JBUSRES.2019.05.024

Tagiuri, R., & Davis, J. (1996). Bivalent attributes of the family firm. *Family Business Review, 9*(2), 199–208. https://doi.org/10.1111/j.1741-6248.1996.00199.x

Ufficio Studi Mediobanca. (2018). *Indagine sul settore vinicolo*. Mediobanca.

Yin, R. K. (2018). *Case study research and applications* (6th ed.). Paper Knowledge. Toward a Media History of Documents, 414.

Chapter 7
The Role of Local Roots on the Economic Performance and Corporate Social Responsibility of Family Firms: A Quantitative Analysis

7.1 Family Firms in Italy

Italian capitalism is essentially a family affair. Behind the largest industrial groups and banks, family firms have traditionally been the leading players. Family-owned and managed firms represent a key component of the Italian entrepreneurial fabric, not only numerically but also for their contribution to GDP and employment. In Italy, it is estimated there are around 784,000 family firms, accounting for more than 85% of the total number and contributing to approximately 70% of the employment, in line with the major European economies. For instance, family firms account for more than 80% of total businesses in France, 90% in Germany, and 83% in Spain.[1] The Global Family Business Index[2] that analyses the 500 largest family-owned businesses in the world, ranks Italy in fourth position with 19 firms, preceded by the USA (with 119 firms), Germany (79), France (32), and before Hong Kong (18), India (178), and Switzerland (16). Table 7.1 displays the Italian family firms ranked in the Global Family Business Index.

Two main features set apart Italian family firms. First, less reliance on external managers: 66% of the Italian family firms are fully managed by family members compared to 26% in France and only 10% in the UK. The board of directors of nearly 30% of the total is made up entirely of family members, albeit with signs of greater

[1]These estimates are provided by the Associazione Italiana delle Aziende Familiari (AIDAF, the Italian Association of Family Firms), which gathers almost 220 firms representing almost 15% of the Italian GDP. The AIDAF carries out three main activities: First, education of both family and non-family members; second, political activity at both national and European level for the formation of a normative framework supportive of family businesses and third, exchange of ideas and experiences among affiliated firms.

[2]The index is developed by the Center for Family Business at the University of St. Gallen (Switzerland) in cooperation with Ernst & Young (EY) and ranks global family enterprises according to their revenues. For more information, see: https://familybusinessindex.com/#impressum

S. Amato, A. Patuelli, *Family Firms and Local Roots*, CSR, Sustainability, Ethics & Governance, https://doi.org/10.1007/978-3-031-31793-4_7

Table 7.1 Italian family firms according to the Global Family Business Index

									Board		CEO	
GFBI rank	Company	Type	Founding year	Revenues	Employees	Industry	Family	Shareholding	No. of directors	Family members	Gender	Family
3	EXOR SpA	Public	1927	145.3	343,415	Financial Services	Agnelli	53.0%	9	3	♂	Yes
71	Edizione Srl	Private	1955	22.5	103,251	Consumer	Benetton	100%	7	3	♂	No
105	Ferrero International Sa	Private	1946	14.9	37,122	Consumer	Ferrero	100%	5	2	♂	No
161	Esselunga SpA	Private	1957	10.2	25,109	Consumer	Caprotti	100%	10	1	♂	No
251	Marcegaglia Spa	Private	1959	6.6	6.6	Energy	Marcegaglia	100%	2	2	♂	Yes
279	Webuild S.p.A.	Public	1906	6.1	29,162	Government & Infrastructure	Salini	45.2%	15	2	♂	Yes
280	Saras SpA (aka Saras Group)	Public	1962	6.1	1687	Energy	Moratti	40.2%	12	5	♂	No
312	Cremonini SpA	Private	1963	5.4	18.5	Consumer	Cremonini	100%	6	3	♂	Yes
318	De Agostini SpA	Private	1901	5.3	12,626	Telecom, Media, and Technology	Drago and Boroli	74.9%	11	5	♂	Yes
350	Fininvest S.p.A.	Private	1978	4.7	15,608	Telecom, Media, and Technology	Berlusconi	97.0%	8	4	♂	No
373	Menarini Group (aka A. Menarini Diagnostics Srl)	Private	1886	4.5	17	Health Sciences & Wellness	Aleotti	100%	6	2	♀	No

409	Gruppo Barilla	Private	1877	4.1	8481	Consumer	Barilla	100%	9	4	♂	No
413	Buzzi Unicem SpA	Public	1907	4.0	9.82	Advanced Manufacturing & Mobility	Buzzi	51.5%	12	4	♂	Yes
425	A.I.A. Agricola Italiana Alimentare Spa	Private	1967	3.9	690	Consumer	Veronesi	100%	3	0	♂	No
444	Chimet S.p. A.	Private	1976	3.6	131	Energy	Squarcialupi	72.0%	4	1	♂	No
452	Grimaldi Group SpA	Private	1947	3.5	16	Advanced Manufacturing & Mobility	Grimaldi	100%	4	2	♂	Yes
474	Api Anonima Petroli Italiana Spa	Private	1933	3.4	15	Energy	Peretti	100%	9	4	♂	No
490	MD S.p.A.	Private	1994	3.3	7.5	Consumer	Podini	100%	9	4	♀	Yes
495	CIR S.p. A.—Compagnie Industriali Riunite	Public	1976	3.3	18,648	Health Sci-ences & Wellness	De Benedetti	44.7%	12	4	♀	No

Source: adapted from Global Family Business Index 2021

openness in recent years.[3] Second, longevity, with centenary family firms are still active today (Corbetta & Salvato, 2012).[4]

Family capitalism has shown a certain vitality and adaptability throughout Italian industrial history. The "first capitalism" of the late nineteenth century, which saw the emergence of first large private companies led by historic entrepreneurial families. The "third capitalism" of the early 1960s was based on the industrial districts, with the family business model representing a distinctive trait of such local productive systems (Cucculelli & Storai, 2015; Markusen, 1996),[5] mainly concentrated in the traditional industries specialized in the so-called "4 Fs" of the *Made in Italy*[6] (Intesa San Paolo, 2019). In between, the "second capitalism" in the 1930s, primarily dominated by the state ownership with the Istituto per la Ricostruzione Industriale (IRI, Institute for Industrial Reconstruction), the Italian public holding company established to rescue and restructure the banking system and the private companies that went bankrupt during the Great Depression (1929–1939). Finally, the "fourth capitalism" of the 1990s was dominated by the medium-sized enterprise—firms with a workforce between 50 and 499 employees and a sales volume between 15 and 330 million euros[7]—that constitutes a kind of *Mittelstand all'Italiana* (an Italian "middle-way"). Wedded, at least initially, to local environments, medium-sized enterprises exploit their geographic and familial roots and draw on well-honed mercantile traditions to establish a sizeable presence abroad, hence the expression of "pocket multinationals" (LoRomer, 2003). At the origin and evolution of the firms of the fourth capitalism is the transformation of the industrial districts through a strengthening of the local hierarchical structure (Chiarvesio et al., 2010). Italian enterprises of the fourth capitalism base their strategy on internationalization and innovation, flexibility, and adaptability to market changes (Schilirò, 2012). As far as firm's ownership is concerned, family firms of the fourth capitalism are deemed to be "enlightened" insofar as they allow external managers into the firm to solve structural weaknesses, thus becoming a "growth factor rather than a regressive factor" (Coltorti, 2013, p. 2055).

[3]This is the result of the XIII report of the AUB Observatory promoted by AIDAF, UniCredit, and Bocconi University on all Italian family-owned firms with revenues equal to or greater than 20 million euros. It is worth noting, that the board of directors made up entirely of family members amounts to nearly 45% for the smaller firms with revenues between 20 million and 50 million of euros.

[4]Of the world's 100 oldest businesses, 15 are Italian. The oldest Italian family firms are the following: Fonderie Pontificie Marinelli (founded in the year 1000), Barone Ricasoli (1141), Barovier and Toso (1295), Torrini (1369), and Marchesi Antinori (1385).

[5]Cucculelli and Storai (2015) is the most comprehensive study on family firms and industrial districts. Based on a dataset of 62,153 private companies, they found that 85.6% of district firms are family owned.

[6]*Made in Italy* identifies the main manufacturing sectors of Italian export backbone of the national manufacturing system. These are referred to 4 Fs, standing for Fashion, Food, Factory automation, Furniture, and Design.

[7]This definition is given by the Research Unit of Mediobanca. For more information, please see: https://www.mediobanca.com/en/index.html

7.2 Data and Variables

The empirical analysis was carried out with secondary data from several sources. First, financial data and information on ownership and management are drawn from the Aida-Bureau Van Dijk (BvD) dataset.[8] Second, patent information is obtained from Orbis Intellectual Property (OIP).[9] Third, information on affiliation to the so-called "Contratto di rete" (Network agreement) was retrieved from the Italian Chamber of Commerce and Industry (ICCI).[10] Fourth, information on foreign sales is drawn from a unique database coming from the Italian National Institute of Statistics (Istat). Fifth, information on ISO14001 environmental certification was retrieved from Accredia.[11] Finally, publicly available municipality-level information is retrieved once again from Istat.

This study focuses on 97,657 active firms in Italy for the year 2019 operating in the manufacturing sector (NACE Rev.2 codes at two-digit 10–33).[12]

The dependent variables are *Productivity*—measured as the natural logarithm of a firm's value-added per employee (van Oort et al., 2012)—and *ISO14001*, a dummy variable coded "1" if the firm has an ISO14001 environmental management certification, "0" otherwise.

Three explanatory variables are employed in the empirical studies of this chapter. First, a dummy variable (*Family firm*), which takes value "1" if at least two members of the firm's governance, whether seated either on the board of directors (BoD) or in the top management team (TMT), carry the same family name, and "0" otherwise.[13] Second, we followed the study of Ren et al. (2021) to capture the firm's local roots. Accordingly, a dummy variable (*Local roots*) was created, which takes value "1" if the managers' hometown is in the same municipality as the enterprise headquarters,

[8] Aida-BvD is a comprehensive dataset that collects information on limited companies located in Italy. A complete set of economic and financial variables—with up to 10 years of history—such as revenues, costs, number of employees, tangible and intangible assets, legal status, sector of activity, and location are provided.

[9] OIP links global patent data to companies and corporate groups. Specifically, 115 million patents are related to information on about 300 million companies so that an extensive patent portfolio for a given company is provided.

[10] Network agreement consists of a legal instrument through which participants realize aggregations and mutual cooperation, while maintaining their autonomy and legal identity. Introduced in the Italian legal system with the Law no. 33 of 9 April 2009, the "contratto di rete" can be stipulated by entrepreneurs regardless of their respective nature (i.e., individual businesses, companies and public entrepreneurs, also non-commercial) as a type of collaboration the aim of which is to realize shared projects and objectives, and increase innovation and competitiveness.

[11] Accredia is the sole national accreditation body appointed by the Italian government in compliance with the application of the European Regulation 765/2008. Please visit www.accredia.it to learn more.

[12] NACE represents the European standard classification of productive economic activities.

[13] This definition stems from the so-called "demographic approach" to define family firms, which considers the family's involvement as a sufficient condition to capture its effect on the organization (Basco, 2013).

and "0" otherwise. The rationale of this variable is that having a local manager running the business ends up embedding the firm in the local context as both the manager and the firm share the same relational space (Hess, 2004; Oinas, 1997). Finally, *Geographic isolation* is the degree to which a firm is located alone or apart from other firms in a place. Typically, geographically isolated locations face decreased access to local, informal knowledge spillovers and less exposure to diversity (Fitjar & Rodríguez-Pose, 2017). Such isolation hinders the diffusion of knowledge and information and the exchange of critical outputs, thus resulting in locational disadvantages (Fitjar & Rodríguez-Pose, 2011). For instance, Wang et al. (2020) found a negative association between geographical isolation and firm performance. Following Wang et al. (2020), *Geographic isolation* is defined as the inverted value of local density, that is, the number of firms located in the same geographical area—defined at the level of local labor markets (LMAs)[14]—plus one. More specifically:

$$\text{Geographic isolation} = \frac{1}{(\text{Local density} + 1)}$$

Hence, two firms are viewed as being located in the same place if their headquarters are based in municipalities belonging to the same LMA.

Several firm- and municipality-level characteristics are controlled to deal with unobserved heterogeneity. Table 7.2 summarizes the variables employed in the empirical analysis.

7.3 Descriptive Statistics and Univariate Results

Table 7.3 displays the descriptive statistics for the whole sample. Only 3.2% of firms in the sample have an ISO14001 environmental management system. While family firms account for almost 30% of firms in the data, 23% have a local manager in charge of the business. Firms are, on average, 21 years old; only 2% have filed a patent, and 39% are exporters. Almost 16% are located in inner areas, while 18% are located in the south of Italy.

Table 7.4 shows the difference in means between family and non-family firms. Family firms are, on average, more productive than non-family counterparts and the percentage of firms with an ISO14001 certification is higher in the case of family

[14] Labor Market Areas (LMAs, "local labour systems—SLL" in Italy) are sub-regional geographical areas where the bulk of the labour force lives and works, and where establishments can find the main part of the labour force. They respond to the need for meaningfully comparable sub-regional labour market areas for the reporting and analysis of statistics. LMAs are defined on a functional basis, the key criterion being the proportion of commuters who cross the LMA boundary on their way to work. Based on the latest census carried out in 2011, there were 611 LMAs in Italy . For more information see: www.istat.it

Table 7.2 Variable description

Variable	Description	Source
Dependent variable		
Productivity	Value added per employee taken in logarithm	Aida-BvD
ISO14001	Dummy variable coded "1" if the firm *i* has an ISO14001 environmental management certification, "0" otherwise	ACCREDIA
Independent variable		
Family firm	Dummy variable coded "1" if the firm *i* at least two individuals in the firm's governance structure carry the same surnames, "0" otherwise	Aida-BvD
Local roots	Dummy variable coded "1" if management birthplace is in the same municipality as the firm's headquarters, "0" otherwise	Aida-BvD
Geographic isolation	Inverted value of firm density plus one	Aida-BvD
Control variables		
Size	Number of total employees taken in logarithm	Aida-BvD
Age	Number of years since firm's establishment	Aida-BvD
Intangibles	Intangibles fixed assets per employee	Aida-BvD
Patent	Dummy variable coded "1" if firm has filed a patent, "0" otherwise	Orbis IP
Leverage	Shareholder equity on total assets	Aida-BvD
Liquidity	Cash and cash equivalents on total assets	Aida-BvD
Exporter	Dummy variable coded "1" if firm *i* sells abroad, "0" otherwise	Istat
Network agreement	Dummy variable coded "1", if the firm *i* is part of a network, "0" otherwise	Italian Commercial Register
Group	Dummy variable coded "1" if firm *i* is part of a business group, "0" otherwise	Aida-BvD
Industry-tech	Categorical variable according to the level of industry technology intensity based on Eurostat taxonomy: (1) Low-tech; (2) Medium-low; (3) Medium-high; (4) High-tech	Aida-BvD
Inner	Dummy variable coded "1" if the municipality is an intermediate area, remote area, and ultra-remote area, "0" otherwise	Istat
Density	Resident population-total area square kilometers ratio of the municipality taken in logarithm	Istat
HHI	Inverse of the Hirschman-Herfindahl Index taken in logarithm	Aida-BvD
LQ	Location quotient expressed as number of jobs in industry *i* and municipality *j*	Aida-BvD
South	Dummy variable coded "1" if the firm is located in the South of Italy, "0" otherwise	Aida-BvD

firms (5.2% compared to 2.5% for non-family firms). The proportion of firms with a local manager is higher in the case of non-family firms, while non-family firms are older and less innovative than their non-family counterparts.

Table 7.5 shows the correlation matrix. Family firm status is positively associated with productivity and an ISO14001 certification. Local roots are negatively associated with productivity and positively with the ISO14001 certificate. Geographic

Table 7.3 Summary statistics for the whole sample

Variable	Obs.	Mean	Std. Dev.	Min	Median	Max
Productivity[a]	*97,657*	3.841	0.671	−4.710	3.870	11.393
ISO14001	*97,657*	0.032	0.178	0	0	1
Family firm	*97,657*	0.296	0.456	0	0	1
Local roots	*97,657*	0.232	0.422	0	0	1
Geographic isolation	*97,657*	0.003	0.008	0.000	0.001	0.333
Size[a]	*97,657*	2.302	1.240	0	2.302	10.396
Age	*97,657*	21.027	16.246	1	18	154
Intangibles	*97,657*	5.892	15.515	0	0.770	115.220
Patent	*97,657*	0.021	0.142	0	0	1
Leverage	*97,657*	0.292	0.303	−46.473	0.253	1
Liquidity	*97,657*	0.122	0.149	0	0.064	1
Export	*97,657*	0.391	0.488	0	0	1
Network agreement	*97,657*	0.024	0.154	0	0	1
Group	*97,657*	0.623	0.485	0	1	1
Industry-tech	*97,657*	1.9	0.83	1	2	4
Inner	*97,657*	0.158	0.365	0	0	1
Density[a]	*97,657*	6.344	1.262	0.415	6.3	9.411
HHI[a]	*97,657*	4.302	2.02	0	4.141	16.197
LQ	*97,657*	3.734	6.850	0.002	1.439	117.277
South	*97,657*	0.180	0.384	0	0	1

Note: [a] Expressed in natural logarithm

Table 7.4 Difference of means

			Test for difference of means	
Variable	Non-family firm	Family firm	Difference of means	t-Statistics
Productivity[a]	3.769	4.013	−0.244	−52.645***
ISO14001	0.025	0.052	−0.027	−22.0***
Local roots	0.253	0.182	0.071	24.07***
Size[a]	2.126	2.721	−0.595	70.217***
Age	18.192	27.78	−9.588	−87.396***
Intangibles	5.959	5.734	0.224	2.06**
Patent	0.015	0.031	−0.016	−15.875***
Leverage	0.268	0.348	−0.08	−37.454***
Liquidity	0.122	0.124	−0.002	−2.017**
Export	0.345	0.501	−0.156	−46.15***
Network agreement	0.021	0.032	−0.011	−10.329***
Group	0.685	0.473	0.212	63.678***
Industry-tech	1.894	1.914	−0.019	−3.4***
Observations	*68,775*	*28,882*		

Note: [a] Expressed in natural logarithm. Level of statistical significance * $p < 0.10$, ** $p < 0.05$, *** $p < 0.01$

Table 7.5 Correlation matrix

Variables	VIF	(1)	(2)	(3)	(4)	(5)	(6)	(7)	(8)	(9)	(10)
(1) Productivity	–	1.000									
(2) ISO14001	1.11	0.139*	1.000								
(3) Family firm	1.18	0.166*	0.070*	1.000							
(4) Local roots	1.04	−0.058*	0.014*	−0.077*	1.000						
(5) Geographic isolation	1.24	−0.069*	0.002	−0.025*	0.023*	1.000					
(6) Size	1.44	0.289*	0.284*	0.219*	−0.025*	−0.039*	1.000				
(7) Age	1.26	0.260*	0.119*	0.269*	−0.001	−0.041*	0.338*	1.000			
(8) Intangibles	1.05	0.131*	0.057*	−0.007*	0.002	−0.012*	0.031*	−0.018*	1.000		
(9) Patent	1.08	0.119*	0.126*	0.051*	0.006*	−0.020*	0.227*	0.080*	0.112*	1.000	
(10) Leverage	1.14	0.239*	0.056*	0.119*	0.003	−0.016*	0.085*	0.213*	−0.019*	0.048*	1.000
(11) Liquidity	1.11	0.083*	−0.040*	0.006*	−0.001	−0.020*	−0.106*	−0.026*	−0.116*	−0.008*	0.252*
(12) Export	1.18	0.260*	0.122*	0.146*	−0.030*	−0.044*	0.345*	0.172*	0.083*	0.113*	0.078*
(13) Network agreement	1.02	0.049*	0.055*	0.033*	−0.001	0.012*	0.108*	0.052*	0.027*	0.048*	0.004
(14) Group	1.08	0.045*	0.064*	−0.200*	0.029*	−0.032*	0.085*	−0.083*	0.059*	0.062*	−0.015*
(15) Industry_Tech	1.10	0.207*	0.070*	0.011*	−0.041*	−0.069*	0.083*	0.056*	0.058*	0.112*	0.072*
(16) Inner	1.32	−0.058*	0.005	−0.007*	−0.006	0.339*	−0.019*	−0.044*	−0.027*	−0.019*	−0.014*
(17) Density	1.41	0.040*	−0.002	−0.033*	0.097*	−0.356*	−0.009*	0.014*	0.046*	0.021*	0.007*
(18) HHI	1.26	0.012*	0.027*	−0.023*	0.063*	−0.164*	−0.013*	0.022*	0.065*	0.023*	0.012*
(19) LQ	1.30	0.002	0.046*	0.030*	−0.018*	0.185*	0.124*	0.038*	0.002	0.007*	−0.003
(20) South	1.16	−0.228*	−0.002	−0.165*	0.150*	0.177*	−0.136*	−0.184*	−0.032*	−0.050*	−0.060*

(continued)

Table 7.5 (continued)

Variables	VIF	(11)	(12)	(13)	(14)	(15)	(16)	(17)	(18)	(19)	(20)
(11) Liquidity	–	1.000									
(12) Export	–	−0.015*	1.000								
(13) Network agreement	–	−0.027*	0.053*	1.000							
(14) Group	–	−0.022*	0.045*	0.008*	1.000						
(15) Industry_Tech	–	0.055*	0.103*	0.009*	0.056*	1.000					
(16) Inner	–	−0.021*	−0.043*	0.012*	−0.030*	−0.068*	1.000				
(17) Density	–	0.033*	0.019*	−0.028*	0.047*	0.082*	−0.437*	1.000			
(18) HHI	–	−0.010*	0.021*	−0.007*	0.033*	0.082*	−0.187*	0.290*	1.000		
(19) LQ	–	−0.039*	0.065*	0.025*	−0.008*	−0.219*	0.175*	−0.224*	−0.392*	1.000	
(20) South	–	−0.018*	−0.158*	0.016*	−0.038*	−0.127*	0.152*	−0.041*	−0.013*	0.063*	1.000

Note: Number of observations: *97,657*. Mean VIF = 1.18. Level of statistical significance $^{*}p < 0.05$

isolation is negatively related to productivity. Again Table 7.5 displays the variance inflation factor (VIF), which rules out multicollinearity issues in the data. Indeed, all VIF coefficients are below the tolerance level of 10 (O'Brien, 2007).

7.4 Family Firms, Local Roots, and Economic Performance

7.4.1 Family Firms and Productivity

Productivity represents a critical source of firm competitiveness and growth (Gupta et al., 2013). For instance, only the most productive firms are able to overcome the sunk costs associated with internationalization (Brancati et al., 2018). Size (Raspe & van Oort, 2011), innovation (Hall et al., 2009), and human capital (Aiello et al., 2014) are viewed as determinants of firm productivity.

Productivity represents a much-debated and controversial issue in family business studies. The existing empirical evidence is somewhat inconclusive as regards whether family firms are more (Martikainen et al., 2009; Sraer & Thesmar, 2007) or less (Barth et al., 2005; Classen et al., 2014) productive than their non-family counterparts. Table 7.6 summarizes the most relevant studies dealing with family firm productivity.

Several theoretical arguments—mainly under the stewardship and agency theories—have been put forward to explain the productivity divergence between family and non-family firms. On the one hand, because of their strong identification with the firm and emotional involvement, family leaders act in the long-run interests of the business and all its stakeholders, that "may engender a number of strategic outcomes that bring superior returns in the long term" (Cucculelli et al., 2014, p. 327). Family firms are deemed to create a unique working environment that promotes employee loyalty, dedication, and commitment, reducing transaction costs (Martikainen et al., 2009). Family firms' superior ability to sustain implicit labor contracts and the perceived organizational solidarity may be reciprocated by employees (Damiani et al., 2018). Hence, these stewardship arguments predict a positive association between the family firm status and productivity.

On the other, although family involvement in the business may reduce principal-agent costs (Schulze et al., 2001), specific agency issues may emerge. Among these, the private benefits of control (e.g., special dividends and excessive compensation for family management) (Barbera & Moores, 2013), talent misallocation, given that executives are usually chosen from family members rather than a pool of external talented managers, nepotism (Creemers et al., 2022), and misalignment of interests between family owners and non-family employees (Neckebrouck et al., 2018). These agency arguments, alongside a certain reluctance toward innovation and internationalization (Bugamelli et al., 2018) and a tendency to minimize risk (Cucculelli et al., 2014), predict a negative association between the family firm status and productivity.

Table 7.6 Empirical studies on family firms and productivity

Authors	Journal/Book	Theoretical framework	Family firm definition	Sample	Country	Main results
Amato et al. (2023)	Small Business and Enterprise Development	Productivity spillovers	Families as Global Ultimate Owner (GUO) and GUO also manager	Secondary data	Italy	Family firm status is negatively associated with productivity. Closeness to family firms is a source of negative externalities. However, the adverse effect vanishes when nearby family firms are also innovators
Barbera and Moores (2013)	Small Business Economics	Agency theory/ Socioemotional wealth	If the respondent considers the business to be a family business	Survey data	Australia	Family labor and capital yield diverse output contributions compared with their non-family counterparts. Specifically, family labor output contributions are significantly higher, and family capital output contributions are significantly lower
Barth et al. (2005)	Journal of Corporate Finance	/	At least 33% of the shares in the firm are owned by one person or by one family	Survey data	Norway	Family-owned firms are less productive than non-family counterparts. However, family-owned firms managed by a manager from outside the owner's family are equally productive as non-family-owned firms
Basco et al. (2021)	Family business and regional development	Regional familiness approach	At least two family members hold managerial positions	Survey data	Spain	Municipality size negatively moderates the productivity of family-managed firms in so far as family-managed firms achieve higher productivity gains in smaller municipalities

Chrisman et al. (2017)	Family Business Review	Agency theory	Two or more members of the same family own the majority of the business	Survey data	USA	Overall, labor productivity in family firms is lower than in non-family firms but the productivity gap between family and non-family firms is reduced when incentive compensation programs are in place
Christensen-Salem et al. (2021)	Journal of Family Business Strategy	Socioemotional wealth theory	Family ownership was identified using three steps and relying on local experts	Survey data	Brazil	Family firm status is negatively associated with labor productivity. Employee-perceived organizational caring has a positive relationship with a change in labor productivity in family firms
Classen et al. (2014)	Small Business Economics	/	The same family holds at least 50% of the company shares	Survey data	Germany	Given the level of product and process innovation, however, family SMEs underperform regarding labor productivity in comparison to non-family SMEs
Creemers et al. (2022)	Journal of Family Business Strategy	Agency theory/ Stewardship theory	Either a one family or a group of families owns more than 50% of the company shares	Survey data	Chile	Family ownership is the source of productivity advantages for firms located in the lower tail of the labor productivity distribution, whereas it has a negative effect on labor productivity in the upper tail compared to non-family counterparts
Cucculelli et al. (2014)	Journal of Small Business Management	Agency theory	The majority of firm's shares are owned by an individual of a family who runs the company	Survey data	Italy	Family-run firms are less productive than firms run by outside managers. This difference tends to vanish when the age of the firms is considered. When considering family-owned firms only, there is

(continued)

Table 7.6 (continued)

Authors	Journal/Book	Theoretical framework	Family firm definition	Sample	Country	Main results
						no difference in performance between outside managers and family managers
Damiani et al. (2018)	Journal of Small Business Management	Agency theory/ Stewardship theory	The firm is owned or controlled by an individual or a family	Survey data	Italy	Family-owned firms have lower labor productivity than their non-family counterparts. However, enterprises under family governance achieve greater labor productivity gains than their non-family counterparts when they adopt firm-level bargaining
Hu et al. (2018)	Management and Organization Review	Agency theory/ Organizational justice perspective	More than 50% of the shares in the firm are owned by the family	Survey data	China	Family involvement in middle management, is negatively associated with labor productivity. Furthermore, this negative relationship exists only when the CEO is a family member rather than a professional (outside) manager, when the size of the firm is large rather than small, or when the firm is located in regions with low rather than high labor mobility
Martikainen et al. (2009)	The Quarterly Review of Economics and Finance	/	Ownership of the founding family and/or the presence of family members on the BoD	Secondary data	USA	Family firms are more productive than non-family counterparts. The superior performance of family firms is due to their more efficient use of labor and capital resources

Morikawa (2013)	Journal of Economics and Business	/	Family ownership at different percentages under 5%/50% or over	Survey data	Japan	The annual productivity growth rate of family firms is lower than that of non-family firms. The difference in performance between family and non-family firms is found to be limited to unlisted firms
Neckebrouck et al. (2018)	Academy of Management Journal	Agency theory/ Stewardship theory	A family holds more than 50% of the shares of the firm, and at least two board members with the same surname	Secondary data	Belgium	The labor productivity of family firms is lower than that of non-family counterparts
Sraer and Thesmar (2007)	Journal of the European Economic Association	/	The founder or a member of the founder's family is a blockholder of the company (more than 20% of the voting rights)	Secondary data	France	Founder-led family firms display higher labor productivity than non-family counterparts. Labor productivity is lower in family firms run by non-family (professional) managers

Despite the wealth of empirical evidence, the debate on family firms' productivity has been mostly "context-less," meaning that the "circumstances, conditions, situations, or environments that are external to the respective phenomenon and enable or constrain it" has been largely overlooked (Welter, 2011, p. 167). In particular, the research has neglected—with a few notable exceptions (Basco et al., 2021; Hu et al., 2018)—one particular dimension, that is "where" the phenomenon of interest occurs. Against this background, the location where the enterprise is conducted may unveil new facets on the productivity differentials of family and non-family firms. A critical issue may be whether and to what extent family firms are in a better position to capitalize on local roots, especially when located in isolated areas. Indeed, for family firms place bonds may turn out to be a source of advantages in acquiring, developing, and allocating tangible and intangible resources, outweighing the drawbacks of geographic isolation (Backman & Palmberg, 2015; Baù et al., 2019).

7.4.2 *Econometric Approach*

Given the hierarchical structure of the data, with units (firms) that are nested in groups (locations), this study relies on multilevel or hierarchical modeling. In a multilevel setting, variables at different levels are not simply add-ons to the same single-level equation but modeled simultaneously (van Oort et al., 2012). There are two main advantages associated with multilevel models. First, they offer a natural way to assess contextuality. In a multilevel approach, the investigation of location on firm performance assumes that firms operating in the same locality are likely to be more similar—due to cluster-specific factors—than those operating in differing locations (Aiello et al., 2014). Second, multilevel analysis allows the incorporation of unobserved heterogeneity into the model by including random intercepts and random slopes, thereby allowing relationships to vary across locations through the inclusion of random coefficients, while "traditional" regression models are designed to model the mean, multilevel models center on modeling variances explicitly (Raspe & van Oort, 2011).[15]

The dependent variable Y refers to firm i and depends on a set X of variables measured at firm level and on a set Z of variables defined at local level j as follows:

[15] By controlling for spatial dependence, multilevel modeling also allows us to overcome the ecological and atomistic fallacies.

$$\begin{aligned}Y_{ij} = {} & \gamma_{00} + \beta_1 \text{Family firm}_{ij} + \beta_2 \text{Local roots}_{ij} + \beta_3 \text{Geographic isolation}_{jt-1} \\ & + \lambda C_{ijt-1} + \sum\nolimits_{f=1}^{k} \delta_f W_{fijt-1} + \sum\nolimits_{h=1}^{v} \zeta_h Z_{hjt-1} + \sum\nolimits_{p=1}^{q} \eta_p S_{pijt-1} \\ & + \xi \text{South} + \left(e_{ij} + u_{0j}\right)\end{aligned} \tag{7.1}$$

where Y is the labor productivity of the *i-th* firm operating in location *j*; γ_{00} is a weighted average of the intercept across all locations (overall mean). β_1, β_2, and β_3 represent the direct effect of the variables of interest on the response variable; C is a matrix containing all two- and three-way interaction terms for the three main regressors; λ is the corresponding coefficients. *W* is a set of firm-level control variables and δ the corresponding coefficients. *Z* represents a set of local-level control variables and ζ the related coefficients. *S* is a set of industrial dummies and η is the corresponding coefficients. *South* is the regional dummy and ξ the associated coefficient; e_{ij} is a random error term defined at firm level which is assumed to have a normal distribution with mean zero and variance $\left(\sigma_e^2\right)$; u_{0j} is a random error term defined at local-level capturing the variability in the intercept across locations, which is assumed to have a multivariate normal distribution with an expected value of zero and variances $\left(\sigma_{u0}^2\right)$ independent from e_{ij} . To lessen endogeneity, we lag both the *Geographic isolation* and the control variables by one period.

The "empty model," that is a model without covariates, allows the decomposition of *Y* into two components: the variance of the lowest level errors e_{ij} $\left(\sigma_e^2\right)$, the so-called within-group variance and the variance of the highest-level errors u_{0j} $\left(\sigma_{u0}^2\right)$, the between-group variance. The proportion of total variance explained by each level is given by the intra-class correlation (ICC):

$$\text{ICC} = \frac{\sigma_{u0}^2}{\left(\sigma_{u0}^2 + \sigma_e^2\right)} \tag{7.2}$$

7.4.3 Empirical Findings

Results are displayed in Table 7.7. Model (1) refers to the empty model specified in Eq. (7.1) that allows us to evaluate how much of the variability in productivity might be attributable to unobserved factors operating at firm and location levels. Model (2) includes the control variables and the explanatory variables, while Models 3–6 are the interaction terms. The likelihood test compares the empty model with the standard linear regression. The test is significant, which justifies the use of multilevel modeling. The ICC value in Model 1 indicates that nearly 12% of firm productivity is explained by location, while the remaining 88% is to firm-specific characteristics. In other words, local context matters for productivity, but to a lesser extent than internal attributes.

By looking at the explanatory variables in Model (2), we can see that the coefficient of *Family firm* is positive and statistically significant (β = 0.06; $p < 0.01$), which suggests that family managed firms are more productive than

Table 7.7 Regression results: Family firms, local roots, and productivity

	Model (1)	Model (2)	Model (3)	Model (4)	Model (5)	Model (6)
Fixed part						
Size		0.080^{***}	0.080^{***}	0.080^{***}	0.080^{***}	0.080^{***}
		(0.002)	(0.002)	(0.002)	(0.002)	(0.002)
Age		0.005^{***}	0.005^{***}	0.005^{***}	0.005^{***}	0.005^{***}
		(0.000)	(0.000)	(0.000)	(0.000)	(0.000)
Intangibles		0.005^{***}	0.005^{***}	0.005^{***}	0.005^{***}	0.005^{***}
		(0.000)	(0.000)	(0.000)	(0.000)	(0.000)
Patent		0.083^{***}	0.083^{***}	0.083^{***}	0.083^{***}	0.083^{***}
		(0.014)	(0.014)	(0.014)	(0.014)	(0.014)
Leverage		0.332^{***}	0.332^{***}	0.332^{***}	0.332^{***}	0.332^{***}
		(0.007)	(0.007)	(0.007)	(0.007)	(0.007)
Liquidity		0.329^{***}	0.329^{***}	0.329^{***}	0.329^{***}	0.329^{***}
		(0.013)	(0.013)	(0.013)	(0.013)	(0.013)
Export		0.176^{***}	0.176^{***}	0.176^{***}	0.176^{***}	0.176^{***}
		(0.004)	(0.004)	(0.004)	(0.004)	(0.004)
Network agreement		0.079^{***}	0.079^{***}	0.079^{***}	0.079^{***}	0.079^{***}
		(0.012)	(0.012)	(0.012)	(0.012)	(0.012)
Group		0.037^{***}	0.037^{***}	0.037^{***}	0.037^{***}	0.037^{***}
		(0.004)	(0.004)	(0.004)	(0.004)	(0.004)
Inner		-0.022^{***}	-0.022^{***}	-0.022^{***}	-0.022^{***}	-0.022^{***}
		(0.007)	(0.007)	(0.007)	(0.007)	(0.007)
Density		0.001	0.001	0.001	0.001	0.001
		(0.003)	(0.003)	(0.003)	(0.003)	(0.003)
South		-0.224^{***}	-0.223^{***}	-0.223^{***}	-0.223^{***}	-0.223^{***}
		(0.007)	(0.007)	(0.007)	(0.007)	(0.007)
Family firm		0.060^{***}	0.052^{***}	0.051^{***}	0.051^{***}	0.053^{***}
		(0.004)	(0.005)	(0.005)	(0.005)	(0.005)

Local roots		−0.027***	−0.037***	−0.037***	−0.037***	−0.035***
		(0.005)	(0.005)	(0.005)	(0.006)	(0.006)
Geographic isolation		−0.516*	−0.519*	−0.642**	−0.605*	−0.457
		(0.270)	(0.270)	(0.300)	(0.333)	(0.340)
Family firm*Local roots			0.040***	0.040***	0.040***	0.031***
			(0.010)	(0.010)	(0.010)	(0.011)
Family firm*Geographic isolation				0.509	0.499	−0.074
				(0.539)	(0.541)	(0.608)
Local roots*Geographic isolation					−0.136	−0.681
					(0.535)	(0.597)
Family firm* Local roots*Geographic isolation						2.726**
						(1.323)
Constant	3.808***	3.196***	3.200***	3.200***	3.200***	3.199***
	(0.005)	(0.018)	(0.018)	(0.018)	(0.018)	(0.018)
Random part						
Variance (location)	0.054	0.008	0.008	0.008	0.008	0.008
Firm (location)	0.407	0.336	0.336	0.336	0.336	0.336
Intra-class correlation (ICC)						
Location	0.118	0.023	0.023	0.023	0.023	0.023
Firm	0.882	0.977	0.977	0.977	0.977	0.977
Log likelihood	−96938.123	−86078.185	−86070.607	−86070.161	−86070.129	−86068.004
LR test	–	21719.88***	15.16***	0.89	0.06	4.25**
LR test vs. linear model	5314.85***	604.86***	604.30***	604.50***	604.56***	604.44***
Industry	Yes	Yes	Yes	Yes	Yes	Yes
Groups	5553	5553	5553	5553	5553	5553
Observations	*97,657*	*97,657*	*97,657*	*97,657*	*97,657*	*97,657*

Note: Standard errors in parentheses Level of statistical significance * $p < 0.10$, ** $p < 0.05$, *** $p < 0.01$

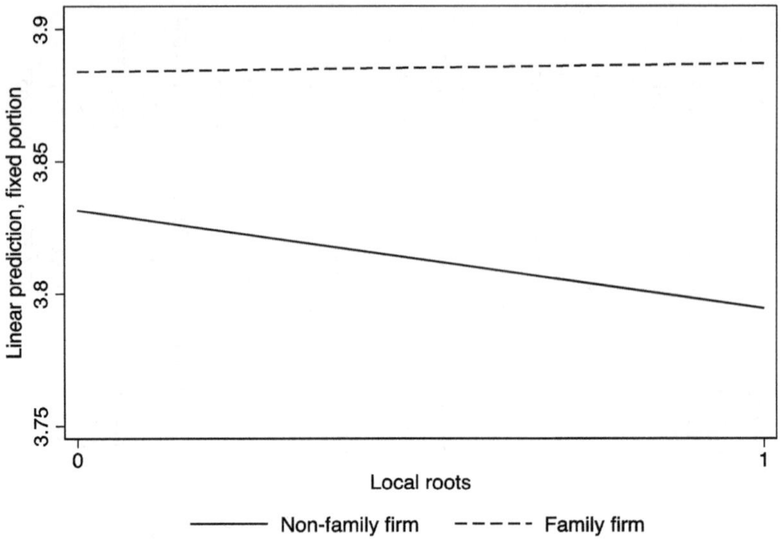

Fig. 7.1 Two-way interaction *Family firm*Local roots*

non-family counterparts. The coefficient of *Local roots* is negative and statistically significant ($\beta = -0.027$; $p < 0.01$), implying that place connections are detrimental to firm productivity. The coefficient of *Geographic isolation* is also negative and significant at 10% level, suggesting that location in isolated areas works against firm productivity. This result is consistent with the work of Wang et al. (2020) carried out in Canada.

Model (3) displays the interaction *Family firm*Local roots* to disentangle the effect of family firm status on productivity conditional on whether or not it is rooted in a particular area. The coefficient of the interaction term is positive and statistically significant ($\beta = 0.040$; $p < 0.01$), suggesting that family firms have productivity advantages compared to their non-family counterparts when rooted in the local *milieu*. Specifically, the productivity differential of locally rooted family firms is equal to 0.092.[16] Family firms in isolation do not seem to benefit from local roots. The productivity premium is indeed negligible, equal to 0.003, but not statistically significant.[17] For a more straightforward interpretation of this result, the interaction is plotted in Fig. 7.1, which shows that the productivity gap between family and non-family firms widens when both are rooted in a local context.

[16] We derive the controlled difference in the logarithm of the dependent variable between locally rooted family firms and locally rooted non-family firms as (β_1 + β_3), which is equal to 0.052 + 0.040 = 0.092.

[17] We derive the controlled difference in the logarithm of the dependent variable between locally rooted family firms and non-locally rooted family firms as (β_3 + β_1), which is equal to 0.04–0.037 = 0.003.

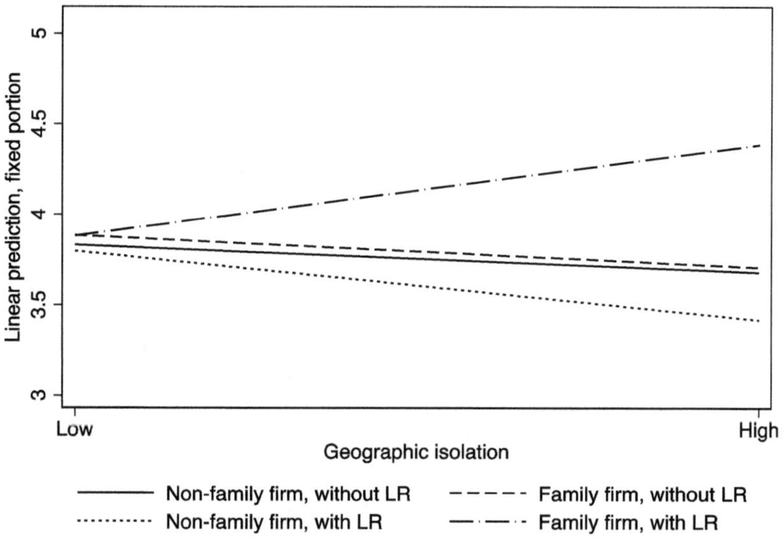

Fig. 7.2 Three-way interaction *Family firm*Local roots*Geographic isolation*

The interaction *Family firm*Geographic isolation* in Model (4) tests whether family and non-family firms are affected by geographic isolation in different ways. However, there is no evidence of this. Indeed, the interaction term is positive but not statistically significant. Likewise, locally rooted firms do not seem to differ according to the geographic isolation. The interaction term *Local roots*Geographic isolation* is in fact negative but not statistically significant. Finally, Model (6) displays the interaction term *Family firm*Local roots*Geographic isolation* to test whether and to what extent locally rooted family firms outperform non-family counterparts according to the level of geographic isolation. The coefficient of the interaction term is positive and statistically significant ($\beta = 2.726$; $p < 0.05$). Figure 7.2 plots the interaction for a more straightforward interpretation of this result.

Locally rooted family firms display a higher productivity level than non-family counterparts—whether rooted or not—and this productivity gain heightens as the geographic isolation increases. Hence, local roots allow family firms to cancel out the drawbacks of geographic isolation, obtaining productivity advantages compared to non-family firms. Geographic isolation magnifies the importance of local roots for family firms. Trust-based and reciprocal ties among family members and between the family firm and the local community, serve as a conduit to identify and exploit tangible (e.g., human capital and financial resources) and intangible resources (e.g., knowledge and information), positively affecting firm productivity in geographically isolated areas. Thus, embedded ties between the firm and the locality and socially proximate relationships between family members keep the firm afloat, overcoming the constraints of geographical isolation. This result is in line with previous studies (e.g., Adjei et al., 2016; Steiner & Atterton, 2015). Conversely, for non-family firms, local roots seem to compound the detrimental effect of geographic isolation on productivity.

7.5 Family Firms, Local Roots, and Corporate Social Responsibility

7.5.1 ISO 14001 Environmental Management Systems

ISO 14001:2015 sets out the requirements for an environmental management system (EMS) that an organization can use to enhance its environmental performance. ISO 14001:2015 helps the organization achieve the intended outcomes of its environmental management system, which provides value for the environment, the organization itself, and interested parties. It applies to any organization, regardless of size, type, and nature, and to the environmental aspects of its activities, products, and services that the organization determines to control or influence, over a life cycle. The ISO 14001:2015 internationally recognized standard is based on a voluntary approach and rewarded with a certification, providing a real quality guarantee, from an approved external body.

The reasons for compliance may be customer pressure and economic, that is, to obtain cost savings and increase productivity (Kocollari, 2018). Ethical motivations, based on ecological awareness, social obligations, and values, may also encourage firms to implement a certified environmental management system (González-Benito & González-Benito, 2005). Beside these, a certified environmental management system may also serve as a signaling device, informing others—such as buyers and regulators—that the adopter is managing its environmental impact efficiently (Johnstone & Labonne, 2009). Thus, firms may implement certified EMS in order to gain the confidence of the institutions and social groups in the socio-economic environment (González-Benito & González-Benito, 2005).

The ISO 14001 standard is based on four principles represented by the Plan-Do-Check-Act (PDCA) cycle, which is the operating principle of all ISO management system standards:

- *Plan* the environmental objectives in line with the organization's environmental policy.
- *Do*, implement a plan of action.
- *Check* the impact of the actions implemented and compliance with environmental regulations via an audit.
- *Act* to improve the process by carefully thought-out fine tuning.

Although it is not a legal obligation, implementation of ISO 14001 has a dual impact on the organization. First, it limits the environmental footprint of business operations regarding waste reduction, CO_2 emissions, and water/energy utilization. For instance, it has been shown that the adoption of ISO 14001 is associated with improving firms' environmental performance (Arimura et al., 2008). Especially for resource-constrained firms such as the SMEs, the ISO 14001 certification is conducive to higher environmental performance when combined with participation in external networks that facilitate its implementation (Graafland, 2018). Second, by enhancing processes and operations, ISO 14001 offers many financial and economic benefits, thus improving organizational competitiveness (Hojnik & Ruzzier, 2017). Against this background, empirical evidence shows that ISO 14001 certified firms have higher market value than those that do not (Al-Najjar & Anfimiadou, 2012).

7.5.2 *Econometric Approach*

To investigate the decision to certify the environmental management system according to the ISO 14001 standard concerning the family firm and local roots, we estimate the following model:

$$\begin{aligned} P(\text{ISO14001}_{ij}=1) &= \gamma_{00} + \beta_1 \text{Family firm}_{ij} + \beta_2 \text{Local roots}_{ij} \\ &+ \beta_{3ij}\left(\text{Family firm}_{ij} * \text{Local roots}_{ij}\right) + \sum\nolimits_{f=1}^{k} \delta_f \text{W}_{fijt-1} \\ &+ \sum\nolimits_{h=1}^{v} \zeta_h \text{Z}_{hjt-1} + \sum\nolimits_{p=1}^{q} \eta_p \text{S}_{pijt-1} + \xi \text{South} + \left(e_{ij} + u_{0j}\right) \end{aligned} \tag{7.3}$$

where Y is a dichotomic variable which takes value "1" if the firm has an ISO14001 environmental management system certification, "0" otherwise; γ_{00} is a weighted average of the intercept across all locations (overall mean). β_1 and β_2 represent the direct effect of the variables of interest on the response variable; β_3 is the coefficient of the interaction term; W is a set of firm-level control variables and δ the corresponding coefficients. Z represents a set of local-level control variables and ζ the related coefficients. S is a set of industrial dummies and η is the corresponding coefficients. *South* is the regional dummy and ξ the associated coefficient; e_{ij} is a random error term defined at the firm level which is assumed to have a normal distribution with mean zero and variance (σ_e^2); u_{0j} is a random error term defined at local-level capturing the variability in the intercept across locations, which is assumed to have a multivariate normal distribution with an expected value of zero and variances (σ_{u0}^2) and independent from e_{ij}. To lessen endogeneity issues, the control variables are lagged by one period.

Equation (7.3) is estimated by using a linear probability model (LPM), which represents a particular case of OLS regression, especially suited to obtaining consistent and unbiased coefficients in the case of a dichotomous response variable (Wooldridge, 2010). One advantage of OLS over logistic models (e.g., Probit/Logit) is that it eases the interpretation of the coefficients, which represent the marginal effect and the interaction term directly. Their interpretation is somewhat problematic with logistic models due to unclear signs or incorrect standard errors (Greene, 2010).

Additionally, the marginal effect obtained from OLS model is very close to those obtained from non-linear models (Wooldridge, 2010). Finally, robust standard errors are estimated to deal with heteroscedasticity.

For the sake of clarity, the interaction term is interpreted by group comparisons (Amato et al., 2022; Dinh et al., 2022). Given the existence of as many groups as possible combinations, a specific reference group is identified. The sign and statistical significance of the marginal effect of a given group in comparison with the reference group provides straightforward evidence of differences across groups. Thus, to investigate the difference, in terms of ISO 14001 adoption, between family and non-family firms with respect to having local roots, the groups *Non-family firm*without Local roots*, *Non-family firm*with Local roots*, and *Family firm*without Local roots* are compared with the reference group *Family firm*with Local roots*.

7.5.3 Empirical Findings

Results are displayed in Table 7.8. Model (1) refers to the empty model, while Model (2) displays the explanatory and the control variables. The coefficient of *Family firm* is positive and statistically significant ($\beta = 0.006$; $p < 0.01$), which suggests that all things being equal, family firms have a higher propensity to implement the ISO 14001 EMS. The coefficient of *Local roots* is also positive and significant ($\beta = 0.005$; $p < 0.01$). This result proves that place-attached firms have stronger environmental concerns, making them more willing to certify their environmental management systems, than firms without strong connections with their local area. Moreover, from a glance at the control variables, it emerges that the more productive, larger, and more innovative firms are more likely to implement the ISO 14001 environmental management system. The same is true for exporting firms and those belonging to formal networks and business groups. Regarding the territorial control variables, location in inner areas does not seem to affect the probability of implementing the ISO 14001 environmental management system voluntarily. Conversely, local specialization (*LQ)* is positively associated with the likelihood of adopting the ISO 14001 environmental management system ($\beta = 0.001$; $p < 0.01$). Firms located in the south of Italy are more environmentally friendly, as shown by the sign and significance of the *South* coefficient ($\beta = 0.026$; $p < 0.01$).

Model (3) displays the interaction terms to test whether the probability of implementing the ISO 14001 environmental management system differs between family and non-family firms depending on place attachment. The interaction term *Non-family firm*With Local roots* compares place-attached non-family firms with their family counterparts as reference group. The coefficient of the interaction term is negative and statistically significant ($\beta = -0.017$; $p < 0.01$), which suggests that place-attached non-family firms have a lower probability of certifying their environmental management systems than place-attached family firms. For a more straightforward interpretation of this result, the interaction is plotted in Fig. 7.3. As

Table 7.8 Regression results: Family firms, local roots, and ISO14001

	Model (1)	Model (2)	Model (3)
Fixed part			
Productivity		0.011***	0.011***
		(0.001)	(0.001)
Size		0.033***	0.033***
		(0.000)	(0.000)
Age		0.000***	0.000***
		(0.000)	(0.000)
Intangibles		0.000***	0.000***
		(0.000)	(0.000)
Patent		0.069***	0.069***
		(0.004)	(0.004)
Leverage		0.008***	0.008***
		(0.002)	(0.002)
Liquidity		−0.016***	−0.016***
		(0.004)	(0.004)
Export		0.007***	0.007***
		(0.001)	(0.001)
Network agreement		0.021***	0.021***
		(0.003)	(0.003)
Group		0.014***	0.014***
		(0.001)	(0.001)
Inner		0.003	0.003
		(0.002)	(0.002)
Density		−0.003***	−0.003***
		(0.001)	(0.001)
HHI		0.004***	0.004***
		(0.000)	(0.000)
LQ		0.001***	0.001***
		(0.000)	(0.000)
South		0.026***	0.026***
		(0.002)	(0.002)
Family firm		0.006***	
		(0.001)	
Local roots		0.005***	
		(0.001)	
*Family firm*With Local roots as reference group*			
Non-family firm*Without Local roots			−0.019***
			(0.002)
Non-family firm*With Local roots			−0.017***
			(0.003)
Family firm*Without Local roots			−0.015***
			(0.003)

(continued)

Table 7.8 (continued)

	Model (1)	Model (2)	Model (3)
Constant	0.031***	−0.131***	−0.112***
	(0.012)	(0.005)	(0.006)
Random part			
Variance (location)	0.017	0.013	0.013
Firm (location)	0.174	0.166	0.166
Intra-class correlation (ICC)			
Location	0.01	0.01	0.01
Firm	0.99	0.99	0.99
Log pseudolikelihood	32808.337	37918.365	37929.031
LR test	–	10220.06***	21.33***
LR test vs. linear model	201.20***	82.63***	82.71***
Industry	Yes	Yes	Yes
Groups	5553	5553	5553
Observations	*97,657*	*97,657*	*97,657*

Note: Standard errors are in parentheses. Level of statistical significance * $p < 0.10$, ** $p < 0.05$, *** $p < 0.01$

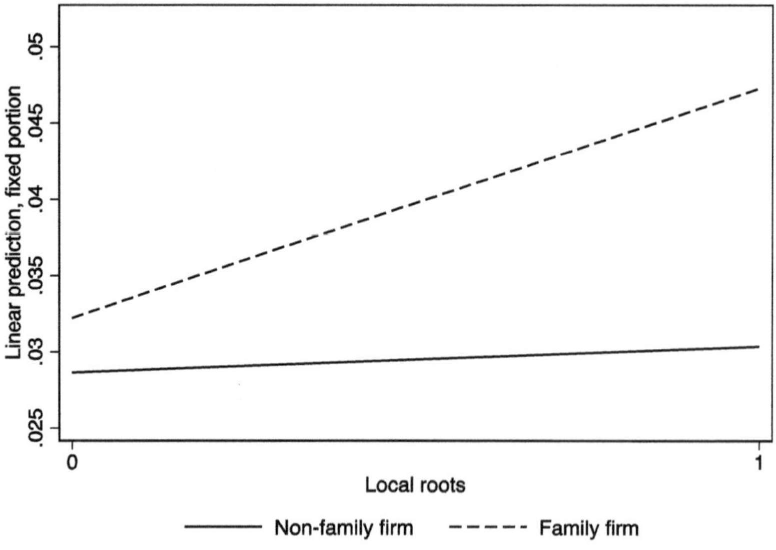

Fig. 7.3 Two-way interaction *Family firm*Local roots*

non-family firms are not affected by place connections,[18] local roots exert a sizeable influence on family firms' probability of implementing the ISO 14001

[18]The coefficient of the interaction term *Non-family*With Local roots* with *Non-family*Without Local roots* as reference group is positive ($\beta = 0.002$) but not statistically significant.

environmental management system, thereby underpinning their ecological commitment. This result confirms family firms as a distinctive type of place-based enterprise (PBE) that is "deeply, intricately, and intimately connected with and rooted in places [. . .]. . .. . .and more likely than other enterprises to engage in socially and environmentally sustainable performance" (Shrivastava & Kennelly, 2013, p. 94). The findings are in line with previous studies investigating the pro-social (Amato et al., 2023) and environmental behavior (Berrone et al., 2010; Dekker & Hasso, 2016) of locally rooted family firms.

7.6 Concluding Remarks

Family firms represent an essential feature of Italian capitalism, with the most important entrepreneurial histories inextricably linked to family dynasties. In spite of criticism related to the small size, inefficiency, and lack of innovation, family firms still play a crucial role in the Italian economy as an engine of entrepreneurship and drivers of transformation of industries and territories. This chapter has provided an empirical quantitative analysis of a large sample of Italian manufacturing firms to answer two main research questions. First, whether and, if so, to what extent local roots enable family firms to mitigate spatial disadvantages related to geographic isolation. The focus is on productivity, a long-lasting issue in family business research given the inconclusive empirical evidence and Italy's gradual decline in productivity, arguably at the root of the abiding stagnation of the "belpaese." The findings reveal that family firms are more productive than their non-family counterparts, and local roots allow them to overcome the constraints of isolation. By imbuing with trust, reciprocity, and closeness the local networks, family firms are better positioned to identify and exploit rare resources, thus counteracting the disadvantages of geographical isolation. Being isolated but deeply rooted in the local area, also amplifies the relevance of family ties compensating for the lack of agglomeration economies.

The second research question is whether family and non-family firms differ regarding environmental orientation in CSR strategies, measured by the voluntary adoption of ISO 14001 certificates. The findings show local roots prompt family firms to take an ecological stance, such as implementing a certified environmental management system. Family members' place attachment leads to greater concern for the local environment, which leads family firms to pay more attention to the ecological implications of economic activity and the need for environmental sustainability.

References

Adjei, E. K., Eriksson, R. H., & Lindgren, U. (2016). Social proximity and firm performance: The importance of family member ties in workplaces. *Regional Studies, Regional Science, 3*(1), 303–319. https://doi.org/10.1080/21681376.2016.1189354

Aiello, F., Pupo, V., & Ricotta, F. (2014). Explaining total factor productivity at firm level in Italy: Does location matter? *Spatial Economic Analysis, 9*(1), 51–70. https://doi.org/10.1080/17421772.2013.863428

Al-Najjar, B., & Anfimiadou, A. (2012). Environmental policies and firm value. *Business Strategy and the Environment, 21*(1), 49–59. https://doi.org/10.1002/bse.713

Amato, S., Pieroni, V., Lattanzi, N., & Vitali, G. (2022). Are family firms good neighbours? A spatial analysis of Italian technology-intensive firms. *Journal of Small Business and Enterprise Development, 29*(4), 663–693. https://doi.org/10.1108/JSBED-06-2021-0242

Amato, S., Patuelli, A., Basco, R., & Lattanzi, N. (2023). Family firms amidst the global financial crisis: A territorial embeddedness perspective on downsizing. *Journal of Business Ethics, 183* (1), 213–236. https://doi.org/10.1007/s10551-021-04930-0

Arimura, T. H., Hibiki, A., & Katayama, H. (2008). Is a voluntary approach an effective environmental policy instrument?: A case for environmental management systems. *Journal of Environmental Economics and Management, 55*(3), 281–295. https://doi.org/10.1016/j.jeem.2007.09.002

Backman, M., & Palmberg, J. (2015). Contextualizing small family firms: How does the urban-rural context affect firm employment growth? *Journal of Family Business Strategy, 6*, 247–258. https://doi.org/10.1016/j.jfbs.2015.10.003

Barbera, F., & Moores, K. (2013). Firm ownership and productivity: A study of family and non-family SMEs. *Small Business Economics, 40*(4), 953–976. https://doi.org/10.1007/s11187-011-9405-9

Barth, E., Gulbrandsen, T., & Schønea, P. (2005). Family ownership and productivity: The role of owner-management. *Journal of Corporate Finance, 11*(1–2), 107–127. https://doi.org/10.1016/j.jcorpfin.2004.02.001

Basco, R. (2013). The family's effect on family firm performance: A model testing the demographic and essence approaches. *Journal of Family Business Strategy, 4*(1), 42–66. https://doi.org/10.1016/j.jfbs.2012.12.003

Basco, R., Amato, S., Gómez-Ansón, S., & Calabrò, A. (2021). Urbanization economies, proximity dimensions and productivity: A family firm perspective. In R. In Basco, R. Stough, & L. Suwala (Eds.), *Family business and regional development*. Routledge. https://doi.org/10.4324/9780429058097

Baù, M., Chirico, F., Pittino, D., Backman, M., & Klaesson, J. (2019). Roots to grow: Family firms and local embeddedness in rural and urban contexts. *Entrepreneurship Theory and Practice, 43* (2), 360–385. https://doi.org/10.1177/1042258718796089

Berrone, P., Cruz, C., Gomez-Mejia, L. R., & Larraza-Kintana, M. (2010). Socioemotional wealth and corporate responses to institutional pressures: Do family-controlled firms pollute less? *Administrative Science Quarterly, 55*(1), 82–113. https://doi.org/10.2307/27856089

Brancati, R., Marrocu, E., Romagnoli, M., & Usai, S. (2018). Innovation activities and learning processes in the crisis: Evidence from Italian export in manufacturing and services. *Industrial and Corporate Change, 27*(1), 107–130. https://doi.org/10.1093/icc/dtx022

Bugamelli, M., Lotti, F., Amici, M., Ciapanna, E., Colonna, F., D'Amuri, F., Giacomelli, S., Linarello, A., Manaresi, F., Palumbo, G., Scoccianti, F., & Sette, E. (2018). *Productivity growth in Italy: A tale of slow-motion change*. Occasional Papers - Questioni di economia e finanza (No. 422). Bank of Italy.

Chiarvesio, M., Di Maria, E., & Micelli, S. (2010). Global value chains and open networks: The case of Italian industrial districts. *European Planning Studies, 18*(3), 333–350. https://doi.org/10.1080/09654310903497637

Chrisman, J. J., Devaraj, S., & Patel, P. C. (2017). The impact of incentive compensation on labor productivity in family and nonfamily firms. *Family Business Review, 30*(2), 119–136. https://doi.org/10.1177/0894486517690052

Christensen-Salem, A., Mesquita, L. F., Hashimoto, M., Hom, P. W., & Gomez-Mejia, L. R. (2021). Family firms are indeed better places to work than non-family firms! Socioemotional wealth and employees' perceived organizational caring. *Journal of Family Business Strategy, 12* (1), 100412. https://doi.org/10.1016/j.jfbs.2020.100412

Classen, N., Carree, M., van Gils, A., & Peters, B. (2014). Innovation in family and non-family SMEs: An exploratory analysis. *Small Business Economics, 42*(3), 595–609. https://doi.org/10.1007/s11187-013-9490-z

Coltorti, F. (2013). Italian industry, decline or transformation? *A Framework. European Planning Studies, 21*(12), 2037–2077. https://doi.org/10.1080/09654313.2012.722972

Corbetta, G., & Salvato, C. (2012). *Strategies for longevity in family firms. Strategies for longevity in family firms*. Palgrave Macmillan. https://doi.org/10.1057/9781137024589

Creemers, S., Peeters, L., Quiroz Castillo, J. L., Vancauteren, M., & Voordeckers, W. (2022). Family firms and the labor productivity controversy: A distributional analysis of varying labor productivity gaps. *Journal of Family Business Strategy*, (March 2021), 100515. https://doi.org/10.1016/j.jfbs.2022.100515

Cucculelli, M., & Storai, D. (2015). Family firms and industrial districts: Evidence from the Italian manufacturing industry. *Journal of Family Business Strategy, 6*(4), 234–246. https://doi.org/10.1016/j.jfbs.2015.07.002

Cucculelli, M., Mannarino, L., Pupo, V., & Ricotta, F. (2014). Owner-management, firm age, and productivity in Italian family firms. *Journal of Small Business Management, 52*(2), 325–343. https://doi.org/10.1111/jsbm.12103

Damiani, M., Pompei, F., & Ricci, A. (2018). Family firms and labor productivity: The role of enterprise-level bargaining in the Italian economy. *Journal of Small Business Management, 56* (4), 573–600. https://doi.org/10.1111/jsbm.12306

Dekker, J., & Hasso, T. (2016). Environmental performance focus in private family firms: The role of social embeddedness. *Journal of Business Ethics, 136*(2), 293–309. https://doi.org/10.1007/s10551-014-2516-x

Dinh, T. Q., Calabrò, A., Campopiano, G., & Basco, R. (2022). The impact of politically connected CEOs and boards of directors on firm performance: A study of Vietnamese family and nonfamily firms. *Entrepreneurship: Theory and Practice, 46*(5), 1284–1316. https://doi.org/10.1177/1042258720985477

Fitjar, R. D., & Rodríguez-Pose, A. (2011). Innovating in the periphery: Firms, values and innovation in Southwest Norway. *European Planning Studies, 19*(4), 555–574. https://doi.org/10.1080/09654313.2011.548467

Fitjar, R. D., & Rodríguez-Pose, A. (2017). Nothing is in the air. *Growth and Change, 48*(1), 22–39. https://doi.org/10.1111/grow.12161

González-Benito, J., & González-Benito, O. (2005). An analysis of the relationship between environmental motivations and ISO14001 certification. *British Journal of Management, 16* (2), 133–148. https://doi.org/10.1111/j.1467-8551.2005.00436.x

Graafland, J. J. (2018). Ecological impacts of the ISO14001 certification of small and medium sized enterprises in Europe and the mediating role of networks. *Journal of Cleaner Production, 174*, 273–282. https://doi.org/10.1016/j.jclepro.2017.10.322

Greene, W. (2010). Testing hypotheses about interaction terms in nonlinear models. *Economics Letters, 107*(2), 291–296. https://doi.org/10.1016/j.econlet.2010.02.014

Gupta, P. D., Guha, S., & Krishnaswami, S. S. (2013). Firm growth and its determinants. *Journal of Innovation and Entrepreneurship, 2*(15), 1–14. https://doi.org/10.1186/2192-5372-2-15

Hall, B. H., Lotti, F., & Mairesse, J. (2009). Innovation and productivity in SMEs: Empirical evidence for Italy. *Small Business Economics, 33*(1), 13–33. https://doi.org/10.1007/s11187-009-9184-8

Hess, M. (2004). "Spatial" relationships? Towards a reconceptualization of embeddedness. *Progress in Human Geography, 28*(2), 165–186. https://doi.org/10.1191/0309132504ph479oa

Hojnik, J., & Ruzzier, M. (2017). Does it pay to be eco? The mediating role of competitive benefits and the effect of ISO14001. *European Management Journal, 35*(5), 581–594. https://doi.org/10.1016/j.emj.2017.07.008

Hu, Q., Zhang, Y., & Yao, J. (2018). Family involvement in middle management and its impact on the labor productivity of family firms. *Management and Organization Review, 14*(2), 249–274. https://doi.org/10.1017/mor.2018.5

Intesa San Paolo. (2019). Economia e finanza dei distretti industriali. *Rapporto annuale* - n. 11.

Johnstone, N., & Labonne, J. (2009). Why do manufacturing facilities introduce environmental management systems? Improving and/or signaling performance. *Ecological Economics, 68*(3), 719–730. https://doi.org/10.1016/j.ecolecon.2008.06.003

Kocollari, U. (2018). *Strategic corporate responsibility. The social dimension of firms*. G. Giappichelli Editore-Routledge. https://doi.org/10.4324/9780429446863

LoRomer, D. (2003). Il Quarto Capitalismo: Un profilo italiano [The fourth capitalism: An Italian profile]. *Business History Review, 77*(3), 566–568. https://doi.org/10.2307/30041222

Markusen, A. (1996). Sticky places in slippery space: A typology of industrial districts. *Economic Geography, 72*(3), 293–313. https://doi.org/10.2307/144402

Martikainen, M., Nikkinen, J., & Vähämaa, S. (2009). Production functions and productivity of family firms: Evidence from the S&P 500. *Quarterly Review of Economics and Finance, 49*(2), 295–307. https://doi.org/10.1016/j.qref.2007.11.001

Morikawa, M. (2013). Productivity and survival of family firms in Japan. *Journal of Economics and Business, 70*, 111–125. https://doi.org/10.1016/j.jeconbus.2012.11.001

Neckebrouck, J., Schulze, W., & Zellweger, T. (2018). Are family firms good employers? *Academy of Management Journal, 61*(2), 553–585. https://doi.org/10.5465/amj.2016.0765

O'Brien, R. M. (2007). A caution regarding rules of thumb for variance inflation factors. *Quality and Quantity, 41*(5), 673–690. https://doi.org/10.1007/s11135-006-9018-6

Oinas, P. (1997). On the socio-spatial embeddedness of business firms. *Erdkunde, 51*(1), 23–32. https://doi.org/10.3112/erdkunde.1997.01.03

Raspe, O., & van Oort, F. G. (2011). Firm heterogeneity, productivity and spatially bounded knowledge externalities. *Socio-Economic Planning Sciences, 45*(1), 38–47. https://doi.org/10.1016/j.seps.2010.08.002

Ren, S., Cheng, Y., Hu, Y., & Yin, C. (2021). Feeling right at home: Hometown CEOs and firm innovation. *Journal of Corporate Finance, 66*, 101815. https://doi.org/10.1016/j.jcorpfin.2020.101815

Schilirò, D. (2012). Italian medium-sized enterprises and the fourth capitalism. *Journal of Applied Economic Sciences, 7*(4), 437–446. Online at https://mpra.ub.uni-muenchen.de/41399/

Schulze, W. S., Lubatkin, M. H., Dino, R. N., & Buchholtz, A. K. (2001). Agency relationships in family firms: Theory and evidence. *Organization Science, 12*(2), 99–116. https://doi.org/10.1287/orsc.12.2.99.10114

Shrivastava, P., & Kennelly, J. J. (2013). Sustainability and place-based enterprise. *Organization and Environment, 26*(1), 83–101. https://doi.org/10.1177/1086026612475068

Sraer, D., & Thesmar, D. (2007). Performance and behavior of family firms: Evidence from the French stock market. *Journal of the European Economic Association, 5*(4), 709–751. https://doi.org/10.1162/JEEA.2007.5.4.709

Steiner, A., & Atterton, J. (2015). Exploring the contribution of rural enterprises to local resilience. *Journal of Rural Studies, 40*, 30–45. https://doi.org/10.1016/j.jrurstud.2015.05.004

van Oort, F. G., Burger, M. J., Knoben, J., & Raspe, O. (2012). Multilevel approaches and the firm-agglomeration ambiguity in economic growth studies. *Journal of Economic Surveys, 26*(3), 468–491. https://doi.org/10.1111/j.1467-6419.2012.00723.x

Wang, L., Helms, W. S., & Li, W. (2020). Tapping into agglomeration benefits by engaging in a community of practice. *Strategic Organization, 18*(4), 617–644. https://doi.org/10.1177/1476127019852726

Welter, F. (2011). Contextualizing entrepreneurship—Conceptual challenges and ways forward. *Entrepreneurship: Theory and Practice, 35*(1), 165–184. https://doi.org/10.1111/j.1540-6520.2010.00427.x

Wooldridge, J. M. (2010). *Econometric analysis of cross section and panel data*. The MIT Press.

Chapter 8
Conclusions

Family business research has mainly focused on explaining how the interaction between two domains, namely the family and the business, shapes a firm's behavior and outcomes, thus making family firms unique. More recently, a new stream of research investigating the interplay between family firms and geographical space has unfolded, disclosing new facets of the family business phenomenon. Exploring the "family firm-territory nexus" means understanding the distinctive way these businesses are affected by and able to influence the geographical space where the firm's economic activity and the family's social life both take place. This nexus is such that the peculiarities of the family firm enmesh with the peculiarities of a given territory. This book took part in this debate by untangling the micro-territorial foundations of family firms. Specifically, the main research questions this book addressed revolved around what makes families deeply "anchored" or embedded in their home territory and the influence of local ties on family firms' economic performance and corporate social responsibility.

Local embeddedness, encompassing the nature, breadth, and depth of business relationships with the local context, represents the main construct employed by regional and economic geography scholars—and, more recently, family business scholars—to describe the firm's conditioning of and reliance upon its immediate surroundings. However, local embeddedness accounts only for the outer layer binding family firms to the local *milieu*, eclipsing the socioemotional connections of family members as individuals and the owning family as the dominant coalition to their home territory. As such, this book disentangles the deepest, hidden, and intangible layer anchoring family firms to their location, that is, the family's place attachment, embodying the affective bonds with its own territory. Place surges as a socio-physical basin—imbued with meanings and emotional engagement—framing the family's life as a social group and economic actor. By embedding the firm in the local *milieu*, the family's place attachment depicts the "local roots" of the firm and, therefore, the intensity with which family firms are loosely anchored, socially and economically, in a particular location.

S. Amato, A. Patuelli, *Family Firms and Local Roots*, CSR, Sustainability, Ethics & Governance, https://doi.org/10.1007/978-3-031-31793-4_8

This book embraced an interdisciplinary approach to conceptualizing family firms' local roots. Theoretical insights and constructs from regional economics, economic geography, business management, and environmental psychology found a synthesis to scrutinize family firms from a territorial perspective. By crossing the disciplines' traditional boundaries, interdisciplinarity allows us to understand and navigate the complexity of the family business phenomenon. The book did so by unpacking family place attachment, a construct from environmental psychology, and linking it with the firm's local embeddedness, a popular construct in regional economics and economic geography. As such, the individual/group and organizational connections to a particular place were considered together, with the former to a large extent molding and nourishing the latter. As to the research methods, the authors' purposive choice relied on both quantitative and qualitative approaches—and thus, deductive and inductive reasoning—to explore family firms' local roots.

This book brings three main empirical findings. First, local roots allow family firms to cope with the hurdles of geographical isolation. The results show family firms located in geographically isolated areas have higher economic performances than their non-family counterparts. Second, family firms display a higher probability of adopting environmental management systems than non-family firms. Such an ecological stance is further amplified when family firms are place attached. Third, the case study shows that the family firm plays a crucial role in keeping the family and younger generations attached to the territory, while corporate social responsibility actions to protect the local area are a natural consequence of the family's place attachment.

This book makes several contributions. By bringing space into the investigation of family firms' behavior and outcomes, this book contributes to family business research, advancing the current knowledge of the territorial dimension of family firms. Making family business research more "context-sensitive" allows additional family firms' distinctive features to emerge. This book points out that the performance differentials between family and non-family firms—a largely explored research query—also depend upon the characteristics of the local operating context and connections to it. Further, this book enriches the ongoing debate on the territorial base of family firms' corporate social responsibility. The findings provide further support for family firms as place-based enterprises, that is a particular type of firm deeply committed to pro-environmental initiatives such as the voluntary adoption of environmental management systems certificates. The sense of belongingness and togetherness toward the local *milieu* prompt the owning family to balance the firm's survival and success with the social and environmental well-being of the local community where the family and the firm dwell. Additionally, the book highlights the underlying mechanisms of why family firms are more attached to the place than non-family firms. Thus, the study contributes to understanding how place attachment originates, develops, and is maintained over time, suggesting a model to interpret the individual, family, and firm relationships with their home territory.

This book also contributes to regional studies and efforts to connect them with family business studies. While space arises as an independent production factor and generator of distinctive static and dynamic advantages—or disadvantages—for the economic agents located within it, the influence of space is uneven, depending on some firm-specific characteristics. The empirical studies of this book corroborate the evidence of the family firm status as a meaningful source of firms' heterogeneity. Place-attached family firms appear to be less affected than family counterparts by the adverse consequences of geographical isolation. Additionally, location has a stronger conditioning effect on the pro-environmental behavior of family firms than non-family firms. Thus, discriminating according to firm type—family versus non-family firms—would disclose new facets of the influence of space on outcomes and behavior.

This book contains a number of policy implications. Any policy intervention aiming at correcting the imbalances or boosting the well-being of territories should consider that family firms are deeply enmeshed, entangled, and engaged with the assets, vocations, and identities of their local area. Cluster initiatives are generally viewed as a lever for stimulating, through agglomeration economies, the competitiveness of firms, and indirectly, of territories. However, this book has shown that local roots allow family firms to prosper in geographically isolated areas. In other words, strong connections within the family and between it and the place compensate for the lack of agglomeration economies arising from the spatial concentration of the economic activity. Additionally, the distinctive pro-environmental stance of place-attached family firms suggests that policy-makers should target family enterprises as drivers of the ecological transition of particular territories. Paths of ecological transformation may indeed emerge spontaneously in territories with a high density of "rooted" family firms. In such territories, the place attachment of the owning families may turn into a spatial loyalty of the firm, which is reflected in pro-environmental choices toward the home territory. Conversely, territories with a low presence of indigenous family firms may need an alternative incentive scheme to adapt, improve and prioritize sustainable patterns of production and consumption. Additionally, the family firm has been found to be a "glue" that keeps the family and younger generations attached to the place. Thus, policy-makers should be aware of the role of family firms in keeping families and individuals linked to specific places, including traditional rural and peripheral areas.

Our work, however, has limitations that could pave the way for further research at the intersection between families, firms, and territories. First, the manager's birthplace-firm's headquarters co-location was used to capture the firm's local roots, whereas future studies could measure the family's place attachment dimensions underlying the firm's embeddedness in the local *milieu*. Second, given that the quantitative studies used relied on a demographic approach to define family firms, future studies should test the consistency of the results with multiple definitions of family firms, integrating the components of involvement and essence approaches accounting for "soft" factors, such as the family's vision and intentions. Third, as we only explored the influence of local roots on the economic performance and corporate social responsibility of family firms *vis-à-vis* non-family firms, there is room for future research to shed some light on the role of place connections in shaping family firms' innovation patterns, namely the "innovation through tradition," and the growth in international markets. A key issue would be how local roots inform family firms' international strategies. Fourth, there is room for the academic community to explore the "family firm-territory nexus" by looking at heterogenous family firms, differing according to characteristics such as the firm's age, size, and the generation in charge of the business, among others. Thus, future studies may untangle multiple configurations of family firms mirroring various nuances of family firm-territory bonds. Fifth, this book disentangles family firms' local roots, also conjecturing their "uprooting." Empirical research may investigate the forces and contingencies impairing the family's place attachment and, by extension, the firm's local embeddedness. Sixth, the empirical studies in this book adopt a micro-level perspective, but future research could extend this by means of a meso-level perspective (e.g., local or regional level) to explore the role of the collective aggregate actions of rooted family firms (i.e., "density") as a source of local resilience following exogenous shocks. Finally, the family firm-territory "nexus" stands out as a promising opportunity for investigation with qualitative research. In fact, while the literature has mostly explored the consequences of place attachment, less attention has been paid to understanding how place attachment originates. Qualitative studies could explore the complexities of this phenomenon, for a better understanding of the underlying forces.

MIX
Papier aus verantwortungsvollen Quellen
Paper from responsible sources
FSC® C105338

If you have any concerns about our products,
you can contact us on
ProductSafety@springernature.com

In case Publisher is established outside the EU,
the EU authorized representative is:
Springer Nature Customer Service Center GmbH
Europaplatz 3, 69115 Heidelberg, Germany

Printed by Libri Plureos GmbH
in Hamburg, Germany